BASIC TEACHINGS
of the
BUDDHA

Glenn Wallis

BASIC TEACHINGS *of the* BUDDHA

A NEW TRANSLATION AND COMPILATION, *with* A GUIDE TO READING THE TEXTS

THE MODERN LIBRARY

NEW YORK

2007 Modern Library Paperback Edition

Published in the United States by Modern Library, an imprint of
The Random House Publishing Group, a division
of Random House, Inc., New York.

MODERN LIBRARY and the TORCHBEARER Design are
registered trademarks of Random House, Inc.

LIBRARY OF CONGRESS CATALOGING-IN-PUBLICATION DATA

Tipiṭaka. English. Selections.
Basic teachings of the Buddha: a new translation and compilation, with a guide
to reading the texts / by Glenn Wallis.
p. cm.
Includes index.
ISBN 978-0-8129-7523-9
1. Gautama Buddha—Teachings. 2. Buddhism—Doctrines. I. Wallis, Glenn.
II. Title.
BQ1172.E5W35 2007
294.3'82—dc22 2006038051

Printed in the United States of America

www.modernlibrary.com

To Charles Hallisey, my teacher

Marco Polo describes a bridge, stone by stone. "But which is the stone that supports the bridge?" Kublai Khan asks.

"The bridge is not supported by one stone or another," Marco answers, "but only by the line of the arch that they form." Kublai Khan remains silent, reflecting. "Why do you speak to me of the stones? It is only the arch that matters to me."

Polo answers, "Without stones there is no arch."

—ITALO CALVINO, *Invisible Cities*

CONTENTS

THE TEXTS

GUIDE TO READING THE TEXTS

INTRODUCTION

A man of genius or a work of love and beauty will not come to order, can not be compounded by the best rules, but is always a new and incalculable result, like health. Don't rattle your rules in our ears; we must behave as we can.

—RALPH WALDO EMERSON

For millennia throughout Asia, the Buddha has been known as an "enlightened" figure whose vast wisdom illuminates the way to a life of meaning and genuine satisfaction. At present, in the West, his teachings are increasingly viewed by adherents, physicists, psychologists, and philosophers alike as exceptionally lucid descriptions of our human situation, and his prescribed practice of meditation as an effective means of awakening to that situation with clarity and equanimity.

The purpose of the present volume is to present the core teachings of the Buddha and, in so doing, engage the reader in an exploration of the Buddha's genius and of the beauty of his work. But since, as Emerson says, such a person and such a work never result from the limitations wrought by received convention, a book purporting to bring these two *to order* has some explaining to do. Anyone with even a passing familiarity with the subject knows that Buddhism comes in a staggering variety of cultural, doctrinal, and historical inflections. "Buddhism," it seems, may be qualified endlessly, evoking with equal ease images of flamboyant ritualism, luxuriant creativity, byzantine philosophizing, and tranquil contemplation. Just browse the shelves at your local bookstore: there is chanting Buddhism, meditating Buddhism, painting Buddhism, therapy Buddhism, martial arts Buddhism, Hollywood Buddhism, motorcycle maintenance Buddhism; there is Māhāyana Buddhism, Theravāda Buddhism, Vajrayāna Buddhism, Zen, Vipassana, Tantric, Dzogchen, Pure Land Buddhism; there is

Japanese, Tibetan, American, Thai, and [insert country name here] Buddhism. Now, for $19.99, for a limited time only (let's hope), you can have Buddhism-in-a-box Buddhism!

How can we sort this all out? There are two crucial factors mitigating against the streamlining of "Buddhism" that many readers presumably desire. First, contrary to Christianity, Judaism, and Islam, Buddhism is not a "religion of the book." There is no single volume that contains the teachings of the Buddha. The Buddha, in fact, wrote nothing at all. He wandered around a four-hundred-square-mile area of eastern India for forty-five years, verbally clarifying for others the nature of what he referred to as his "awakening"—his liberating insight into the nature of human existence. Eventually codified by the community of his followers in India and committed to writing in Sri Lanka, China, and beyond (this process is explained later), this nearly half century of teaching amounts to a virtual library of books. The second factor working against an easy solution to the present-day multiplicity of Buddhisms is the fact that although the Buddha became a renowned teacher with a substantial following during his lifetime, he never centralized his authority. Scholars speculate that the Buddha modeled his practitioner community on the power-sharing republican political structure of his own people, the Śākyas of northeastern India (see "Pronunciation of Sanskrit and Pāli Words"). In any case, shortly before he died, the Buddha insisted that no one assume the role of authority when he was gone. Hence, without a popelike figure to lay down the law, two predictable results manifested: the community splintered into numerous divergent sects and schools, and doctrinal disputes and variations in practice proliferated. The result of twenty-five hundred years of such diffusion is precisely the confusing cacophony of Buddhist voices beckoning us today from bookshelves and practice centers.

Can these voices be harmonized? Can so many Buddhisms be reconciled to the point of the *basic*, as the title of the present volume suggests? Do they all share some underlying commonality? If we want to claim that the varieties of Buddhism are fundamentally identical, as indeed many scholars and practitioners alike do, then an additional difficulty appears: What criteria will we use to locate that point of commonality? Remember the Greek mathematician Archimedes? He said that if he were given but a single fixed point on which to stand, he could move the

Earth off its foundation. Imagine that—is there such a point? Standing on the Earth, he would just revolve along with it; stepping off the Earth in order to gain a footing, he would fall into empty space. Similarly, we cannot locate a fixed vantage point—an Archimedean point—from which to make normative claims about Buddhism as a totality. We must formulate our claims either from within a particular tradition or from the outside altogether. The first stance is, from the perspective of the whole, too limited, while the second stance is, from the perspective of each particular tradition, too broad. This being the case, isn't the very notion of "basic teachings of the Buddha" vacuous?

THE JOURNEY OF THE BUDDHA'S TEACHINGS

In the simplest terms, the basic teachings of the Buddha consist of his forty-five-year-long effort to clarify to others what he considered to be the essential knowledge (*buddhi*) for human well-being. He referred to his own insight into this knowledge as an "awakening" (*bodhi*). Hence, his followers eventually gave him the epithet *buddha*, "one who is awakened." It is of course from this appellation that we get the term "Buddhism." But how do we get from one man's specific teachings to myriad forms of Buddhism? The story of how the Buddha's basic teachings gave rise to the multiple doctrinal, linguistic, ritual, cultural, and institutional traditions that call themselves "Buddhist" is, of course, filled with minute, complex detail. The details, moreover, must be culled from several scholarly disciplines, including philology, archaeology, sociology, history, and anthropology, to name but a few. In the present section, I hope to convey to the reader an impression of the process whereby the Buddha's teachings became so many Buddhisms.

PART ONE: FROM SEARCH TO COMMUNITY

The first part of the story covers the period from the Buddha's search for consequential knowledge to the codification of his teachings concerning this knowledge. This account is somewhat reconstructive and speculative in nature, though grounded in common sense and some historical data.*

* Readers interested in an extended biography of the Buddha can see John Strong, *The Buddha: A Short Biography* (Oxford: Oxford University Press, 2001).

After a six-year period of seeking out and training under reputable teachers, Siddhattha Gotama (ca. 480–400 B.C.E.; Sanskrit: Siddhārtha Gautama), the young man who would become known as the Buddha, isolated himself in a forest grove and strenuously applied himself to practice. Unlike for followers of the dominant social and religious group of the day, the Vedic Brahmans, "practice" for Gotama did not entail sacrificial and devotional actions aimed at coercing the divine forces held to be arrayed throughout the cosmos. Gotama had been inspired by adherents of the relatively new groups of practitioners who referred to themselves as *śramaṇas*, "seekers, wandering ascetics." Although there were significant differences among these *śramaṇa* groups, they shared a rejection of the presuppositions that underlay Vedic Brahmanism. These presuppositions included the status of the Vedas—the scriptural basis of Brahmanical knowledge and customs—as dogmatic revelation, the inviolability of the caste system (with Brahmans at the top), the presence of "divine" (*deva*) power, and the efficacy of rituals (created and administered by Brahmans) to manipulate these powers toward desired ends. Gotama saw merit, rather, in the ideas circulating among the *śramaṇa* communities concerning the causal role played by human thought, speech, and action (*karma*); the destructive influence of ignorance (*avidya*) regarding the nature of reality; the prospect of incessant painful existence (*saṃsāra*); and the possibility of releasing oneself from this human pain and dissatisfaction (*mokṣa, nirvāṇa*). Most important, perhaps, Gotama shared the basic orientation of the *śramaṇas* away from speculative supernaturalism and toward the actual establishment of human happiness here and now. This orientation would point as well to the necessity of meditation, rather than to devotion or sacrifice, as the primary practice in which to engage. Hence, sitting in his forest grove, under the shelter of a tree, Siddhattha Gotama exerted himself in meditation.

The fruit of his efforts was clear insight into the nature of reality. With this insight, Gotama could see the role that his mind played in shaping the various phenomena—sights, sounds, scents, tastes, feelings, and thoughts—that constituted his lived experience, or reality. He saw clearly a way out of the debilitating effects of what seemed to be ceaseless mental-physical-emotional reactivity to the incessant deluge of phenomena.

When his understanding was thorough and his knowledge complete, Gotama, like some, though not all, *śramaṇas,* made the decision to teach others what he had discerned about existence. So he spent the rest of his long life, an additional forty-five years, walking around a section of eastern India talking to, debating with, and teaching men and women—carpenters, barbers, farmers, shepherds, wandering ascetics, philosophers, princes, and even kings.

Over time the Buddha, similar to many teachers even today, likely developed specific formulae in order to stabilize the expression of his teachings and to ease reception and memorization for those who listened. As his body of teachings expanded and his followers increased, the Buddha, furthermore, probably organized and classified his teachings into basic sections and subsections to ensure safe (mnenomic) storage and to facilitate accurate transmission. This stabilization was even more crucial in an environment such as the Buddha's, of oral, rather than written, expression, storage, and transmission.

During his lifetime, the Buddha's followers, or, literally, "listeners" (Sanskrit: *śrāvaka*), formed into a substantial group. This group was known as the *bhikkhu saṅgha,* "the community of mendicants." As the *bhikkhus* dispersed throughout India to teach, they carried with them this roughly codified idiom of the teachings, refashioning it into the local vernaculars of those who would gather to listen. Laypeople, too, became part of the larger *saṅgha,* supporting the *bhikkhus* materially. Soon, as merchants and traders, these laypeople would contribute to the spread of the teachings throughout Asia.

Some Buddhist traditions hold that shortly after the Buddha's death the *bhikkhu saṅgha* convened a council to determine the wording and fix the organization of his teachings. Such a council, or "communal recitation" (*saṅgiti*), seems commonsensical when we reflect on the fact that the *śramaṅas* ("wanderers"), *bhikkhus* ("begging mendicants"), and *parivrajakas* ("peripatetics") who constituted the Buddha's community had, even during his lifetime, carried the teachings far and wide into the diverse cultural, geographical, and linguistic regions of ancient India. It is certainly not difficult to imagine both the emotional and the practical necessity of a communal gathering after an event as pivotal as the master's passing. In any case, tradition holds that three months after the death of the Buddha, some five hundred *bhikkhus* gathered in Rajagaha in eastern India to hear and approve recitations of both the rules governing the community (*vinaya*) and the teachings proper (*suttas*). Before each recitation, the reciting *bhikkhu* would say, "This is what I heard," indicating that he was recalling actual discourses he had personally heard the Buddha deliver. After each recitation the attending *bhikkhus* would debate the accuracy of the recitation and, eventually, confirm the wording. It is in this manner that the Buddha's teachings were stringently codified and the earliest Buddhist canon established. Since some schools' accounts of the first council mention rehearsal of a third category of teachings, we refer to the Buddhist canon from this date forward as the *tripiṭaka* (Pāli: *tipiṭaka*), "the three baskets," namely, *vinaya*, *sutta*, and *abhidhamma*. (These categories are explained further later.)

PART TWO: FROM CANON TO TRANSMISSION

The second part of the story of the Buddha's teachings covers the period from this initial codification to the present day. This story courses through the numerous fragmentations, proliferations, and cultural transmutations that the Buddhist schools and communities have undergone throughout history. Its telling is complex and meandering; it requires a careful analysis of the rich data of the sort mentioned in the previous section. Here, I can hope to give only a general impression of this process.*

Buddhist communities proliferated after the death of the Buddha. One primary reason for this development was the fact that the Buddha encouraged his followers to wander far and wide "for the welfare of the human multitude," teaching others according to their needs and in their local vernaculars. (Some communities, such as the Vedic Brahmans, cultivated technical languages, such as Sanskrit, for their teachings.) Another factor giving rise to the increase of Buddhist communities was the new tendency of the *bhikkhus* to reside permanently in settlements and monasteries, not just during the rainy season, as had been their way in the Buddha's day. The apparent ability of the Buddha's followers to attract patronage certainly contributed to this new state of affairs. The result of these developments was the simultaneous increase in the number of communities adhering

* Readers interested in a full account might want to consult Richard Robinson, Willard L. Johnson, and Thanissaro Bhikkhu, *Buddhist Religions: A Historical Introduction* (Belmont, Calif.: Wadsworth Publishing, 2004).

to the Buddha's teachings and the institutionalization of these communities.

So by one hundred years or so after the Buddha's death, there were numerous Buddhist communities, distinct, in varying degrees, from one another, dotting the Indian landscape. It isn't hard to imagine the kinds of differences that would have arisen concerning interpretation of doctrine and implementation of the monastic regulations, not to mention the variations in letter and spirit introduced by diverse languages, geographical regions, and cultures. And all along, different groups of "reciters" (*bhāṇakas*) were preserving the body of orally transmitted teachings. These *bhāṇakas* were the *bhikkhus* assigned particular teachings to memorize and, when requested, recite. It is true that the *bhāṇakas* periodically checked their versions of the teachings with other *bhāṇakas;* nonetheless, differences arose and positions hardened. (To get a sense of the forces of instability and change inherent in this system, just think of the "telephone" game you played in grade school.) Tradition holds that a second council was convened in Vaisali around one hundred years after the first council to resolve the points of contention that had arisen. Although the differences under investigation largely involved monastic regulations, these concerns were apparently serious enough to be pushing the various communities toward schism.

And indeed, it is around this time that we may speak of independent Buddhist schools (*nikāyas,* literally "groups") with diverse doctrinal orientations and distinct institutional infrastructures. Tradition holds that there were some eighteen such schools by the time the millennium came to a close. Sometimes we can glean certain points of contention within the early Buddhist world from the names of these schools. There was, for instance, the Sarvāstivāda sect, which held that "all things exist" (*sarvam asti*), that is, that past and future phenomena have actual material existence. There was the Sautrāntika, who looked to the dialogues of the Buddha (*sūtras*) as the final arbiter or end (*anta*) of doctrinal authority. There was the Lokottaravāda, which had the doctrine (*vāda*) that the Buddha possessed supernatural (*lokottara*) qualities. Sometimes we can see the importance of a teacher lineage in a sect's name, such as the Dharmaguptaka ("followers of Dharmagupta"), or the provenance of the sect, such as the Haimavata ("from the Himālaya region"). Finally, there was the Theravāda (Sanskrit: Sthaviravāda). The Theravāda is the variety of Buddhism that became dominant in Sri Lanka, Thailand, Burma, Cambodia, and Laos. Theravāda's self-understanding as a conservative tradition is revealed in the designation itself: "those who subscribe to the doctrine (*vāda*) of the elders (*thera*)." Indeed, throughout the centuries down to the present day, Theravāda has resisted the more substantive innovations that were developed within other Buddhist communities. Of the "eighteen schools" (the number shouldn't be taken literally), only the Theravāda has survived to the present day—although not without its own internal schisms.

The Theravāda is a particularly important Buddhist school for reasons other than its longevity and relative conservatism. According to Theravādin historical accounts, the great Indian emperor Asoka (270–232 B.C.E., that is, before the Common Era; replaces B.C., "before Christ") sent his son Mahinda, a Buddhist *bhikkhu,* to Sri Lanka as an ambassador of "the beneficial teachings" (*dharma*). There, Mahinda converted King Tisya and founded the first *bhikkhu saṅgha* on the island. (Similarly, Asoka's daughter is held to have founded the first order of *bhikkhunis,* or nuns.) With royal patronage underwriting the building of monasteries and supporting the *saṅgha,* Theravāda easily gained a powerful foothold in Sri Lanka and indeed has continued to flourish there to this very day.

But the histories report the occurrence of a potentially devastating event in the year 29 C.E. When Mahinda came to Sri Lanka, he brought with him the entire Buddhist canon (presumably via accompanying *bhāṇakas*). The traditional view (there is no actual evidence) is that the version of the canon transmitted by Mahinda was precisely that which was recited at the first council. Tradition holds, furthermore, that this original version was pristinely transmitted, memorized, mnemonically stored, and further transmitted for the next two hundred years, when the very existence of Buddhism on the island was threatened.

A Theravādin historical, or really quasi-historical, text, the *Dīpavaṃsa,* relates that during the reign of King Vaṭṭagāmaṇi Abaya (29–17 C.E.), the kingdom was devastated by civil war. Realizing the precariousness of the Buddha's teachings—dependent, as they were, on the health of the monks and nuns who preserved them—and fearing their irretrievable loss, the monks recorded the teachings on birch bark and safely stored them away for future generations. It is interesting to note that one sense of the term *sutta,* which is cognate with the

English word "suture," is "to stitch together, to sew, to weave." (Our English term "text" also reveals the close relationship between ideas and textiles.)

The traditional view is that this version of the canon preserved both the original language and the original wording of the Buddha's teachings. As we will see, the matter is not so simple. But in Sri Lanka, at least, the teachings of the Buddha had found a safe, secure home.

In the rest of Asia, however, the story of the Buddha's teachings developed further. After the turn of the millennium and into the Middle Ages, contentious issues similar to those affecting the earliest communities would eventually give birth to two revolutionary developments within Buddhism. The first of these distinctly new directions is known as the Mahāyāna. Again, its very name—"the great (*mahā*) vehicle (*yāna*)"—reveals its adherents' view that it represents a monumental expansion from the older sects—which they referred to collectively, and pejoratively, as the Hināyana, "the small vehicle"—in both the doctrine and social application of Buddhism. Mahāyāna emerged at the beginning of the first millennium and spread to regions in northern India and beyond, to Tibet, China, Korea, Japan, and Vietnam. The second great innovation flourished in India from the sixth to the twelfth centuries, after which Buddhism largely disappeared from the subcontinent. This revolutionary form of Buddhism is known as Vajrayāna, "the diamond (*vajra*) vehicle (*yāna*)," in reference to its claim to be in possession of practices that lead the practitioner to the indestructible (adamantine, or diamond-like) mind of a *buddha*. The popularity of the Vajrayāna in India corresponds precisely to the period when Tibetans were scouring India in search of Buddhist teachings, texts, and teachers to bring back to Tibet. In some cases they found what they sought in the great monasteries of eastern India; in other cases, in isolated forests, deserted charnel grounds, and mountain retreats. Thus, it is in Tibetan communities—now largely exiled in India, Europe, and North America—that the several varieties of Vajrayāna have been preserved.

Both of these new forms of Buddhism were characterized by creative literary developments. In Mahāyāna *sūtras* and Vajrayāna *tantras*, ingenious fashionings of ancient doctrines and practices were worked out and fresh, often startling, innovations developed. In contrast, the Theravāda endeavored to preserve what it understood to be the ancient forms of the teachings as expressed in their most ancient formulation, namely, the *suttas.* So, the threefold grouping of Buddhism into Theravāda, Mahāyāna, and Vajrayāna as a means of arranging the many Buddhist sects and schools into basic family types can be used to organize the thousands of volumes that constitute Buddhist literature. Such a division is borne out in the three great collections of Buddhist literature, referred to by scholars as the Pāli canon, the Chinese canon, and the Tibetan canon. (These collections are discussed further shortly.)

So, as time went on, the Buddha's teachings meandered throughout ancient and medieval India, transmuting into the countless local vernaculars they encountered along the way. Who knows which ones and how many? They moved northward along the upper and lower Silk Roads, through Gandhara, Kashmir, Gilgit, and Tunhuang, coursing through China, Mongolia, Korea, and Japan. They traveled over the sea routes to the southeast, into Thailand, Burma, Laos, Cambodia, Vietnam, and Indonesia, coursing through Tibet and Nepal in the medieval period, through cultures high and low, through languages, time, and space, into the modern era, through England, Germany, France, and North America. In every instance, what counted as "the Buddha's teachings" transformed into the idiom of those who stood on the meandering pathway of those teachings, open-armed in acceptance. Really, this incessant meandering was wholly predictable. After all, what should we expect when a teacher, such as the Buddha, insists from the outset that his disciples go forth, no two in the same direction, and instruct others "in their native tongue"? Being in the service of "the welfare of the human multitude," how could the Buddha's teachings *not* exhibit such fluidity?

—

It may create some perspective for the reader of a book titled *Basic Teachings of the Buddha*—a book, moreover, that presents a mere sixteen texts—to provide some hard numbers relating to the three abovementioned Buddhist canons. These numbers concern works held by the traditions to be "the word of the Buddha" (*buddhavacana*) only:

Pāli canon: 5,434 texts (classified as "teaching discourses," or *suttas*), plus fifteen book-length works (classified as "short works," or *khuddaka*, ranging between roughly nine modern printed pages and five hundred);

Chinese canon: 151 texts (translations of the previously mentioned *suttas,* but called *āgamas,* or "traditions"), 612 Mahāyāna works (*sūtras*), 572 Vajrayāna works (*tantras*);

Tibetan canon: 270-text *sūtra* section in 30 oversize-format volumes (includes a few *sutta* translations), 33 additional volumes of Mahāyāna *sūtras,* 300-plus *tantras* in 30 volumes.

(The canons include much more than the teachings of the Buddha. There are in addition some 300 volumes of monastic regulations, philosophical works, narrative texts, histories, commentaries, and even treatises on drama, medicine, and poetics.)

Tedious text-critical examinations of these canons by scholars yield a significant fact: through centuries of transmission, different canonical versions of the same text rarely reveal any but the most inconsequential differences. These differences mainly involve minor alterations in style, organization, and orthography. Furthermore, a comparative reading of the Mahāyāna *sūtras* and Vajrayāna *tantras* would lead most readers to conclude that even these works constitute innovations not so much in doctrinal substance as in style and tenor. There will always be exceptions to this consistency, but I believe that a careful analysis of Buddhist literature as a whole will generally show that "the basic teachings of the Buddha" somehow always remain the basic teachings of the Buddha.

THE IDIOM AND MEANING OF THE BUDDHA'S TEACHINGS

Idiom

The Buddha purportedly asked those who would explore his teachings to examine both their idiom and their meaning. Narrowly construed, the idiom and meaning of the teachings are closely bound up with the phraseology and significance indicated by the Buddha himself and roughly replicated, we may assume, by his earliest disciples. But, contrary to the traditional view, we do not know what that wording was; in fact, we do not even know in which *language* the Buddha uttered those words. None of the versions of the teachings as we now have them is in a language that the Buddha would have spoken, and each reveals considerable editing over a considerable span of time. So, the original—though without a doubt continuously developing—idiom and meaning being unavailable to us for examination, we must apply broader definitions of these terms.

For the purposes of the present book, the task of determining what counts as the proper phraseology of the teachings removes us some four centuries and fifteen hundred miles from our source (the Buddha in India), to the island of Sri Lanka. It was here, as explained in the preceding section, that around 29 C.E. the memory of the Buddha's idiom was transferred from actual oral utterance into literature. It is from the wording of this literature that I am deriving "basic teachings of the Buddha."

According to the ancient and venerable Theravādin tradition of Buddhism, this transference coursed directly from the lips of the teacher to the pen of the scribe. But we have seen how tradition, as Henry David Thoreau said of education, "makes a straight canal out of a meandering brook." So the question arises: How can we ever determine that it is at *this* particular point, at *this* particular bend, that a responsible rendering of the Buddha's teaching is to be found?

To answer this question, it may be helpful to take the metaphor further. As a waterway courses through the land, it deposits particularly generous amounts of fertile silt at certain points along the way. This silt provides the conditions for luxuriant vegetation; and this vegetation provides the conditions for vibrant life; so, over time, a civilization emerges there. Similarly, there are rich deposits in the topography of Buddhism; these deposits are the places where idiom and meaning have coursed into memory, and memory into literature.

Meaning

In imploring his followers to set off in separate directions to instruct people in their native tongues, the Buddha set the course for the manifold trajectories of idiom that are exhibited today in the various Buddhist canons. And just as idiom would course into canonical literature, meaning would crystallize into teacher-centric institution.

Today, a historically unprecedented number and variety of Buddhist organizations with roots in Asia have begun to settle and gain acceptance in twenty-first-century America as offering viable options for living and practice. A list of these organizations' charismatic founders would read as a who's who of international Buddhism through the ages:

Atiśa, Dōgen, Nichiren, Shinran, Milarepa, Naropa, Tsongkhapa, Lin Chi, Hōnen, Seung San, Shunryu Suzuki, Ajahn Chah, Buddhadāsa Bhikkhu—the list would fill several pages. The institutions founded by this multitude of Buddhist teachers *all* lay claim to "the meaning of the Buddha." But since intra-Buddhist dialogue is remarkably non-polemic on the surface, this claim of privilege and purity of meaning does its work invisibly, for the most part.

So a historically responsible inquiry into "the meaning of the Buddha" must pick up on one of these institutional trajectories. Questions of the form "What did the Buddha mean by *X*?" can be broached only *via* the traditions—the lineage-based Buddhist institutions—whose texts, teachings, rituals, et cetera, constitute answers to the various questions of meaning. "What did the Buddha mean by *X*?" "Well, according to Dōgen and the Japanese Sōtō Zen tradition . . . On the other hand, according to Buddhaghosa and the Southeast Asian Theravādin traditions . . . And according to Marpa and the Tibetan Kagyü tradition . . ." Buddhist institutions, then, are the arbiters of "the meaning of the Buddha." And, being *arbiters* (the Latin term for "judge"), they can make the rules—can't they?

"No, they can't," I hear the Buddha say.

"Tell them not to rattle their rules in our ears," Emerson concurs.

And I imagine Emerson as my ally, pressing the matter further: "Do you, dear reader, seek a result that is *new and incalculable, like health*? Assuming that you do, and wishing that for you, this book has been conceived in a way that invites you to explore the idiom and meaning of the Buddha *behaving as you can,* as you are, just as you are. Doing so, who knows what (and whose) genius and beauty might come to order?"

Some Conclusions

We can draw several conclusions from the scenarios outlined in the preceding pages.

First, the idiom and meaning of the Buddha's teachings exhibit an equalizing measure of fluidity and stability. Though adaptable across cultural, linguistic, temporal, and geographical lines, a recognizable core of concerns animates the teachings throughout.

Second, our primary means of accessing the Buddha's idiom and meaning—other than a living teacher—is Buddhist literature. And all Buddhist literature, whatever its origins, is just that: literature. It is always words on the page, words in the ear. The terms used by the world's religious traditions, such as "canon," "scripture," "sacred work," "holy book," "the revealed word," are at heart just ways of dressing up crafted human compositions as pristinely "religious." Whether Buddhist, Muslim, Hindu, or Christian, such works are *never* pristine: every page of every "sacred" work is smudged with the handprints of its creators through the ages. This observation is not meant to belittle the claims made by the multitude of humanity concerning their precious texts; it is simply an effort to remind the reader that we are concerned here *in the first instance* with literature, with compositions and writings, pure and simple.

Third, being literature, Buddhist textual material is always *tropological.* That is, it is always an instance of a particular and discernible *turn* (called a *tropos,* from the Greek, in literary studies)—a turn of speech (for the sake of rhetoric, recall, and memorization, for instance), a turn from utterance to narrative (from "what the Buddha said" to "what the Buddha's followers—and followers' followers ad infinitum—said the Buddha said"), a turn from *that* language and culture to *this* (Indian to Chinese to American), a turn from that community's concerns to this community's (mendicant to monk to lay; craftsman to businessperson to academic to you), a turn from the spoken word (*buddhavacana,* "idiom of the Buddha") to the written ("text," "canon," *sutta*).

The fourth conclusion that may be drawn is that the *writer* of a book on Buddhism stands, like Archimedes, on the spinning sphere of history; and the fifth is that the *reader* of a book on Buddhism stands, like Archimedes, on the spinning sphere of history. Although it would be convenient, for the sake of neatness, to do so, I find it impossible to refute the literary critic Harold Bloom's comment in this regard that "no reader [or writer], however professional, or humble, or pious, or disinterested, or 'objective,' or modest, or amiable, can describe any person's relationship to a prior text without taking up a stance no less tropological than that occupied by the text itself." This insight will prove valuable for our purposes here if it prompts the reader to reflect for a moment on the inevitability of such a stance (you within the flow of history) and the nature of your particular stance (we all bring to the material certain interests, hopes, biases). I hope, too, that Bloom's comment will pique in the reader an abiding suspicion toward any author who presents himself or herself, and the Buddhist material, as standing clear of all *turns.*

Finally, the Buddhist canonical collections are particularly rich deposits in the vast *idiomatic* topography of Buddhism. Since the Pāli canon preserves particularly ancient specimens of the Buddha's idiom, in the present volume "the idiom of the Buddha's teachings" means this particular formulation of the teachings. And it is, moreover, on the basis of this wording that I aim to explore "the meaning of the Buddha's teachings."

Why the Pāli Canon?

Why should we use the Pāli texts, the *suttas*, preserved by the Theravādin communities of Sri Lanka and Southeast Asia, as our basis for "the Buddha's idiom" as opposed to, say, the Chinese versions of the same old works, the *āgamas*, or even the later Mahāyāna *sūtras* or Vajrayāna *tantras*? There are three good reasons for this decision.

(1.) The Pāli canon is the only extant *complete Indian* collection of Buddhist texts. While there were certainly other whole collections, most of this literature would have been destroyed by the invading Islamic armies that, by the end of the twelfth century, had devastated the great Indian Buddhist monastic libraries. Since the Pāli collection had been transmitted as far away as Sri Lanka in the third century B.C.E., it was spared this fate. In Sri Lanka, the canon has been preserved with great care down to the present day by the lone surviving sect of ancient Indian Buddhism, namely, the Theravāda. This is not to say that the texts have not undergone alterations over time. In fact, to speak of *a* Pāli canon is somewhat misleading. There are, for instance, Burmese and Thai recensions of the canon—though nonetheless in Pāli—in addition to the Sri Lankan version. There are also plenty of instances of later scribal emendations. In fact, some of these alterations occurred as late as the twelfth century. But again, the insubstantiality of the disagreements between these versions serves more to accentuate the consistency of Buddhist textual transmission since the Buddha's own day than to reveal serious divergence. So, if your aim is to get as close to "the Buddha's idiom" as possible, the Pāli *suttas* are the logical starting point.

(2.) Linguistically, too, the Pāli canon holds an advantage over the Chinese and Tibetan collections. We don't know what the Buddha's mother tongue was. But assuming that he followed his own advice, he would have taught in the local dialects of his listeners. Scholars refer to the vernacular languages spoken at the time of the Buddha as Middle Indo-Aryan, and distinguish it from Sanskrit, which was the learned language of the time. It is a common misconception that Pāli is one such regional vernacular. In fact, the term *pāli* simply means "text." Nowhere in the entire canon itself does the term appear; rather, it apparently derives from the usage in later commentaries on the canonical literature, which referred to the *pālibhāsā*, "the language of the texts." As might be expected from a two-thousand-year transmission history, Pāli, "the language of the texts," also exhibits linguistic features from other Middle Indo-Aryan dialects, as well as attempts to transform certain terms into Sanskrit—a process known as "sanskritization."

How do these points about language bear on my decision to translate from the Pāli? Look at an example close to home. William Blake's language, though fine English, sounds somewhat foreign even to present-day English speakers. Add to this everyday English usage his technical vocabulary, and Blake's language becomes nearly impenetrable. This, though his language is English and only two hundred years old. Now, imagine how Blake comes across in Mongolian. Then, imagine the Mongolian Blake translated into Japanese. Blake's technical vocabulary, which he chose with great care, can really only be roughly approximated in another language. But if I were a Japanese reader of Blake, I would want a translation from English, not from Mongolian. The Pāli *suttas*, of course, are certainly not to the Buddha what *Songs of Innocence* and *Songs of Experience* are to Blake. The *suttas* are *already* a translation—and an edited one at that. But this point adds even more ballast to the decision to look to the Pāli canon as the basis for what has become the multitudinous assortment known today as "the teachings of the Buddha." Simply put, the language of the Pāli canon mediates the conceptual world of ancient Buddhism, and probably of the Buddha himself, to an extent impossible for Chinese and Tibetan, or for that matter, English.

(3.) Just as students of the history of philosophy sometimes quip that the bulk of work done in their discipline is but a footnote to Plato, it is arguable that the bulk of the developments within Buddhism over the centuries are but elaborations on, local adaptations of, and cultural inflections of what we find in the Pāli texts. This goes for central Mahāyāna notions such as emptiness (Sanskrit: *śūnyatā;* Pāli: *sunyatā* and *anattā*) and compassion (Sanskrit and Pāli: *karuṇā*) as well as for foundational Vajrayāna ritual practices such as recitation of *mantras* for subduing hostile forces (Pāli: *mantas* and *parittas*). In this regard, the *suttas* can as a rule be shown to be the fountainhead of subsequent teachings, even those that have been radically developed. With the exception of a remarkably minuscule number of doctrinally anomalous traditions, the chorus of Buddhisms evoked in the first paragraphs of this introduction can, by and large, be traced to this source, to the *suttas* of the Pāli canon.

WHAT IS A *SUTTA*?

But what, precisely, are these *suttas* that I am claiming occupy such a prominent place in Buddhism as the basis of the teachings? The Pāli term *sutta* (the better-known Sanskrit equivalent is *sūtra*) refers to the dialogues that the Buddha engaged in with others. The reader will quickly notice, however, that as dialogues, these discussions are so radically one-sided as to be better viewed as discourses, or sometimes even lectures or speeches. Quite contrary to Socrates' dialogues as recorded by Plato, the Buddha's dialogues as recorded by his followers involve only the most minimal exchange of ideas. Whereas Socrates' interlocutors routinely offer thoughtful rebuttals, and even complex counterarguments, to his positions, the Buddha's conversation partners routinely appear merely as foils for his positions. That is certainly not to say that the Buddha's interlocutors don't pose difficult questions, make legitimate counterarguments, or flat out disagree with the Buddha. They do all of this and more. They do not, however, do so *vigorously enough* to satisfy what most of us, I imagine, would consider the basic requirements of a genuinely engaged discussion partner.

Why do the *suttas* present us with such weak interlocutors? Anyone with even a passing familiarity with Indian culture knows that it has a deep and ancient tradition of robust intellectual debate and religious skepticism. Given that fact, the *suttas* are certainly not full records of the Buddha's discussions with men and women who would have, in reality, often been formidable partners in dialogue: ascetics, mendicants, teachers, philosophers, princes, and kings. But partiality notwithstanding, I am unaware of any good reasons to doubt that the *suttas* do record accurate records of the *teachings* the Buddha imparted to his interlocutors. Herein may lie the reason for the apparent passivity of the conversation partners. The early compilers of the *suttas* were not *interested* in what the interlocutors had to say; their interest lay exclusively in what their teacher, the Buddha, had to say. For these compilers and preservers of the *suttas*, the crux of the matter was in each instance to record *the Buddha's* words. That those words were in response to someone's query or comment was just a natural point of departure, stemming, furthermore, from the fact that the Buddha was very much a public teacher. So while the *suttas* are clearly not verbatim dialogues, they are just as clearly records of the teachings that the Buddha imparted to those with whom he engaged in dialogue.

As we saw earlier, the discussions that the Buddha had with others were first recorded and organized mnemonically and eventually written down on birch bark and literally sewn together as a book. While the woven book (*sutta*, "text") ensures a certain degree of material preservation of the teachings, it does not ensure their vitality. For this to occur, the teachings must be further woven into the hearer-reader's attitude toward living. This rich and complex interweaving of dialogue between the Buddha and a seeker, the physical embodiment of this as a text, and the application of this in the life of the reader constitute the real *sutta*.

The collection of these *suttas*, known as the *piṭaka* (literally "basket"), constitutes the Buddhist canon. The term *piṭaka* is quite apt. Baskets are universally used for storage and preservation; and I have seen that in building construction in India and Nepal, bricks are placed and passed on in baskets even today. Hence, *piṭaka* suggests storage, preservation, and transmission.

To get a sense of the place of the *suttas* within the canon as a whole, it will be useful to consider this overview:

1. *Vinayapiṭaka*. This *piṭaka* contains rules and regulations governing the details of monastic life. Examples of what you will find here include rules governing entrance into the order, the use of medicine, the consumption of food, the wearing of clothes, the utilization of furniture, the daily operation of a community dwelling, and so on.
2. *Suttapiṭaka*. This is the section preserving the *suttas*. It is composed of five collections containing the "ocean of *dhamma*," the doctrines and practices that constitute the idiom or word of the

Buddha (*buddhavacana*). Texts taken from these five sections constitute the heart of the present book. The five collections are:

i. *Dīghanikāya.* The "collection of long" discourses. This section contains 34 lengthy *suttas* that, in many ways, serve as a broad introduction to the teachings. I say this because in the *suttas* themselves, the Buddha is often discussing his teachings with outsiders, those who are unfamiliar with them.

ii. *Majjhimanikāya.* The "collection of middle-length" discourses. This section contains 152 *suttas.* The Buddha is engaged here with numerous types of people from throughout Indian society. Since these people range from accomplished teachers from other orders to unlearned villagers, from his own followers to those who are opposed to him, the teachings in this section take numerous tacks. Nonetheless, while some of the *suttas* here are general and broad in scope, as might be expected, most are extremely detailed, pointing to the Buddhist community as the main recipient.

iii. *Saṃyuttanikāya.* The "collection of connected" discourses of the Buddha. The 2,889 *suttas* of this section are among the most thorough and penetrating of all of Buddhist literature. The insights revealed here are those that are central to the Buddha's teachings on the nature of the person, the phenomenal world, and the relationship between the two. As such, these texts presuppose on the side of the interlocutor extensive experience in the study and practice of the teachings. The final section of this collection, the *Mahāvagga,* "Great Book," contains what the Buddha himself referred to as his core teachings.

iv. *Aṅguttaranikāya.* The "collection of numerical" discourses. The 2,308 *suttas* in this section are more or less summative. They thus appear to recapitulate points made in *suttas* throughout the *Suttapiṭaka* as a way to facilitate quick recall of vital aspects of the teachings. The tactic of numerical sequencing, perhaps, is indicative of this function: "There are two kinds of happiness, namely . . . ," "There are four types of people, namely . . . ," et cetera.

v. *Khuddaka.* The "collection of small" books. This is a group of fifteen individual works that are held to have been added to the *piṭaka* later than the other collections. All of these works are of anonymous authorship. The most well known of these are the *Dhammapada*, the *Jātaka* (stories, largely ethical in nature, of the Buddha's previous lives), and the *Theragāthā* and *Therīgāthā* (poetic expressions of realization by early male and female followers).

3. *Abhidhammapiṭaka.* The "basket of works elaborating on the teachings." This collection consists of seven works that examine specific aspects of the *sutta* material in minute detail. Themes of the various texts include enumeration of the elements (called *dhamma*) of existence, investigation of the unfolding of mental moments or factors; the nature of causation, and a description of personality types. One of the better-known texts in this collection is the *Kathāvatthu*, which contains an account of numerous contested points and views among the earliest schools of Buddhism (of which, at the time, the Theravāda was but one).

—

The themes covered in the *Suttapiṭaka* constitute the core concerns of the Buddha. These themes include those that preoccupy our modern disciplines of psychology (for example, the nature of mind, the processes of perception), religion (the question of supernatural agency, the practice of meditation), ethics (the necessity and means of self-restraint and moderation), and philosophy (the nature of reality, the modes of knowledge). But despite this variety, in the end, the Buddha says, his teachings are like the salty ocean. As vast and various as they are, the teachings contain but a single taste: that of *awakening*. They teach slumbering, deluded, dissatisfied people the means to transform themselves into ones who are bright, clear, and wide awake.

A BUDDHA, A READER, AND A TEXT

In the Beginning: A Buddha, Maybe

Once upon a time, the Buddha was a bombastic braggadocio. Considering that he lived ensconced in his palace as the coddled prince Siddhārtha until he was nearly thirty years old, then isolated himself in remote forest thickets until middle age, what should we expect? He certainly could not have developed any of the skills in interpersonal communication required for an effective "caravan leader" or "pointer of the way," as he would eventually refer to his teaching prowess. No, in the beginning, the fully awakened one was not so obviously "the teacher supreme."

In the beginning, the Buddha sat at the foot of a tree deep in the forest in a state of unutterable delight and ease. Rising after several days, he set out on the road to the deer park on the outskirts of Varanasi. He had determined to locate his five former companions, with whom he had practiced severe asceticism until being abandoned by them as a backslider. The Buddha's intention was to teach the group "the *dhamma*," that is, the insights that led to his own realization of life's ultimate refuge, "unborn unsurpassable peace, unbinding, *nirvāṇa*." Here is the Buddha's own version of what happened next (this firsthand account can be found at *Majjhimanikāya* 26).

> An ascetic named Upaka saw me on the road between Gayā and the place of my awakening, and, on seeing me, spoke to me as follows. "Your faculties are clear, brother. Your complexion is pure and bright. Under whose supervision have you become a seeker? Who is your teacher? Whose teachings do you accept?" When this was said, I replied to Upaka in verse.

"Master of all,
knower of all, am I.
Unstained among
the things of the world,
I abandon all.
With the withering of craving,
I am liberated.
Having realized this condition
completely on my own
to whom should I point as a teacher?

"I have no teacher;
a person like me cannot be found.
In this world with its resplendent beings,
I have no equal.

> "For, in this world,
> I am highly accomplished.
> I am the teacher supreme.
> I, alone, am fully and soundly awakened.
> Cooled am I, and quenched.
>
> "To set in motion
> the wheel of teaching
> I am going to the city of Kasi.
> In a world become blind,
> I beat the drum of the deathless."
>
> Upaka responded, "According to your claims, brother, you must be an infinite conqueror." To which I replied:
>
> "Conquerors are those who, like me,
> have dissolved habituated impulses.
> I have conquered detrimental qualities.
> Therefore, Upaka, I am a conqueror."
>
> When this had been uttered, the ascetic Upaka said, "Maybe, brother," and, shaking his head, he set off on a side road.

"Master of all"? "Knower of all"? Having no peer even among the gods? How would *you* respond to such claims—spoken, no less, in ostentatious verse? *An infinite conqueror! Sure, brother. Whatever, brother. May it be so, bro! Maybe, brother, maybe.* Wouldn't you, too, just shake your head and walk away?

The Buddha's lesson—that a teacher must *earn* his prerogative to teach others—did not end there. Here are his own words:

> Then, wandering gradually, I arrived at Varanasi, at the deer park in Isipatana, where the group of five mendicants were staying. They saw me coming from the distance and, on seeing me, made an agreement with one another as follows:
>
> "Brothers, here comes the seeker Gotama, living luxuriously, slacking in his effort, and backsliding into luxury. He does not deserve to be greeted with words of reverence, or by our rising from our seats, or by us respectfully taking his bowl and outer robe. But a

> seat should nonetheless be prepared. If he wants to, he can sit down."
>
> But as I approached, the five mendicants were unable to keep their agreement. One of them, rising up to greet me, respectfully took my bowl and outer robe. Another prepared a seat. Another put out water for washing my feet. However, they still addressed me by name and as "brother."

The Buddha then told his five former companions that he should no longer be addressed by his given name. He was now an *arahant*—a person who is supremely accomplished. He was now a *tathāgata*—a person who has come to a realization of the nature of reality. He was now a *buddha*—a person who has awakened. But these claims, too, met with skepticism. The Buddha's former companions insisted it simply could not be the case that someone like him might attain such distinction in knowledge and wisdom. The discussion went back and forth in this manner as the Buddha persisted in his claims. Finally, he asked the mendicants to reflect honestly on his present demeanor, saying, "Have I ever spoken like this before?" Signaling a shift in their view of their former companion, the five responded with the sign of deference sought by the Buddha: "No, *bhante,* no, sir." So now the Buddha could begin teaching.

> Listen! The deathless has been realized. I will instruct you. I will teach you the way. Practicing as instructed, by realizing for yourselves here and now through direct insight, you will soon enter on and dwell in the ultimate refuge of the higher life, for the sake of which people properly go from their home into homelessness.

The Buddha says that he then proceeded to instruct the five men over a period of time until each realized for himself an insight so profound and genuine that he could joyfully declare: "My liberation is unshakable!"

In the Midst: A Model Reader

What should we make of the fact that the Buddha's first attempts to teach were met with such skeptical resistance? Something eventually enabled him to convince the group of five former companions that he was indeed an *arahant,* a *tathāgata,* a *buddha,* as he claimed. What was it? Was it something that he said? Was it a change in his demeanor? To answer these questions, as well as the question of their meaning, I would ask you, the reader, simply to look into the midst of things. In doing so, I aim to impart something of the spirit with which you will, I hope, read this book.

Looking into the midst of things, we see, first of all, a model reader. Such a reader is in the midst of the story just presented. This reader is composed of the combined spirit of Upaka and each of the five mendicants. That is, we can see in these literary figures traits that would, if taken to heart, strengthen the empirical reader's reading. One quality that makes this figure a model is the *ability to resist* coming under the spell of flamboyant language. Religious literature is immediately recognizable as religious in large part because of its extravagant language. Such language is *not* inviting the reader to examine closely, much less argue with, the claims that it is conveying.

Recent research in the field of cognitive science suggests that, when coupled with certain social factors, there is a correspondence between the grand language of a religious proclamation and a person's inclination to accept that proclamation as plausible. Our minds are captivated, awestruck, and enchanted by correspondingly captivating, awesome, and charming language. Such language makes a spectacle of itself; it insists on being granted our attention or, more aptly, our devotion. In so doing, it weaves its way into our thinking patterns and lodges there, in much the same manner as a tantalizing piece of gossip courses easily through a social circle.

As provocative and potent as the Buddha's words appear, really he presented Upaka and the group of five with nothing but assertions dressed up in flamboyant guise. Each of these men resisted the seductive pull of such language, eventually compelling the Buddha to take a different tack. Ideally you, too, will resist an easy acceptance of the Buddha's words, examining them at the most basic level of meaning and usage. As we will see, the Buddha himself will insist on this approach; and he will do so for reasons that have everything to do with the very possibility of *your* insight "here and now" into matters of real consequence.

The reader in the midst of the text, then, is a model reader for an additional reason. This reader, while cautious, nonetheless *responds with openness* to the Buddha's prescription for verifying his statements. As reluctant as the five mendicants were to accept the Buddha's claims, they could not simply disregard his confident assertion that they, too, could know for themselves here and now what he himself had realized about human existence. Perhaps the Buddha was so persistent because of his audience: it consisted of people whose lives were oriented principally toward the very "accomplishment" that he was claiming for himself. So, like this model audience, the real reader of this book will, I hope, regard the teachings presented herein as at least potentially verifiable. (In this regard, Upaka represents a reader who does not fulfill the ideal. He turned away before the Buddha could offer a means for verifying his claims.) To do so, the reader must, like the mendicants in the text, be prepared to go from "home into homelessness." The reader must, that is, be open to abandoning the comfort of his or her habitual ways of thinking, speaking, and acting. And the reader must be willing to "practice as instructed," to cultivate the way of being that constitutes the sole purpose of the teachings presented by the Buddha.

In the End: Nothing Is Got for Nothing

Why all of these "musts"? Because in the end "nothing is got for nothing." That is what Emerson said about literature in general. Or, in Umberto Eco's memorable phrase, because books are "lazy machines." In the texts, those already quoted and those to come, the Buddha is placing demands on his audience: his interlocutor is assumed to have specific aspirations and abilities and the willingness to work at developing those qualities. If the interlocutor lacks the capacity for the specific kind of work that is required, then he or she will be incapable of productively receiving the words of the Buddha. Eco says that the process of fruitful reception, or reading, begins only once the reader consciously decides *to see* the intention of the text. This seeing is the beginning of work. The Buddha indeed does not teach the mendicants until they make just such a decision, evidenced by their referring to him finally as *"bhante."*

The model reader, as we saw, is in the text in the guise of an appropriately responding interlocutor. But that reader is a temporally and spatially unbound prototype requiring the collaboration of a *real* reader, an empirical person. Collaboration is the key. An empirical reader is an agent in the real world whose task as a reader is to discern with care the intentions of the text. The text itself, of course, lacks any real instrumental power. It is in this sense that it is aptly compared to a "lazy machine."* The text offers guidance and gives signals, but the reader must do the work of generating real-world effects via these signals. The promise of the *suttas*—the intention of the Buddha's words—is that the effects are, as the Buddha puts it, "conspicuous, palpable, leading the practitioner to *come and see,* and to be personally realized." Personally realized, that is, by a *real person.* Nothing is got for nothing. So, are you willing to do the work?

Throughout the present book, it is to this complex of signals and conjectured intentions that I am referring when I ascribe agency to "the *sutta,*" or to "the text." By "practitioner" I mean that person, both within the text (as interlocutor and as model reader) and without the text (as empirical reader—you), who labors to realize the text's intentions and whom the text, from its side, labors to create.

ON PHYSIOLOGY AND THE EPHEMERAL IMAGE

After the Buddha had taught the *dhamma* to his five former companions, his reputation as a teacher began to spread. Eventually, sixty-one men had gathered around him. This group constituted the beginning of what would become the great Buddhist *saṅgha,* or "community of practitioners," both lay and ordained. The Buddha trained this group until he had determined that they, just like he himself, were "freed from all snares," that is, fully accomplished and thus qualified to teach. Then, with words that would become paradigmatic for the propagation of Buddhism throughout the world, the Buddha dispersed the group:

> Go, wander for the welfare of the human multitude, for the happiness of the human multitude, out of compassion for the world, for the benefit, the good, and the happiness of people and resplendent beings. Let no two of you go in the same direction. Teach both the meaning and the idiom of the *dhamma,* which is good in the beginning, good in the middle, and good in the end. Manifest the com-

* For a closer look at Eco's ideas mentioned here, I recommend Umberto Eco, *Six Walks in the Fictional Woods* (Cambridge, Mass.: Harvard University Press, 1994).

> pletely fulfilled and perfectly purified life of training. There are people who have but little dust in their eyes, who are falling away because they have not heard of the way (*dhamma*). They will understand the teachings (*dhamma*). I, too, will go—to Senānigama in Uruvela—to teach the *dhamma*. (*Saṃyuttanikāya* 1.4.5)

A close look at this passage will throw some light on certain issues at the heart of the present book. It will also allow me to make explicit to you some of my own views concerning the Buddha, the Buddha's teachings, the end of the teachings, and you, the reader of this book. In mentioning these points here, I am really hoping to create the conditions for a dialogue between the reader and the text (both the book as a whole and *suttas* in particular). Partly this effort involves giving my implicit argument—after all, *I* chose which *suttas* to include—a measure of explicit form; partly it involves providing the reader with some grist for debate.

THE BUDDHA

> Of physiology from top to toe I sing.
>
> —WALT WHITMAN, *Leaves of Grass*

> The teaching of Buddhism is nothing special. It is just our human way.
>
> —SHUNRYU SUZUKI, *Zen Mind, Beginner's Mind*

The view that the Buddha was through and through *human* would not, on the face of it, be disputed by most Buddhists throughout history. "A man; extraordinary, but human" is how one teacher has put it. Yet *listen* to a Theravādin Buddhist tell a story about the Buddha, *observe* a Zen or Pure Land practitioner ritually interact with a statue of the Buddha, *watch* a Vajrayāna or tantric practitioner recite *mantras* while gazing at a painted scroll depicting a *buddha* or *bodhisattva*. Do so, and a certain cognitive dissonance is unavoidable: they *say* "human," but they certainly *act* as if the Buddha, that statue, the *mantra*, the icon, even the *teacher*, possessed supernatural qualities.

Why must this obvious point about the Buddha's humanity be made? Well, because our brains seem to push in the other direction.

Who hasn't noticed that religious authorities easily acquire (and assert) an aura of magical efficacy? Recent research in cognitive studies suggests that it is in fact a *natural human tendency* to think about certain figures—priests, monks, gurus, *roshis,* the Buddha, Jesus, Oprah—as possessing "some internal, vaguely defined quality that sets them apart from the common folk."

> The notion of a hidden causal essence that cannot be observed yet explains outward form and behavior, is a crucial feature of our spontaneous, intuitive way of thinking about living species. Here, it is transferred upon a pseudo-natural kind, as it were: a sub-kind of human agents with different essential characteristics.*

An all-too-common result of this imputation of causal essence is that we easily elevate certain humans to an exclusive, even deified, status. The Buddha will ask you to "go against the flow" and resist this human proclivity. He will want to remind you that "it is within this six-foot body, with its mind and its concepts" that he realized and subsequently declared the teachings (*Saṃyuttanikāya* 1.2.26). Can we take a clear-eyed view of the Buddha as a fully embodied *ordinary* human being, as depicted in this statement? It may turn out that such a view is actually *necessary* for an understanding of his teachings.

THE BUDDHA'S TEACHINGS

> All space, all time . . .
> Fill'd with eidólons [ephemeral images] only.
>
> —WALT WHITMAN, *Leaves of Grass*

> Where there is no abiding,
> that's where there is emptiness.
> *Nibbāna* is this emptiness.
>
> —AJAHN CHAH

If the teachings are to be realized and declared within your human body, then they must pertain relentlessly to what unfolds right there.

* Pascal Boyer, "Out of Africa: Lessons from a By-product of Evolution," in Timothy Light and Brian C. Wilson, *Religion as Human Capacity* (Leiden: Brill, 2004), p. 33.

"There" in the narrow sense is "within the body-mind continuum," abbreviated by the Buddha as "the sensorium" (*āyatana*), namely, thinking, seeing, hearing, smelling, tactile feeling, and tasting. "There" in this sense covers our sensory and affective life. "There" also has a broader sense, namely, "the world" (*loka*). The world is just that which unfolds *right there,* before, around, within, concomitant with, us. The central point of the teachings is thus twofold: to enable us to identify the conditions that compel each of us to fashion the particular world that we do at any given moment, and to enable us to realize the primary condition making *just that fashioning* possible. The Buddha called this primary condition *anattā, suññatā,* "zero," "emptiness," "non-substantiality." If interminable flux is the case, with what other "primary condition" could a teaching that purports to end human suffering be concerned?

THE END OF THE TEACHINGS

Unfix'd yet fix'd.
—WALT WHITMAN, *Leaves of Grass*

In the present—let go!
—THE BUDDHA, *Dhammapada* 348

What happens when we realize this "zero point" of reality? Assuming that this realization is purely human in nature and not "spiritual," "transcendental," or otherwise special or spectacular, we can further assume a wide range of possible responses, such as alcoholism, depression, bad poetry, renewed vigor, elation, soaring prose. We could name names of people who have produced some evidence of having realized this basic zero point of human existence, for example, Meister Eckhart, William Blake, St. Teresa of Ávila, the Wizard of Oz. Naming names serves only to show that, first, the realization is human, and second, realization is not enough.

The end of the Buddha's teachings is to drive the careful practitioner incessantly toward the development of a single skill: *nirvāṇa* (Pāli: *nibbāna*)—the capacity to *unbind* oneself from distress-creating habits and qualities, the ability to *let it all go.* I can hear a chorus of concerned queries: "This *nirvāṇa,* the summum bonum of the great Buddhist path, is a mere *skill*? Isn't it a superhuman feat, like talking to

God or piercing the veil of reality, achievable only by the greatest spiritual virtuosos? Learning a foreign language requires *skill*. Building a cabinet requires *skill*. Making chocolate fudge brownies requires *skill*. Can *nirvāṇa* really be in the category of *human skill*?" Try an experiment. Read the *suttas* in this book as if they were grammars, instruction manuals, or recipes. Read them, that is, as if they were providing actual directions entailing an actual outcome. Notice for yourself whether notions such as "spiritual," "religious," "transcendental," and the like apply, or whether it is simply a matter of old-fashioned *labor*, a matter of effort, work, practice, cultivation, and development. A reader encountering some nice words on a page may get a sense of "spiritual uplift" for a moment, but until "laborious skillfulness" becomes the operative term, and not "spiritual uplift," he or she will remain "like a cowherd counting the cows of others," as the Buddha put it (*Dhammapada* 19), cozying up to the matter but not penetrating it.

The passage under investigation supports this view. There, the Buddha allows each member of the group to teach others once he is "freed from all the snares." This phrase is shorthand for becoming an *arahant*. This important Buddhist technical term carries the double meaning of "worthy" and "accomplished." A person is of genuine value to society because he or she has mastered the particular skills that constitute the Buddhist path. In the passage, this accomplishment is cast in terms of being "freed from all the snares." Numbering ten, the snares include belief in an abiding personality, misplaced confidence in the ability of rituals to lead to advanced understanding, ignorance, and conceit. The snares are human creations. Conversely, being freed from the snares is a thoroughly human accomplishment.

Throughout this book, I have assumed the view that the Buddha and his *arahant* followers were models of *human* accomplishment, and were categorically no different from the reader of this book. I think that the Buddha himself is taking this position in his treatment of the group of sixty when he tells them to "manifest" to the human multitude "the completely fulfilled and perfectly purified life of training." This is language that points to skill acquisition, not to unique states of being or supernatural ability.

You

Leaving it to you to prove and define it,
Expecting the main things from you.
—Walt Whitman, *Leaves of Grass*

In the passage leading this section, the Buddha evokes two groups of people: those who should "go, wander . . . out of compassion for the world" and those who constitute "the human multitude" seeking happiness. The first group, which includes the Buddha himself, has realized the fruits of practice directly. The second group benefits from that realization only secondarily, through osmosis presumably (via education, ethical exhortation, encouragement). My assumption about you, the reader of the present book, is that you are looking for actual knowledge, understanding, and realization of these teachings.

DRAWING NEAR TO THE TEXTS

Why These Texts?

In reading the sixteen *suttas* presented in this book, you, the reader, can be confident that you are getting a reliable overview of the concerns at the heart of the Buddha's teachings. It is certainly true that a hundred different authors would present a hundred different combinations of "basic teachings of the Buddha." Given the countless idiosyncratic possibilities behind any particular selection of texts, it is unlikely that any two authors would select the exact same sixteen *suttas* as necessarily basic. But I think it is also unlikely that many Buddhists or Buddhist scholars would have serious qualms with the present selection of *suttas.* In any case, knowing the contents of the *suttas* presented here, you will have a good grasp of the most vital Buddhist principles for living a fulfilled life. And perhaps that grasp is, after all, the decisive test of what constitutes a reliable selection of "basic teachings."

As I stated earlier, the Buddhist canon contains well over five thousand *suttas.* What, then, is my rationale for selecting the sixteen that I have? My selection is based on two criteria: rate of recurrence and relevance. The first criterion takes into account the frequency with which a theme occurs in the dialogues. There are certain issues that the Buddha raises repeatedly in his discourses. On this principle, I have selected several *suttas* dealing with the Buddha's *ideas* concerning the world, the person, the mind, and perception; and with his *prescriptions* for cultivating meditative concentration, mental and emotional calm, present-moment awareness, and the unbinding from tendencies detrimental to human happiness.

There are other *suttas,* however, that contain material on issues on which the Buddha and his interlocutors placed little importance (again, using rate of recurrence as a yardstick). I have, nonetheless, selected some of these texts because they address matters that the contemporary reader *does* (I assume) consider important. I am not making this assumption on the basis of any complex sociological data analysis but rather on my own discussions with others throughout my life. These issues include the problematic nature of the idea of a creator deity, or "God"; the manner of conducting a meaningful conversation; methods for countering depression, anxiety, and despair; cultivation of meaningful relationships; healthy reflection on illness and death; and the very nature of a question.

Using these two criteria for the selection of texts, this book should at the very least prove to be a vibrant guide for studying Buddhism and, if the reader so wishes, for applying its principles to life.

Reading Suggestions

In exploring a text, I find it helpful to pose specific questions. Some of these questions may seem painfully obvious, since they concern basic facets of a text. But, if we are honest, isn't much of our reading unsuccessful? For me, "successful reading" means that I have recognized, literally re-cognized, the material—the ideas, concepts, logic, schemas, claims, and so on. I have made them my own, if only for the sake of temporary consideration. Here are some questions that I find useful:

- What is the text about? If I had to say so in a word, which word?
- With what major theme or themes is it concerned?
- How is the text structured? What would an outline of it look like?
- With which of these dimensions, individually or in combination, is the text concerned: doctrinal, ethical, experiential, mythologi-

cal, ritual, liturgical, social, institutional? Some other one? How is it expressed?

- What does the text demand of me? For example, does it indicate that some sort of practice is required for a thorough understanding? Does it ask me to alter my life in some fundamental way?
- What limitations do I impose on the text? For example, would I be willing to *do* the practices that may be required for a thorough understanding of the text? Would I be willing to alter my life in the ways the text is suggesting?

It is very important to take note of your responses as you read. These responses might include having additional questions, surprise, bafflement, insight, sadness, joy, hope, discouragement, making comparisons with other traditions, disagreement, annoyance, boredom. To this end, the logic of exploration and discovery requires that the reader bring a critical mind to bear on the material. Learning takes place at the point of tension *between* credulous appreciation and wary dismissal. We are all pretty good at the two extremes: yes/no, like/dislike, agree/disagree, accept/reject. Exploration and discovery, however, call for an abandonment of this +/− dichotomy and an occupation of the open middle ground. In my own encounters with Buddhist literature, I have found the German philosopher Hans-Georg Gadamer's idea of the dialectic, the art of questioning, to be of boundless benefit:

> As the art of asking questions, dialectic proves its value because only the person who knows how to ask questions is able to persist in his/her questioning. Questioning involves being able to preserve one's orientation toward openness. The art of questioning is the art of questioning even further. This is then: the art of thinking. It is called dialectic because it is the art of conducting a real dialogue.*

Whatever it is, your response to a word, passage, or text is the very lifeblood of reading. It is in your response that your relationship to the world of the *suttas* is formed, developed, and fulfilled or unfulfilled.

*Hans-Georg Gadamer, *Truth and Method* (New York: Continuum,1994), p. 367.

Sixteen Propositions

The concern at the heart of this book is to provide you, the contemporary reader, with a doctrinally responsible basis for further pursuing the study and practice of the Buddha's teachings.

The sixteen propositions here represent my attempt to make a clearing in the interwoven thicket of texts, doctrines, schemas, technical vocabulary, practices, and so on that compose the immense labyrinth of the Buddha's forty-five-year dispensation. They are meant to bring some basic structure to the considerable material contained in the *suttas.* As I see it, though, these propositions do more than provide structure: they constitute a reliable basis for understanding the heart of the Buddha's teachings. Another author could and most certainly would posit different propositions, thereby laying a different foundation. These sixteen propositions are the result of *my* effort to trace the footprints of the Buddha. They are posited neither by the Buddha nor by any of the schools of Buddhism that preserve his legacy. In that regard and beyond, I have, in the present book, been careful to steer clear of sectarian interpretations of the *sutta* material and sought rather to attend to the texts themselves. Toward that end, I resisted the powerful temptation to consult the vast commentarial traditions of the great Buddhist schools. The result is that the raw material of the *suttas* is presented to the reader and then processed in the section "Guide to Reading the Texts." It is up to the reader to refine the material with the grit of daily life.

The following sixteen propositions can lead you into the heart of the Buddha's teachings. (Each proposition corresponds to the *sutta* of identical number listed in the table of contents.) I am using the picture of a path and journey, perhaps a pilgrimage, as a way to structure the material. The teachings begin by asking you to recognize and explore where you are (Habitat). You are introduced to ideas and perspectives that have a disorienting effect (De-orientation). You are introduced to ideas and perspectives that point you in a different direction (Re-orientation). You are shown the plan for a new habitat (Map). You are given the details of that end (Destination). You are set out on the open journey (Going).

HABITAT

1. We are like ghosts sleepwalking in a desolate and dangerous domain.

DE-ORIENTATION

2. We remain transfixed there, enchanted by pleasure and flamboyant speculation.
3. The most enthralling belief of all is that of supernatural agency.
4. There is a safeguard against this bewitchment: knowing for yourself.

RE-ORIENTATION

5. The means of "knowing for yourself" is immediately available: it is the sensorium.
6. But the modes of perception are miragelike, and the perceived like a magical display.
7. And there is no self, no integral perceiver, behind those modes of perception.
8. To hold on to the miragelike perceiver, the phantom self, is a stultifying burden.

MAP

9. When we reflect on these propositions, four preeminent realities become obvious,
10. as do the emergence and cessation of our incessant "worlding."

DESTINATION

11. Our genuine refuge from this whirlwind of worlding is to be unbound;
12. to eradicate infatuation, hostility, and delusion. Eradicated, quenched, unbound.
13. Binding is concomitant with the fabricated.
14. Unbinding is concomitant with the unfabricated.

GOING

15. Cultivation of present-moment awareness is the means to conspicuous unbinding.
16. Application of this awareness in daily life is concomitant with living as a *buddha:* awakened.

TWO TRAJECTORIES: TOWARD PAIN, TOWARD PEACE

As you read the *suttas,* you may find it helpful to consider the following diagram. The diagram shows two basic trajectories of human existence presented by the Buddha. One trajectory runs through infatuation, hostility, and delusion, and culminates in pain. The other trajectory runs through clear seeing, insight, and present-moment awareness, and culminates in peace. The possibility for changing trajectories occurs at every instant. The diagram should serve as a sort of preliminary guide through the material; therefore, I will not comment further at this point.

FEELING CONDITIONS:
CRAVING, WHICH MANIFESTS IN THOUGHT, SPEECH, ACTION,
AS *GRASPING*, WHICH FOLLOWS A COURSE OF
BECOMING ALONG ONE OF TWO TRAJECTORIES:

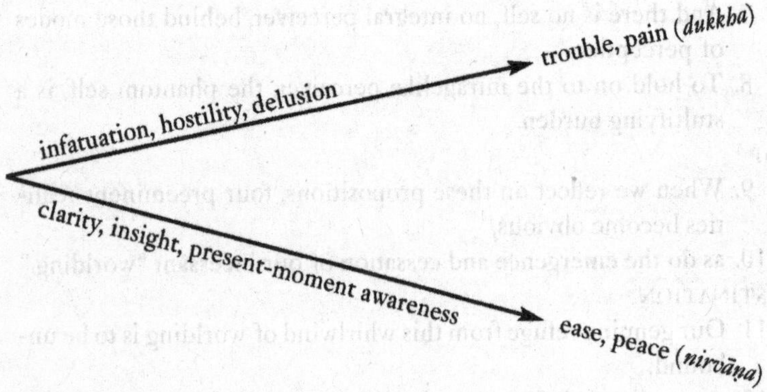

THE TEXTS

SUTTA I

सकुणग्घिसुत्त

The Hawk

Sakuṇagghi Sutta; Saṃyuttanikāya 5.47.6

THE BUDDHA RELATED THIS STORY TO A GROUP OF HIS FOLLOWERS.

Once, in the distant past, a hawk suddenly swooped down and seized a quail. As the quail was being carried away by the hawk, it lamented, "How unfortunate I am, what little merit I possess to have wandered out of my natural habitat into a foreign domain. If I had wandered within my native domain today, within my own ancestral, natural habitat, this hawk would certainly not have been a match for me in battle."

"What is your native domain, quail? What is your own ancestral, natural habitat?" asked the hawk.

The quail answered, "That clod of earth freshly tilled with a plow."

Then the hawk, not boasting about its own strength, not mentioning its own strength, released the quail, saying, "Go, quail; but having gone there, you cannot escape me."

Then the quail, having gone to the clod of earth freshly tilled with a plow, climbed onto the large clod of earth and, standing there, said to the hawk, "Come get me now, hawk, come get me now!"

Now the hawk, not boasting about its own strength, not mentioning its own strength, folded up its wings and suddenly swooped down on the quail. When the quail fully realized that the hawk was coming, it got inside that clod of earth. And the hawk, striking against it, suffered a blow to its chest.

So it is when someone wanders out of his or her natural habitat into a foreign domain. Therefore, do not wander out of your natural habitat into a foreign domain. Death will gain access [1.1]* to the person who has wandered out of his or her natural habitat into a foreign domain, death will gain a footing.

Now, what is for you a foreign domain, outside of your natural habitat? It is the fivefold realm of sensual pleasure [1.2]. Which five? Forms perceptible to the eye, which are pleasing, desirable, charming, agreeable, arousing desire, and enticing; sounds perceptible to the ear, which are pleasing, desirable, charming, agreeable, arousing desire, and enticing; scents perceptible to the nose, which are pleasing, desirable, charming, agreeable, arousing desire, and enticing; tastes perceptible to the tongue, which are pleasing, desirable, charming, agreeable, arousing desire, and enticing; tactile objects perceptible to the body, which are pleasing, desirable, charming, agreeable, arousing desire, and enticing. This is for you a foreign domain, outside of your natural habitat. Death will not gain access to the person who lives within his or her native domain; within his or her own ancestral, natural habitat, death will not gain a footing. Now, what is your native domain, your own ancestral, natural habitat? It is the foundation of present-moment awareness [1.3] in four areas [1.4]. What are the four areas? Now, being ardent, fully aware, and mindful, and having put down longing and discontentment toward the world, live observing the body *in and as the body,* live observing feelings *in and as feelings,* live observing mind *in and as mind,* and live observing mental qualities and phenomena *in and as mental qualities and phenomena.*

This is your native domain, your own ancestral, natural habitat.

* Numbers refer to notes in the Guide.

SUTTA 2

चूळमालुक्यसुत्त

A Brief Talk to Mālukya

Cūḷamālukya Sutta; Majjhimanikāya 63

THIS IS WHAT I HEARD. ONCE, THE FORTUNATE ONE [THE BUDDHA] WAS STAYING IN SĀVATTHĪ, IN JETA'S GROVE IN ANĀTHAPIṆḌIKA'S PARK.

There, the venerable Mālukya was living in solitary seclusion. Mālukya reflected as follows. "There are certain speculative matters that the Fortunate One has left undetermined, set aside, and rejected. Is the world eternal, or is the world not eternal? Is the world infinite, or is the world finite? Is the life force identical to the body, or is the life force different from the body? Does a person who has come to know reality exist after death; not exist after death; both exist and not exist after death; or neither exist nor not exist after death [2.1]? These are the matters that the Fortunate One has not determined. It does not please me or seem right to me that the Fortunate One has not determined these matters. I will approach the Fortunate One and ask him the reason for this refusal. If he determines these matters for me, then I will continue the training. If he does not determine these matters for me, then I will abandon the training and return to the lowly world."

So, in the evening, Mālukya emerged from his solitude and approached the Fortunate One. After exchanging greetings, he sat down and said, "When I was in solitary seclusion, it occurred to me that you have left undetermined, set aside, and rejected certain speculative matters. Is the world eternal, or is the world not eternal? Is the world infinite, or is the world finite? Is the life force identical to the body, or is the life force different from the body? Does a person who has come to know reality exist after death; not exist after death; both exist and not exist after death; or neither exist nor not exist after death? These are the matters that you have not determined.

"It does not please me or seem right to me that you have not determined these matters. So I thought that I would approach you and ask you the reason for this refusal. If you determine these matters for me, then I will continue the training. If you do not determine these matters for me, then I will abandon the training and return to the lowly world. So if you know the answers to these questions, then answer me! If you do not know, then it is straightforward for a person who does not know or see to say, 'I do not know, I do not see.'"

The Buddha replied, "Mālukya, did I ever say to you, 'Come, Mālukya, train with me, I will determine for you whether the world is eternal or not eternal, infinite or finite,' and so on?"

"No, you did not," responded Mālukya.

"In that case, you fool of a man [2.2], who do you think you are, and what is it that you are repudiating?"

The Buddha continued, "Mālukya, if anyone were to say, 'I will not enter the life of training under the Fortunate One until he determines for me whether the world is eternal or not eternal, infinite or finite,' and so on, I would still not determine those matters, and in the meantime that person would die.

"It is, Māḷukya, as if a person would be shot by an arrow [2.3] thickly smeared with poison, and his friends, companions, and relatives would hire a physician to remove the arrow. But that person would say, 'I will not have this arrow removed until I know who shot it; whether he was of the upper, middle, or low class; his name and family; whether he was tall, short, or of medium stature; whether he was black, brown, or light-skinned; whether he lived in such and such a town, village, or city; and until I know whether the bow that was used to shoot the arrow was a longbow or a crossbow; and until I know whether the bowstring that was used to shoot the arrow was made from the swallowwort plant, from *sanha* hemp, sinew, *maruva* hemp, or from the bark of the *khira* tree; and until I know whether the shaft was made from wild or cultivated wood; and until I know whether the feathers on the shaft were those of a vulture, crow, hawk, peacock, or stork; and until I know whether the sinew used to wrap the shaft was from a cattle, water buffalo, deer, or monkey; and until I know whether the arrow that was used to wound me was razor-tipped, curved, tubular, calf-toothed, or oleander.

"All of this would remain unknown to that person, Mālukya, and in the meantime he or she would die. So, too, Mālukya, someone might say, 'I will not enter the life of training under the Fortunate One until he determines for me whether the world is eternal or not eternal, infinite or finite,' and so on. Still, these matters would remain undetermined, and in the meantime that person would die.

"Mālukya, because there is the speculative view *The world is eternal,* the training life cannot be cultivated. And because there is the speculative view *The world is not eternal,* the training life cannot be cultivated. Whether there is the view *The world is eternal* or the view *The world is not eternal,* whether there is the view *The life force is different from the body* or the view *The life force is the same as the body,* and so on, still there is birth, there is aging, there is death; still there is sadness, regret, unease, depression, and anxiety. It is the destruction of all of *this,* in this very world, that *I* make known.

"It is for this reason, Mālukya, that you should bear in mind that which I have not determined, because it is indeterminate, and that which I have determined, because it is determinate. What have I not determined? I have not determined *The world is eternal;* I have not determined *The world is not eternal;* I have not determined *The world is infinite;* I have not determined *The world is finite;* I have not determined *The life force is identical to the body;* I have not determined *The life force is different from the body;* I have not determined *A person who has come to know reality exists after death, A person who has come to know reality does not exist after death, A person who has come to know reality both exists and does not exist after death,* or *A person who has come to know reality neither exists nor does not exist after death.*

"And why, Mālukya, have I not determined these matters? To do so does not lead to what is beneficial, to the beginning of training, to disenchantment, to dispassion, to cessation, to peace, to direct knowing, to awakening, to unbinding. That is the reason that I have not determined these matters.

"And what, Mālukya, *have* I determined? I have determined *This is unease.* I have determined *This is the arising of unease.* I have determined *This is the cessation of unease.* I have determined *This is the path leading to the cessation of unease.*

"And why, Mālukya, have I determined these matters? To do so leads to what is beneficial, to the beginning of training, to disenchantment, to dispassion, to cessation, to peace, to direct knowing, to awakening, to unbinding. That is the reason I have determined these matters.

"It is for this reason, Mālukya, that you should bear in mind that which I have not determined, because it is indeterminate, and that which I have determined, because it is determinate."

This is what the Fortunate One said. Exalted, the venerable Mālukya rejoiced at the words of the Fortunate One.

SUTTA 3

तेविज्जसुत्त

Threefold Knowledge

Tevijja Sutta; Dīghanikāya 13

THIS IS WHAT I HEARD. TRAVELING IN KOSALA WITH A LARGE GROUP OF FIVE HUNDRED MENDICANTS, THE FORTUNATE ONE APPROACHED THE BRAHMAN [3.1] VILLAGE MANASĀKAṬA. THE FORTUNATE ONE STAYED THERE, JUST NORTH OF THE VILLAGE, IN THE MANGO GROVE ON THE BANKS OF THE RIVER ACIRAVATIYĀ. MANY RENOWNED AND WEALTHY RELIGIOUS AUTHORITIES LIVED IN MANASAKĀṬA AT THAT TIME.

Now, Vāseṭṭha and Bhāradvāja were wandering, strolling along the road, when a dispute arose between them concerning the right and wrong paths. The young Brahman Vāseṭṭha said, "*This* is the direct path, this is the straight path that leads to salvation, and leads one who follows it to communion [3.2] with God [3.3]. This is what is proclaimed [3.4] by the Brahman Pokkharasāti."

And the young Brahman Bhāradvāja said: "*This* is the direct path, this is the straight path that leads to salvation, and leads one who follows it to communion with God. This is what is proclaimed by the Brahman Tāruḳkha." But neither could Vāseṭṭha convince Bhāradvāja, nor Bhāradvāja convince Vāseṭṭha.

Then Vāseṭṭha said to Bhāradvāja, "Bhāradvāja, the ascetic Gotama Sakyaputta, who went forth from the Sakya clan, is staying north of Manasākaṭa, in the mango grove on the banks of the river Aciravatiyā. A favorable reputation has preceded the honorable Gotama. It is said that the Fortunate One is worthy, completely awakened, perfected in knowledge and conduct, happy, knowledgeable in the ways of the world, unsurpassed as a trainer of people needing to be tamed, a teacher of humans and resplendent beings, awakened, fortunate. Let's go, Bhāradvāja, to where the ascetic Gotama is. Let's approach him, and ask about this matter. Whatever the ascetic Gotama answers, we will take to heart."

"Very well, friend," consented Bhāradvāja.

So, Vāseṭṭha and Bhāradvāja approached the Fortunate One, exchanged friendly greetings and polite conversation with him, then sat down on one side. Having done so, Vāseṭṭha spoke to the Fortunate One. "We were wandering, friend Gotama, strolling along the road here, when a dispute arose concerning the right and wrong paths. I said, '*This* is the direct path, this is the straight path that leads to salvation, and leads one who follows it to communion with God. This is what is proclaimed by the Brahman Pokkharasāti.' "

Then the young Brahman Bhāradvāja said, "And I said, '*This* is the direct path, this is the straight path that leads to salvation, and leads one who follows it to communion with God. This is what is proclaimed by the Brahman Tārukkha."

"It is in this matter, friend Gotama, that there is an argument, a disagreement, a difference of opinion."

The Buddha replied, "So, Vāseṭṭha, you say this: '*This* is the direct path, this is the straight path that leads to salvation, and leads one who follows it to communion with God. This is what is proclaimed by the Brahman Pokkharasāti.' Bhāradvāja says this: '*This* is the direct path, this is the straight path that leads to salvation, and leads one who follows it to communion with God. This is what is proclaimed by the Brahman Tārukkha.' So what, then, Vāseṭṭha, does the dispute, the argument, the difference of opinion between you, concern [3.5]?"

Vāseṭṭha said, "The right and wrong paths, friend Gotama. Various religious authorities declare various paths. Do they all lead the one who follows them to communion with God? For example, there might be many different paths near a village or a town. Do they all necessarily merge in the village? Similarly, various religious authorities declare various paths. Do they all lead the one who follows them to communion with God?"

"Are you asking whether 'they lead [3.6],' Vāseṭṭha?" asked the Buddha.

"I'm asking whether 'they lead,' friend Gotama," Vāseṭṭha replied.

"Are you asking whether 'they lead,' Vāseṭṭha?" repeated the Buddha.

"I'm asking whether 'they lead,' Gotama," Vāseṭṭha replied.

"Are you asking whether 'they lead,' Vāseṭṭha?" repeated the Buddha.

"I'm asking whether 'they lead,' friend Gotama," Vāseṭṭha replied.

The Buddha said, "Vāseṭṭha, is there even a single religious authority among those versed in their tradition who has seen God face-to-face?"

"Certainly not, friend Gotama," responded Vāseṭṭha.

"Vāseṭṭha, is there even a single teacher among those religious authorities versed in their tradition who has seen God face-to-face?"

"Certainly not, friend Gotama."

"Vāseṭṭha, is there even a single teacher of teachers among those religious authorities versed in their tradition who has seen God face-to-face?"

"Certainly not, friend Gotama."

"Vāseṭṭha, is there anyone among those religious authorities versed in their tradition, going back as far as seven generations of teachers, who has seen God face-to-face?"

"Certainly not, friend Gotama."

"Vāseṭṭha, those ancient visionaries among the religious authorities versed in their tradition, those creators and expounders of the sacred verses that are preserved, sung, and declared, and that the religious authorities of today continually recite and endlessly repeat—did those ancient visionaries say, 'We know, we see where, how, and when God appears'?"

"Certainly not, friend Gotama."

"So, Vāseṭṭha, there is not a single religious authority, teacher of religious authorities, teacher of those teachers going back seven generations, who has seen God face-to-face. Nor did the ancient visionaries declare, 'We know, we see where, how, and when God appears.' So those religious authorities versed in tradition are saying, 'That path, which we neither know nor have seen, we declare to be the path to union; this is the direct path [3.7], this is the straight path that leads to salvation, and leads one who follows it to communion with God.' What do you think, Vāseṭṭha, this being the case, doesn't the talk of those religious authorities turn out to be ridiculous?"

"Certainly, friend Gotama."

"Good, Vāseṭṭha. That which those religious authorities neither know nor see, they nonetheless declare to be the path to union: 'This is the direct path, this is the straight path that leads to salvation, and leads one who follows it to communion with God.' This just is not possible.

"Vāseṭṭha, it is just as if there were a single file of blind men clinging to one another: the first one sees nothing, the middle one sees nothing, and the last one sees nothing. The talk of the religious authorities is similarly nothing but blind talk: the first one sees nothing, the middle one sees nothing, and the last one sees nothing. The talk of these religious authorities turns out to be ridiculous, mere words, vacuous, and desolate [3.8].

"What do you think, Vāseṭṭha, do those religious authorities see the sun and moon, just as other people do? And when the sun and moon rise and set, do they entreat, extol, honor, and worship them with folded hands?"

Vāseṭṭha responded, "Yes, Gotama."

"So, what do you think, Vāseṭṭha, are those religious authorities able to point out the path to union with the sun and moon [3.9], which they see, saying, 'This is the direct path, this is the straight path that leads one who follows it to communion with the sun and moon'?"

"Of course not, friend Gotama."

"So, Vāseṭṭha, those religious authorities are not able to point out the path to union with the sun and moon, which they see. And none of them, nor their teachers going back seven generations, nor the ancient visionaries, can say, 'We know, we see where, how, and when God appears.' So those religious authorities versed in tradition are saying, 'That path, which we neither know nor have seen, we declare to be the path to union; this is the direct path, this is the straight path that leads to salvation, and leads one who follows it to communion with God.' What do you think, Vāseṭṭha, this being the case, doesn't the talk of those religious authorities turn out to be ridiculous?"

"Certainly, friend Gotama."

"Good, Vāseṭṭha. That which those religious authorities neither know nor see, they nonetheless declare to be the path to union: 'This is the direct path, this is the straight path that leads to salvation, and leads one who follows it to communion with God.' This just is not possible.

"Vāseṭṭha, it is as if a man were to say, 'I am going to seek out and love the most beautiful woman [3.10] in the land.' And the people would ask him, 'This "most beautiful woman in the land," do you know which class she belongs to?' Asked this, he would have to answer no. And then the people would ask him, 'This "most beautiful woman in the land" whom you will seek out and love, do you know her name, or her family name, whether she is tall, short, or of medium height; dark, brown, or golden in complexion; or in what village or town or city she lives?' Asked this, he would have to answer no. And then people might say to him, 'So then, you neither know nor see the one whom you seek and desire?' Asked this, he would have to answer, 'Yes, that is correct.'

"Now, what do you think, Vāseṭṭha? This being the case, does not the talk of that man turn out to be ridiculous?"

"Yes, friend Gotama, it does," said Vāseṭṭha.

"In the same way, the claim of the religious authorities to know the path to union with God is just not viable.

"Vāseṭṭha, it is just as if a man were to make a staircase at a crossroads, leading up to a palace [3.11]. And people would say to him, 'This staircase leading to the palace, do you know whether it is for a palace that will face east, south, west, or north, or whether it will be of high, low, or medium size?' Asked this, he would have to answer no. And people would say to him, 'You are making a staircase leading to a palace that you neither know nor see?' And when asked, he would have to answer, 'Yes, that is correct.'

"Now, what do you think, Vāseṭṭha? This being the case, does not the talk of that man turn out to be ridiculous?"

"Yes, friend Gotama, it does," said Vāseṭṭha.

"In the same way, the claim of the religious authorities to know the path to union with God is just not viable.

"Vāseṭṭha, it is just as if there were a river that was so full of water that cows and crows could drink out of it; and a man would come to it, desiring to cross over to the other bank. Standing on the near bank, he calls out to the farther bank, 'Come, farther bank, come [3.12]!'

"What do you think, Vāseṭṭha, would the far bank of the river come to the near bank as a result of his calling, pleading, requesting, and cajoling?"

"Certainly not, Gotama," said Vāseṭṭha.

"Vāseṭṭha, in just the same way do the religious authorities, who persistently neglect the duties of a religious authority and persistently undertake what such an authority should not do, declare, 'We summon the supernatural beings!' That such religious authorities, as a result of their cajoling, should, after death, when the body is dissolved, realize communion with God is simply not reasonable.

"Vāseṭṭha, it is just as if there were a river that was so full of water that cows and crows could drink out of it; and a man would come to it, desiring to cross over to the other bank. This man's arms are bound tightly behind his back with a strong cord.

"What do you think, Vāseṭṭha, could this man go from the near bank of the river to the far bank?"

"Certainly not, friend Gotama," said Vāseṭṭha.

The Buddha continued, "There are five cords of sensory desire, called fetters and binds in the Buddhist discipline. What are the five cords? Forms perceptible to the eye, which are pleasing, desirable, charming, agreeable, arousing desire, and enticing; sounds perceptible to the ear, which are pleasing, desirable, charming, agreeable, arousing desire, and enticing; scents perceptible to the nose, which are pleasing, desirable, charming, agreeable, arousing desire, and enticing; tastes perceptible to the tongue, which are pleasing, desirable, charming, agreeable, arousing desire, and enticing; tactile objects perceptible to the body, which are pleasing, desirable, charming, agreeable, arousing desire, and enticing.

"These five cords of sensory desire are called fetters and binds in the Buddhist discipline. Vāseṭṭha, those religious authorities are enslaved and infatuated by these five cords of sensory desire, enjoying them guiltily, not realizing the danger, and knowing no way out.

"These religious authorities, who persistently neglect the duties of a religious authority and persistently undertake what such an authority should not do, are enslaved and infatuated by these five cords of sensory desire, enjoying them guiltily, not realizing the danger, and knowing no way out. Bound by the binds of sensory desire, the possibility that they would realize communion with God after death, when the body is dissolved, is simply not viable.

"Vāseṭṭha, it is just as if there were a river that was so full of water that cows and crows could drink out of it; and a man would come to it, desiring to cross over to the other bank. But this man would lie down on the near bank, his head covered with a cloth [3.13]. What do you think, Vāseṭṭha, could this man go from the near bank of the river to the far bank?"

"Certainly not, friend Gotama," said Vāseṭṭha.

The Buddha continued, "There are five hindrances [3.14], called 'obstructions, obstacles, coverings, envelopings' in the Buddhist discipline. What are the five hindrances? The impulse toward desire, hostility, heavy lethargy, agitated worry, and debilitating doubt. These are called the five hindrances.

"These religious authorities are obstructed, enveloped, covered, and ensnared by these five hindrances. They persistently neglect the duties of a religious authority and persistently undertake what such an authority should not do. Hindered as they are, the possibility that they would realize communion with God after death, when the body is dissolved, is simply not viable."

The Buddha asked, "What do you think, Vāseṭṭha, have you heard the venerable, accomplished teachers of the religious authorities saying whether or not God is wrapped up in possessions?"

"Not wrapped up in possessions, friend Gotama," said Vāseṭṭha.

"Ill-tempered or composed?" continued the Buddha.

"Composed, friend Gotama."

"Antagonistic or gracious?"

"Gracious, friend Gotama."

"Corrupt or honest?"

"Honest, friend Gotama."

"Domineering or compliant?"

"Compliant, friend Gotama."

"Now, what do you think, Vāseṭṭha, are the religious authorities wrapped up in possessions or not?"

"Wrapped up in possessions, friend Gotama," said Vāseṭṭha.

"Ill-tempered or composed?" continued the Buddha.

"Ill-tempered, friend Gotama."

"Antagonistic or gracious?"

"Antagonistic, friend Gotama."

"Corrupt or honest?"

"Corrupt, friend Gotama."

"Domineering or compliant?"

"Domineering, friend Gotama."

"So," the Buddha continued, "is there then any communion or commonality between the religious authorities—who are wrapped up in possessions, ill-tempered, antagonistic, corrupt, and domineering—and God—who is not wrapped up in possessions, is composed, gracious, honest, and compliant?"

"Certainly not, Gotama," answered Vāseṭṭha.

"Very good, Vāseṭṭha. So the idea that these authorities will realize communion [3.15] with God after death, when the body is dissolved, is simply not viable.

"These authorities, having come to the near shore thinking that they will cross over to the dry bank, sink down and fall into despair. Therefore, this knowledge of the religious authorities is called a desertlike knowledge, a wilderness of knowledge, the ruin of knowledge."

This having been said, Vāseṭṭha spoke to the Fortunate One. "I have heard that you—the ascetic Gotama—know the path [3.16] to communion with God."

The Buddha replied, "What do you think, Vāseṭṭha; is the town of Manasākaṭa near here, and not distant?"

"Yes, friend Gotama, it is near and not distant."

"Now," the Buddha continued, "imagine this. There is a person born and raised in the town of Manasākaṭa. Someone who was just leaving the town asks him about the town road. Would there be any perplexity or hesitation on the part of that person when so asked?"

"Certainly not, Gotama," said Vāseṭṭha.

"And why not?"

"Because that person, born and raised in the town, would know all of the town's paths," said Vāseṭṭha.

"It may be that a person is perplexed and hesitant when asked about the path to the town, but the *tathāgata,* when asked about the province of God/exceptional integrity [3.17] or the way leading to the province of God/exceptional integrity, is neither perplexed nor hesitant. So, Vāseṭṭha, I know God/exceptional integrity and the province of God/exceptional integrity and the way leading to the province of God/exceptional integrity. I have entered and realized the province of God/exceptional integrity, so, yes, I do know that."

This having been said, Vāseṭṭha spoke to the Fortunate One. "I have heard that you—the ascetic Gotama—teach the path to communion with God. Please teach the path to communion with God! Please help God's progeny!"

"Now, listen, and concentrate completely on what I will now say," said the Buddha.

"Yes, I will," replied Vāseṭṭha to the Fortunate One.

The Fortunate One spoke. "Here, a *tathāgata*—a person who has come to know reality—arises in the world, an accomplished person, a perfectly awakened person, adept in conduct and knowledge, going well through life, understanding the world, an unsurpassed guide of people in need of training, a teacher of resplendent beings and humans, an awakened, fortunate one. Having realized directly, come to know thoroughly for himself, he makes this known to the world, to this world with its resplendent beings, with its death and God, with its ascetics and upper class, with its royalty and common people. He elucidates a teaching that is good in the beginning, good in the middle, good at the end, complete and entire in both letter and spirit, a teaching that clearly illuminates the training life."

The Buddha continued, "A person, having heard the teaching, develops confidence in the *tathāgata.* That person reflects as follows. 'The householder's life is filled with pressure and much dust; a mendicant's life is open and spacious. It is not easy for the person living a householder's life to live the life of training to its utmost fulfillment, purity, and splendor. Let me shave my hair and beard, put on the yellow robes of the mendicant, and go from home into homelessness [3.18].' After a short period, he gives away his amassed possessions, great and small; he lets go of his circle of relationships, significant and insignificant; and he shaves his hair and beard, puts on the yellow robes of the mendicant, and goes from home into homelessness.

"Now a mendicant seeker, he lives guarded by the restraints of the rules, grazing in the field of good conduct. Seeing danger even in the slightest faults, he undertakes the training precepts. Skilled in beneficial bodily and verbal conduct, he sustains his life through pure means, perfected in integrity. Watchful at the gateways to the senses, he is skilled in present-moment awareness and attention, and is contented.

"And how, Vāseṭṭha, is the practitioner a mendicant who is perfected in integrity? Having renounced the destruction of life, he is a person who abstains from the destruction of life. He has put down all weapons. He lives as a conscientious and kind person, anxious for the welfare of all sentient beings. In this way he becomes accomplished in integrity.

"Having renounced the taking of what is not given, he is a person who abstains from taking what is not given, who takes only what is given and desires only what is given. So, he spontaneously lives purely and genuinely. In this way he becomes accomplished in integrity.

"Having renounced sexual activity, he is a person who lives distanced from it, as a person who abstains from the sexual practices of the world. In this way he becomes accomplished in integrity.

"Having renounced useless speech, he is a person who abandons useless speech, who speaks according to the case, who is truthful, reliable, trustworthy, and not deceitful toward others. In this way he becomes accomplished in integrity.

"Having renounced malicious speech, he is a person who abstains from malicious speech. Hearing something here, he does not repeat it there in order to create division among others. He is thus a reconciler of those who are divided and an inspirer of those who are together. He is someone who speaks delighting in harmony, taking pleasure in harmony, and creating harmony. In this way he becomes accomplished in integrity.

"Having renounced harsh speech, he is a person who abstains from harsh speech. The words that he speaks are pleasant to the ear and affectionate; they go straight to the heart and are humane, pleasing many people, agreeable to many people. He is a person whose speech has such qualities. In this way he becomes accomplished in integrity.

"Having renounced chatter, he is a person who abstains from chatter. He is a person whose speech is timely, in accordance with the case, beneficial, just, and edifying. He is a person whose speech is a real treasure. In this way he becomes accomplished in integrity.

"And how, Vāseṭṭha, is the practitioner someone who is watchful at the gateways to the senses? Here, a practitioner, on seeing an object with his eyes, does not grasp at its general appearance or its accompanying characteristics. Because desire and dejection, as well as detrimental and unskillful qualities, would overcome him if he lived unrestrained in the eye faculty, he follows the method of restraining this faculty, he protects the eye faculty, he manifests restraint in the eye faculty. And the practitioner does so similarly for the ear and sounds, nose and scents, tongue and tastes, body and tactile objects, mind and thoughts. Maintaining this noble restraint of the senses, he experiences an unimpaired sense of ease within himself. In this way, Vāseṭṭha, he is watchful at the gateways to the senses.

"And how, Vāseṭṭha, is the practitioner someone who is endowed with clear attention and present-moment awareness? Here, he is a person who acts with clear attentiveness when going back or forth, when looking ahead or behind, when bending or stretching, when getting dressed. He acts with clear attentiveness when eating, drinking, chewing, and tasting. He is a person who acts with clear attentiveness when defecating and urinating. When walking, standing, sitting, sleeping, waking, speaking, and remaining silent, he is a person who acts with clear attentiveness. In this way, Vāseṭṭha, the practitioner is someone who is endowed with clear attention and present-moment awareness.

"And how, Vāseṭṭha, is the practitioner someone who is contented? Just as a winged bird flies here and there burdened only by its wings. In this way, Vāseṭṭha, the practitioner is someone who is contented.

"Possessing these noble traits of integrity, restraint of the senses, clear attentiveness and present-moment awareness, and contentment, the practitioner retreats to an isolated place. He sits down in a cross-legged position, holds his body erect, and establishes present-moment awareness in front of him.

"Abandoning his longing for the world, he abides with his mind freed from longing. This causes his mind to be thoroughly purified of longing.

"Abandoning hostility and anger, he abides with a friendly mind, as a person who pulses with compassion for all sentient beings. This causes his mind to be thoroughly purified of hostility and anger.

"Abandoning sluggishness and drowsiness, he abides free from sluggishness and drowsiness, as one who perceives with luminous clarity. Being attentive and mindful causes his mind to be thoroughly purified of sluggishness and drowsiness.

"Abandoning agitation and anxiety, he abides well balanced, as one whose mind is quieted from within. This causes his mind to be thoroughly purified of agitation and anxiety.

"Abandoning indecisiveness, he is a person who abides having overcome indecisiveness. By virtue of his being a person who no longer wonders why or how concerning the development of skillful qualities, his mind is purified of indecisiveness.

"When he recognizes that theses five hindrances have been eliminated, delight arises in the practitioner. Out of this delight emerges joy. Because his mind is filled with joy, his body becomes calm, and a body that is calmed experiences ease. Now, as a result of this ease, his mind becomes concentrated. Disengaged from sensual desire and unskillful qualities, he enters into and abides in the first meditative absorption, which entails applied and sustained cognizance and is born of detachment and filled with joy and ease. He suffuses his body, pervades, fills, and permeates it with joy and ease born of detachment. There is no part whatsoever of his entire body that is not saturated by this joy and ease born of detachment.

"The practitioner persists in gradually suffusing the entire world and all of space with a heart and mind filled with friendliness toward others, vast, expansive, boundless, and peaceful. Just as a powerful trumpeter could with ease make a proclamation known throughout space, the practitioner leaves nothing in the sensuous sphere untouched or unaffected by this heart released through the cultivation of friendliness.

"Then the practitioner persists in gradually suffusing the entire world and all of space with a heart and mind filled with compassion, vast, expansive, boundless, and peaceful. And further, the practitioner persists in gradually suffusing the entire world and all of space with a mind filled with joy, vast, expansive, boundless, and peaceful. And yet further, the practitioner persists in gradually suffusing the entire world and all of space with a heart and mind filled with equanimity, vast, expansive, boundless, and peaceful.

"Just as a powerful trumpeter could with ease make a proclamation known throughout space, the practitioner leaves nothing in the sensuous sphere untouched or unaffected by this heart released through the cultivation of friendliness, compassion, sympathetic joy, and equanimity.

"Vāseṭṭha, *this* is the path to communion [3.19] with God/exceptional goodness."

The Buddha continued, "What do you think, Vāseṭṭha, is a Buddhist practitioner who lives in this manner wrapped up in possessions or not?"

"Not wrapped up in possessions, friend Gotama," said Vāseṭṭha.

"Ill-tempered or composed?"

"Composed, friend Gotama."

"Antagonistic or gracious?"

"Gracious, friend Gotama."

"Corrupt or honest?"

"Honest, friend Gotama."

"Domineering or compliant?"

"Compliant, friend Gotama."

"So, Vāseṭṭha," the Buddha continued, "the practitioner is not wrapped up in possessions, and God is not wrapped up in possessions. Is there then any likeness or unity shared by the practitioner and God?"

"Yes, there is, friend Gotama," said Vāseṭṭha.

"Good, Vāseṭṭha. That a practitioner who is not wrapped up in possessions could, after death, when the body is dissolved, realize communion with God, who is also not wrapped up in possessions—that is a reasonable notion. And it is the same for a practitioner who, like God, is composed, gracious, honest, and possessing self-mastery. That a practitioner possessing such qualities could, after death, when the body is dissolved, realize communion with God, who also possesses such qualities—that is a reasonable notion."

Vāseṭṭha and Bhāradvāja then spoke to the Fortunate One. "Wonderful, wonderful, friend Gotama! It is just as if someone were to set up what had been upset, uncover what had been concealed, divulge the path to someone who had gotten lost, hold up a lamp for the blind so that those with eyes could finally see visible forms. Friend Gotama has illuminated the teaching in various ways. We go for refuge to the fortunate Gotama, and to the teaching and the community of practitioners. May the fortunate Gotama accept us as lay followers who have gone for refuge from this day for the rest of our lives!"

SUTTA 4

केसमुत्तिसुत्त

Discourse in Kesamutta

Kesamutti Sutta; Aṅguttaranikāya 3.65

THIS IS WHAT I HEARD. ONCE, THE FORTUNATE ONE WAS WANDERING IN KOSALA WITH A LARGE GROUP OF MENDICANTS WHEN HE CAME TO A VILLAGE OF THE KĀLĀMAS NAMED KESAMUTTA.

Now, the Kālāmas of Kesamutta heard that the seeker Gotama Sakyaputta, who had left the Sakya clan to enter into a life of mendicancy, had settled in Kesamutta. They said, "A favorable reputation has preceded this honorable Gotama. It is said that he is an accomplished person, a perfectly awakened person, adept in conduct and wisdom. It is certainly good to see an accomplished person like him."

So the Kālāmas of Kesamutta went to the Fortunate One. Some greeted him respectfully and then sat down next to him, some exchanged friendly greetings with him and then sat down, some bowed with their hands together in a gesture of reverence and then sat down, some told him their clan name and then sat down, some remained silent and then sat down. When they were all seated, the Kālāmas of Kesamutta spoke to the Fortunate One.

"Certain mendicants and religious authorities [4.1] come to Kesamutta. They explain and illuminate their own doctrines while cursing, reviling, despising, and emasculating the doctrines of others. Then come other mendicants and religious authorities to Kesamutta. And they explain and illuminate *their* own doctrines while cursing, reviling, despising, and emasculating the doctrines of others. We have doubts and perplexity concerning which of these teachers are speaking truthfully and which are speaking falsely."

The Buddha replied, "Kālāmas, it is understandable that you are uncertain; and it is understandable that you are perplexed. Being uncertain in this matter, you have become perplexed. You should not be convinced by unconfirmed reports, by tradition, by hearsay, by scriptures, by logical reasoning, by inferential reasoning, by reflection on superficial appearances, by delighting in opinions and speculation, by the appearance of plausibility, or because you think, *This person is our teacher* [4.2].'

"Kālāmas, when you know for yourselves [4.3] *These teachings are detrimental, these teachings are faulty, these teachings would be censured by the wise, these teachings, when fully taken up, lead to harm, to trouble*—then, Kālāmas, you should reject those teachings.

"What do you think, Kālāmas," the Buddha continued; "when infatuation, hostility, and delusion [4.4] arise in a person, is it harmful or beneficial?"

"It is harmful," replied the Kālāmas.

"A desirous, offensive, or confused person is overpowered by infatuation, hostility, and delusion. His mind overcome by these qualities, such a person also destroys life, takes what is not freely given, engages in damaging sexual relations, speaks falsely, and incites others to do just the same. Such a person is subject to harm and trouble for a long time."

And the Kālāmas replied, "That is true, sir."

The Buddha continued, "Now, what do you think, Kālāmas, are these qualities beneficial or detrimental?"

The Kālāmas responded, "Detrimental."

"Are they with or without fault?"

"With fault."

"Would they be censured or approved of by the wise?"

"They would be censured by the wise," answered the Kālāmas.

The Buddha continued, "When fully carried out, do they or do they not lead to harm and trouble? Now, how is it in such a case?"

"Fully carried out, they lead to harm and trouble. That is how it seems to us to be in such a case."

"Yes, Kālāmas! And it is for this reason that I have advised you as I have not to be convinced by unconfirmed reports, by tradition, by hearsay, by scriptures, by logical reasoning, by inferential reasoning, by reflection on superficial appearances, by delighting in opinions and speculation, by the appearance of plausibility, or because you think, *This person is our teacher.* It is for this reason that I said that when you know for yourselves *These teachings are detrimental, these teachings are faulty, these teachings would be censured by the wise, these teachings, when fully taken up, lead to harm, to trouble,* you should reject those teachings."

The Buddha continued, "You should not be convinced by unconfirmed reports, by tradition, by hearsay, by scriptures, by logical reasoning, by inferential reasoning, by reflection on superficial appearances, by delighting in opinions and speculation, by the appearance of plausibility, or because you think, *This person is our teacher.*

"Kālāmas, when you know for yourselves *These teachings are beneficial, these teachings are without fault, these teachings would be approved of by the wise, these teachings, when fully taken up, lead to welfare, to ease*—then, Kālāmas, you should live embracing those teachings.

"What do you think, Kālāmas; when infatuation, hostility, and delusion do not arise in a person, is it harmful or beneficial?"

"It is beneficial."

"A non-desirous, non-offensive, or non-confused person is not overpowered by infatuation, hostility, and delusion. His mind not overcome by these qualities, such a person does not destroy life, does not take what is not freely given, does not engage in damaging sexual relations, does not speak falsely, and does not incite others to behave in such ways. Such a person is subject to well-being and ease for a long time."

And the Kālāmas replied, "That is true, sir."

The Buddha continued, "Now, what do you think, Kālāmas, are these qualities beneficial or detrimental?"

The Kālāmas responded, "Beneficial."

"Are they with or without fault?"

"Without fault."

"Would they be censured or approved of by the wise?"

"They would be approved of by the wise," said the Kālāmas.

The Buddha continued, "When fully carried out, do they or do they not lead to well-being and ease? Now, how is it in such a case?"

"Fully carried out, they lead to well-being and ease. That is how it seems to us to be in such a case."

"Yes, Kālāmas! And it is for this reason that I have advised you as I have not to be convinced by unconfirmed reports, by tradition, by hearsay, by scriptures, by logical reasoning, by inferential reasoning, by reflection on superficial appearances, by delighting in opinions and speculation, by the appearance of plausibility, or because you think, *This person is our teacher.* It is for this reason that I said that when you know for yourselves *These teachings are beneficial, these teachings are without fault, these teachings would be accepted by the wise, these teachings, when fully taken up, lead to well-being, to ease,* you should live embracing those teachings."

The Buddha continued, "Kālāmas, the superlative practitioner, who, thus embracing beneficial teachings, becomes free from desire, free from hostility, without confusion, attentive, and mindful, dwells gradually pervading the world with a heart suffused with friendliness. He dwells pervading the entire cosmos with a vast, expansive, boundless heart [4.5] suffused with friendliness, free from hostility, free from ill will.

"The practitioner dwells gradually pervading the world with a heart suffused with compassion. He dwells pervading the entire cosmos with a vast, expansive, boundless heart suffused with compassion, free from hostility, free from ill will.

"The practitioner dwells gradually pervading the world with a heart suffused with joy. He dwells pervading the entire cosmos with a vast, expansive, boundless heart suffused with joy, free from hostility, free from ill will.

"The practitioner dwells gradually pervading the world with a heart suffused with equanimity. He dwells pervading the entire cosmos with a vast, expansive, boundless heart suffused with equanimity, free from hostility, free from ill will.

"The practitioner, thus manifesting the four boundless qualities, becomes a person whose heart is kind and gentle, open and clear. For such a person, the four comforts [4.6] are realized here and now:

"*If there is an afterlife, and if there is such a possibility as the ripening of positive and negative actions, then, after the dissolution of my body following death, I will be reborn in positive circumstances in the resplendent world beyond the starry vault.* This is the first comfort realized by the practitioner.

"*If there is not an afterlife, and if there is no such a thing as the ripening of positive and negative actions, then I will take care of myself here and now, well at ease, undisturbed, without hostility or ill will.* This is the second comfort realized by the practitioner.

"*If something harmful is done to someone who has himself done harm, then I do not wish harm on that person or on anyone else. How, then, can trouble touch me, since I did not perform the harmful action?* This is the third comfort realized by the practitioner.

"*If no harm is done to someone who has himself done harm, then in both cases I view myself as untainted.* This is the fourth comfort realized by the practitioner."

The Kālāmas replied, "Wonderful, wonderful, sir! It is just as if someone were to set up what had been upset, uncover what had been concealed, divulge the path to someone who had gotten lost, hold up a lamp for the blind so that those with eyes could finally see visible forms. The Fortunate One has illuminated the teaching in various ways. We go for refuge to the Fortunate One, and to the teaching and the community of practitioners. May the Fortunate One accept us as lay followers who have gone for refuge from this day for the rest of our lives!"

SUTTA 5

सब्बसुत्त

The All

Sabba Sutta; Saṃyuttanikāya 4.25.23

THIS WAS SPOKEN BY THE BUDDHA AT SĀVATTHĪ.

I will teach you the all. Listen to what I say.

What is the all? The eye and forms, the ear and sounds, the nose and scents, the tongue and tastes, the body and tactile objects, the mind and thoughts. This is called the all.

Someone might say, "I reject this all, I will declare another all." But because that is simply a groundless assertion, such a person, when asked about it, would not be able to explain, and would, moreover, meet with distress. What is the reason for that distress [5.1]? Because *that* all is not within his or her sensorium [5.2].

SUTTA 6

फेणपिण्डूपसुत्त

Like a Ball of Foam

Pheṇapiṇḍūpama Sutta; Saṃyuttanikāya 3.22.95

ONCE, THE FORTUNATE ONE WAS STAYING AT AYODHYA, ON THE BANKS OF THE GANGES RIVER. THERE, HE ADDRESSED SOME MENDICANTS.

Imagine that a large ball of foam were to float out of the Ganges River, and that a person with good vision would look at it, reflect on it, and carefully examine it. Looked at in such a manner, it would appear as empty, hollow, and insubstantial. For, what substance could there be in a ball of foam? In the same way, whatever appearance there may be—whether in the past, present, or future; internal or external; subtle or massive; inconsequential or exalted; close at hand or in the distance—you should look at it, reflect on it, and carefully examine it. Looked at in such a manner, it will appear as empty, hollow, and insubstantial. For, what substance could there be in an appearance [6.1]?

Imagine that in autumn, when massive rain is falling, a water bubble appears on the surface of a puddle and then dissolves. A person with good vision would look at it, reflect on it, and carefully examine it. Looked at in that manner, it would appear as empty, hollow, and insubstantial. For, what substance could there be in a water bubble? In the same way, whatever feeling there may be—whether in the past, present, or future; internal or external; subtle or massive; inconsequential or exalted; close at hand or in the distance—you should look at it, reflect on it, and carefully examine it. Looked at in that manner, it will appear as empty, hollow, and insubstantial. For, what substance could there be in a feeling [6.2]?

Imagine that at noon, late in the summer months, a shimmering mirage appears. A person with good vision would look at it, reflect on it, and carefully examine it. Looked at in that manner, it would appear as empty, hollow, and insubstantial. For, what substance could there be in a mirage? In the same way, whatever perception there may be—whether in the past, present, or future; internal or external; subtle or massive; inconsequential or exalted; close at hand or in the distance—you should look at it, reflect on it, and carefully examine it. Looked at in that manner, it will appear as empty, hollow, and insubstantial. For, what substance could there be in a perception [6.3]?

Imagine that a person, needing heartwood, searching for wood, wandering around looking for heartwood, takes a sharp ax and goes into a forest. There, the person would see the trunk of a plantain tree [6.4], straight, fresh, of enormous height. He would cut the root, then cut the top, then cut off the outer bark. Cutting off the outer bark of the tree, the person would not find even soft wood, much less heartwood. A person with good vision would look at the tree's woodless core, reflect on it, and carefully examine it. Looked at in that manner, it would appear as empty, hollow, and insubstantial. For, what substance could there be in the trunk of a plantain tree? In the same way, whatever conceptual fabrications there may be—whether in the past, present, or future; internal or external; subtle or massive; inconsequential or exalted; close at hand or in the distance—you should look at them, reflect on them, and carefully examine them. Looked at in that manner, they will appear as empty, hollow, and insubstantial. For, what substance could there be in conceptual fabrications [6.5]?

Imagine that a magician or a magician's apprentice were to conjure up a magical illusion in the city square. A person with good vision would look at it, reflect on it, and carefully examine it. Looked at in that manner, it would appear as empty, hollow, and insubstantial. For, what substance could there be in a magical illusion? In the same way, whatever cognizance there may be—whether in the past, present, or future; internal or external; subtle or massive; inconsequential or exalted; close at hand or in the distance—you should look at it, reflect on it, and carefully examine it. Looked at in that manner, it will appear as empty, hollow, and insubstantial. For, what substance could there be in cognizance [6.6]?

Seeing in this manner, as a learned superlative practitioner, you become disenchanted [6.7] with appearances, disenchanted with feeling, disenchanted with perception, disenchanted with conceptual fabrications, disenchanted with cognizance. Being disenchanted, you are free from infatuation. Because of this dispassion, you are liberated. Being liberated, the knowledge is present: *I am liberated.* And you clearly know: *Generation is exhausted. The exalted life has been lived. What had to be done was done. There is no further becoming in this state.*

THIS IS WHAT THE BUDDHA SAID. HAVING DONE SO, THE TEACHER FURTHER SAID THE FOLLOWING:

As was pointed out by the kinsman of the sun [6.8],
appearance is like a ball of foam; feeling, like a water bubble;
perception is like a mirage; conceptual fabrications like a plantain tree;
and cognizance is like a magical display.
However you reflect on it or carefully examine the matter,
to whomever looks at it with care, each is empty and hollow.
As for the body, the one with extensive insight has taught
three matters concerning its abandonment.
Seeing these, you will cast away your physical form.
The body, when devoid of vitality, heat, and cognizance,
lies there, discarded, food for some other being, without volition.
Such is the continuum, this illusory charmer of the childlike.
Although it is said that the continuum is a slayer, no substance is found here.
That is how you should regard the aggregates of being,
day and night, energetically, ardently, mindfully.
You should dissolve all bonds, make a refuge for yourself,
and live as if your head were ablaze,
yearning for the way that is never-vanishing.

SUTTA 7

अनत्तलक्खणसुत्त

Evidence of Selflessness

Anattālakkhaṇa Sutta; Saṃyuttanikāya 3.22.59

THE FORTUNATE ONE WAS ONCE STAYING AT VARANASI IN THE DEER PARK [7.1] AT ISIPATANA. THERE, HE ADDRESSED THE GROUP OF FIVE MENDICANTS [7.2].

The body [7.3] does not constitute a self [7.4]. If the body constituted a self, then it would not give us trouble [7.5], and it would be possible to manipulate the body by making determinations such as *Let my body be this way, let my body not be that way.* So, because the body does not constitute a self, it *does* give us trouble, and it *is not* possible to manipulate the body by making determinations such as *Let my body be this way, let my body not be that way.*

Feeling does not constitute a self. If feeling constituted a self, then it would not give us trouble, and it would be possible to manipulate feeling by making determinations such as *Let my feeling be this way, let my feeling not be that way.* So, because feeling does not constitute a self, it *does* give us trouble, and it *is not* possible to manipulate feeling by making determinations such as *Let my feeling be this way, let my feeling not be that way.*

Perception does not constitute a self. If perception constituted a self, then it would not give us trouble, and it would be possible to manipulate perception by making determinations such as *Let my perception be this way, let my perception not be that way.* So, because perception does not constitute a self, it *does* give us trouble, and it *is not* possible to manipulate perception by making determinations such as *Let my perception be this way, let my perception not be that way.*

Conceptual fabrications do not constitute a self. If conceptual fabrications constituted a self, then they would not give us trouble, and it would be possible to manipulate conceptual fabrications by making determinations such as *Let my conceptual fabrications be this way, let my conceptual fabrications not be that way.* So, because conceptual fabrications do not constitute a self, they *do* give us trouble, and it *is not* possible to manipulate conceptual fabrications by making determinations such as *Let my conceptual fabrications be this way, let my conceptual fabrications not be that way.*

Cognizance does not constitute a self. If cognizance constituted a self, then it would not give us trouble, and it would be possible to manipulate cognizance by making determinations such as *Let my cognizance be this way, let my cognizance not be that way.* So, because cognizance does not constitute a self, it *does* give us trouble, and it *is not* possible to manipulate cognizance by making determinations such as *Let my cognizance be this way, let my cognizance not be that way.*

THE BUDDHA THEN QUESTIONED THE FIVE MENDICANTS.

"What do you think, are the body, feeling, perception, conceptual fabrications, and cognizance permanent or impermanent [7.6]?"

The five mendicants replied, "Impermanent."

"And is that which is impermanent distressful [7.7] or gratifying?"

"Distressful."

"And is it correct to see that which is impermanent, distressful, and subject to change in terms of *This is mine, I am this, this is my self*?"

"Certainly not," said the five mendicants.

"Therefore," the Buddha continued, "whatever body there is—whether past, present, or future; internal or external; subtle or massive; inconsequential or exalted; close at hand or in the distance—every body should be seen with thorough understanding for what it is: *This is not mine, I am not this, this is not my self* [7.8].

"Similarly, whatever feeling, perception, conceptual fabrications, and cognizance there are—whether past, present, or future; internal or external; subtle or massive; inconsequential or exalted; distant or near—each of these should be seen with thorough understanding for what it is: *This is not mine, I am not this, this is not my self.*

"Seeing in this way, as a trained practitioner, you become disenchanted with the body, feeling, perception, conceptual fabrications, and cognizance. Being disenchanted, you are free from infatuation. Because of this dispassion, you are liberated. When you are liberated, the knowledge is present: *I am liberated.* And you clearly know: *Generation is exhausted. The exalted life has been lived. What had to be done was done. There is no further becoming in this state.*"

This is what the Fortunate One said. Exalted, the five mendicants rejoiced at the words of the Fortunate One. As this exposition was being spoken, the five mendicants' minds were freed from the habituated impulses through letting go.

SUTTA 8

भरासुत्त

The Burden

Bharā Sutta; Saṃyuttanikāya 3.22.22

THIS IS WHAT I HEARD [8.1]. THE FORTUNATE ONE WAS ONCE STAYING IN SĀVATTHĪ, IN JETA'S GROVE IN ANĀTHAPIṆḌIKA'S PARK. THERE, HE SPOKE TO A GROUP OF MENDICANTS.

I will teach you about the burden. I will teach you about the bearer of the burden, the taking up of the burden, and the putting down of the burden. Listen to what I say.

What, then, is the burden? To this, it should be said, *The five existential functions subject to grasping* [8.2]. Which five? The materiality function subject to grasping; the feeling function subject to grasping; the perception function subject to grasping; the conceptual fabrication function subject to grasping; and the cognizance function subject to grasping. This is what is called the burden.

And what is the bearer of the burden? To this, it should be said, *The person* [8.3]. This person named so-and-so, from such and such a family. This is what is called the bearer of the burden.

And what is the taking up of the burden? It is this craving that leads to further being, accompanied by passion and delight, seeking pleasure here and there. It is, namely, craving for sensual pleasures, craving for becoming, and craving for non-becoming. This is what is called the taking up of the burden.

And what is the putting down of the burden? It is the complete dissolution and cessation of precisely that craving, the relinquishment and rejection of it, freedom from it, non-attachment to it. This is what is called putting down the burden.

THIS IS WHAT THE FORTUNATE ONE SAID. AND WHEN HE HAD FINISHED, HE SPOKE FURTHER, AS FOLLOWS.

> Such burdens are the five existential functions subject to grasping.
> And the bearer of the burden is the person.
> Taking up the burden in this world is painful.
> Putting down the burden is happiness.
> Having put down the heavy burden,
> you should not take up another burden.
> Craving eradicated, together with its root,
> you are sated and quenched.

SUTTA 9

धम्मचक्कप्पवत्तनसुत्त

Turning the Wheel of the Teaching

Dhammacakkappavattana Sutta; Saṃyuttanikāya 5.56.11

THIS IS WHAT I HEARD. THE FORTUNATE ONE WAS ONCE STAYING AT VARANASI, IN THE DEER PARK [9.1] AT ISIPATANA. THERE HE ADDRESSED THE GROUP OF FIVE MENDICANTS [9.2] AS FOLLOWS.

"There are two extremes that are not to be embraced by a person who has set out on the path. Which two? The practice of clinging to sensory pleasure in sensory objects. This practice is lowly, common, ordinary, dishonorable, and unprofitable. And the practice of exhausting oneself with austerities. This practice is distressful, dishonorable, and unprofitable.

"Not tending toward either of these extremes, a *tathāgata* [9.3]—a person who has come to know reality—has completely awakened to the middle way [9.4]. The middle way engenders insight and understanding, and leads to calmness, to direct knowledge, to full awakening, to unbinding. So what is that middle way completely awakened to by a *tathāgata*? It is precisely this preeminent eight-component course [9.5]; namely, sound view, sound inclination, sound speech, sound action, sound livelihood, sound effort, sound awareness, and sound concentration. This is the middle way, realized by a *tathāgata*, which gives rise to vision and knowledge, and leads to calmness, to direct knowledge, to full awakening, to unbinding.

"Now, this is unease [9.6]. It is a preeminent reality [9.7]. Birth is unsettling, aging is unsettling, illness is unsettling, death is unsettling, association with what is displeasing is unsettling, separation from what is pleasing is unsettling, not getting what is wanted is unsettling. In short, the five existential functions subject to grasping [9.8] are unsettling.

"This is the origination of unease. It is a preeminent reality. It is this craving [9.9] that leads to further being, accompanied by passion and delight, seeking pleasure here and there. It is, namely, craving for sensual pleasures, craving for being, and craving for non-being.

"This is the cessation of unease [9.10]. It is a preeminent reality. It is the complete dissolution and cessation of precisely that thirst, the relinquishment and rejection of it, freedom from it, non-attachment to it.

"This is the way leading to the cessation of unease. It is a preeminent reality. It is this preeminent eight-component course; namely, sound view, sound inclination, sound speech, sound action, sound livelihood, sound effort, sound awareness, and sound concentration.

"When I realized *This is unease,* there arose in me vision, insight, discernment, knowledge, and clarity concerning things that have not been previously heard. When I realized *This unease is to be fully recognized,* there arose in me vision, insight, discernment, knowledge, and clarity concerning things that have not been previously heard. When I realized *This unease has been fully recognized,* there arose in me vision, insight, discernment, knowledge, and clarity concerning things that have not been previously heard.

"When I realized *This is the origin of unease,* there arose in me vision, insight, discernment, knowledge, and clarity concerning things that have not been previously heard. When I realized *The arising of unease is to be abandoned,* there arose in me vision, insight, discernment, knowledge, and clarity concerning things that have not been previously heard. When I realized *The arising of unease has been abandoned,* there arose in me vision, insight, discernment, knowledge, and clarity concerning things that have not been previously heard.

"When I realized *This is the cessation of unease,* there arose in me vision, insight, discernment, knowledge, and clarity concerning things that have not been previously heard. When I realized *The cessation of unease is to be realized,* there arose in me vision, insight, discernment, knowledge, and clarity concerning things that have not been previously heard. When I realized *The cessation of unease has been realized,* there arose in me vision, insight, discernment, knowledge, and clarity concerning things that have not been previously heard.

"When I realized *This is the path leading to the cessation of unease,* there arose in me vision, insight, discernment, knowledge, and clarity concerning things that have not been previously heard. When I realized *The path leading to the cessation of unease is to be cultivated,* there arose in me vision, insight, discernment, knowledge, and clarity concerning things that have not been previously heard. When I realized *The path leading to the cessation of unease has been cultivated,* there arose in me vision, insight, discernment, knowledge, and clarity concerning things that have not been previously heard.

"As long as [9.11] my insight and vision concerning these four preeminent realities just as they are, in their three sequences and twelve aspects [9.12], was not completely purified, I did not claim to have fully realized unsurpassed, complete awakening in this world with its resplendent beings, God, and death, with its seekers and priests, its supernatural beings and humans. But as soon as my insight and vision concerning these four preeminent realities just as they are was completely purified, then did I claim to have fully realized unsurpassed, complete awakening. The insight and vision arose in me: *Unwavering is my release; this is the final birth, there is now no further becoming.*"

That is what the Fortunate One said. Exalted, the group of five mendicants delighted at the words of the Fortunate One. And while this discourse was being spoken, there arose for the venerable Koṇḍañña this dustless, stainless insight: *All that is subject to origination is subject to cessation.*

And when the Fortunate One had set in motion the wheel of teaching, the resplendent earth-dwelling beings cried out, "At Varanasi, in the deer park at Isipatana, the Fortunate One has set in motion the unexcelled wheel of the teaching, which cannot be stopped by any seeker or priest, any resplendent being, by God or death, or by anyone in the world!" Hearing the resplendent earth-dwelling beings' cry, resplendent beings throughout the cosmos cried out in the exact fashion.

Thus, at that moment, at that instant, at that second, the cry extended as far as the *brahmā* realm, and this ten thousand–fold cosmos trembled, shook, and violently quaked, and an immeasurable, great radiance appeared in the cosmos, exceeding the brilliant majesty of the resplendent beings themselves.

Then the Fortunate One exclaimed this inspired utterance: "So you really know, Koṇḍañña! So you really know!" And that is how the venerable Koṇḍañña acquired the name Añña-Koṇḍañña—Koṇḍañña-Who-Knows [9.13].

SUTTA 10

गोतमसुत्त

Gotama's Discourse

Gotama Sutta; Saṃyuttanikāya 2.1.10

Before my awakening, when I was still an aspirant to awakening and not yet a fully awakened person, it occurred to me: *How troubled is this world! It is born, it decays, and it dies. It falls away and then appears yet again. And people understand but little about the escape from unease, from aging-and-death. When will an escape from this unease, this aging-and-death, be understood?*

From this consideration, it occurred to me: *There being what, does aging-and-death come to be? By means of what condition is there aging-and-death?* Because of my complete attentiveness to this matter, I came, through penetrative insight, to full comprehension [10.1]: *There being birth* [10.2], *aging-and-death comes to be. Aging-and-death is founded on birth.*

From this consideration, it occurred to me: *There being what, does birth come to be? By means of what condition is there birth?* Because of my complete attentiveness to this matter, I came, through penetrative insight, to full comprehension: *There being existence* [10.3], *birth comes to be. Birth is founded on existence.*

From this consideration, it occurred to me: *There being what, does existence come to be? By means of what condition is there existence?* Because of my complete attentiveness to this matter, I came, through penetrative insight, to full comprehension: *There being grasping* [10.4], *existence comes to be. Existence is founded on grasping.*

From this consideration, it occurred to me: *There being what, does grasping come to be? By means of what condition is there grasping?* Because of my complete attentiveness to this matter, I came, through penetrative insight, to full comprehension: *There being craving* [10.5], *grasping comes to be. Grasping is founded on craving.*

From this consideration, it occurred to me: *There being what, does craving come to be? By means of what condition is there craving?* Because of my complete attentiveness to this matter, I came, through penetrative insight, to full comprehension: *There being feeling* [10.6], *craving comes to be. Craving is founded on feeling.*

From this consideration, it occurred to me: *There being what, does feeling come to be? By means of what condition is there feeling?* Because of my complete attentiveness to this matter, I came, through penetrative insight, to full comprehension: *There being contact* [10.7], *feeling comes to be. Feeling is founded on contact.*

From this consideration, it occurred to me: *There being what, does contact come to be? By means of what condition is there contact?* Because of my complete attentiveness to this matter, I came, through penetrative insight, to full comprehension: *There being the six sense fields* [10.8], *contact comes to be. Contact is founded on the six sense fields.*

From this consideration, it occurred to me: *There being what, do the six sense fields come to be? By means of what condition are there the six sense fields?* Because of my complete attentiveness to this matter, I came, through penetrative insight, to full comprehension: *There being the mind-body entity* [10.9], *the six sense fields come to be. The six sense fields are founded on the mind-body entity.*

From this consideration, it occurred to me: *There being what, does the mind-body entity come to be? By means of what condition is there the mind-body entity?* Because of my complete attentiveness to this matter, I came, through penetrative insight, to full comprehension: *There being cognizance* [10.10], *the mind-body entity comes to be. The mind-body entity is founded on cognizance.*

From this consideration, it occurred to me: *There being what, does cognizance come to be? By means of what condition is there cognizance?* Because of my complete attentiveness to this matter, I came, through penetrative insight, to full comprehension: *There being fabrications* [10.11], *cognizance comes to be. Cognizance is founded on fabrications.*

From this consideration, it occurred to me: *There being what, do fabrications come to be? By means of what condition are there fabrications?* Because of my complete attentiveness to this matter, I came, through penetrative insight, to full comprehension: *There being ignorance* [10.12], *fabrications come to be. Fabrications are founded on ignorance.*

> So, with ignorance as the condition, there are fabrications.
> With fabrications as the condition, there is cognizance.
> With cognizance as the condition, there is the mind-body entity.
> With the mind-body entity as the condition, there are the six sense fields.
> With the six sense fields as the condition, there is contact.
> With contact as the condition, there is feeling.
> With feeling as the condition, there is craving.
> With craving as the condition, there is grasping.
> With grasping as the condition, there is existence.
> With existence as the condition, there is birth.
> With birth as the condition, there is aging-and-death.

Thus is the emergence of this entire mass of unease. It occurred to me, *This is the emergence, this is the emergence.* And there arose in me an eye for previously unheard of matters, there arose in me direct knowledge, penetrative insight, wisdom, and clear seeing.

From this consideration, it occurred to me: *There not being what, does aging-and-death not come to be? From the cessation of what does aging-and-death come to cessation?* Because of my complete attentiveness to this matter, I came, through penetrative insight, to full comprehension: *When there is not birth, aging-and-death does not come to be. The cessation of aging-and-death comes from the cessation of birth.*

From this consideration, it occurred to me: *There not being what, does birth not come to be? From the cessation of what does birth come to cessation?* Because of my complete attentiveness to this matter, I came, through penetrative insight, to full comprehension: *When there is not existence, birth does not come to be. The cessation of birth comes from the cessation of existence.*

From this consideration, it occurred to me: *There not being what, does existence not come to be? From the cessation of what does existence come to cessation?* Because of my complete attentiveness to this matter, I came, through penetrative insight, to full comprehension: *When there is not grasping, existence does not come to be. The cessation of existence comes from the cessation of grasping.*

From this consideration, it occurred to me: *There not being what, does grasping not come to be? From the cessation of what does grasping come to cessa-*

tion? Because of my complete attentiveness to this matter, I came, through penetrative insight, to full comprehension: *When there is not craving, grasping does not come to be. The cessation of grasping comes from the cessation of craving.*

From this consideration, it occurred to me: *There not being what, does craving not come to be? From the cessation of what does craving come to cessation?* Because of my complete attentiveness to this matter, I came, through penetrative insight, to full comprehension: *When there is not feeling, craving does not come to be. The cessation of craving comes from the cessation of feeling.*

From this consideration, it occurred to me: *There not being what, does feeling not come to be? From the cessation of what does feeling come to cessation?* Because of my complete attentiveness to this matter, I came, through penetrative insight, to full comprehension: *When there is not contact, feeling does not come to be. The cessation of feeling comes from the cessation of contact.*

From this consideration, it occurred to me: *There not being what, does contact not come to be? From the cessation of what does contact come to cessation?* Because of my complete attentiveness to this matter, I came, through penetrative insight, to full comprehension: *When there are not the six sense fields, contact does not come to be. The cessation of contact comes from the cessation of the six sense fields.*

From this consideration, it occurred to me: *There not being what, do the six sense fields not come to be? From the cessation of what do the six sense fields come to cessation?* Because of my complete attentiveness to this matter, I came, through penetrative insight, to full comprehension: *When there is not the mind-body entity, the six sense fields do not come to be. The cessation of the six sense fields comes from the cessation of the mind-body entity.*

From this consideration, it occurred to me: *There not being what, does the mind-body entity not come to be? From the cessation of what does the mind-body entity come to cessation?* Because of my complete attentiveness to this matter, I came, through penetrative insight, to full comprehension: *When there is not cognizance, the mind-body entity does not come to be. The cessation of the mind-body entity comes from the cessation of cognizance.*

From this consideration, it occurred to me: *There not being what, does cognizance not come to be? From the cessation of what does cognizance come to cessation?* Because of my complete attentiveness to this matter, I came, through penetrative insight, to full comprehension: *When there are no fabrications, cognizance does not come to be. The cessation of cognizance comes from the cessation of fabrications.*

From this consideration, it occurred to me: *There not being what, do fabrications not come to be? From the cessation of what do fabrications come to cessation?* Because of my complete attentiveness to this matter, I came, through penetrative insight, to full comprehension: *When there is not ignorance, fabrications do not come to be. The cessation of fabrications comes from the cessation of ignorance.*

So, with the cessation of ignorance, the cessation of fabrications.
With the cessation of fabrications, the cessation of cognizance.
With the cessation of cognizance, the cessation of the mind-body entity.
With the cessation of the mind-body entity, the cessation of the six sense fields.
With the cessation of the six sense fields, the cessation of contact.
With the cessation of contact, the cessation of feeling.
With the cessation of feeling, the cessation of craving.
With the cessation of craving, the cessation of grasping.
With the cessation of grasping, the cessation of existence.
With the cessation of existence, the cessation of birth.
With the cessation of birth, the cessation of aging-and-death.

Thus is the cessation of this entire mass of unease. It occurred to me, *This is cessation, this is cessation.* And there arose in me an eye for previously unheard of matters, there arose in me direct knowledge, penetrative insight, wisdom, and clear seeing.

SUTTA 11

परायनसुत्त

Destination

Parāyana Sutta; Saṃyuttanikāya 4.43.44

THE BUDDHA SPOKE AS FOLLOWS.

I will teach the destination and the path leading to the destination. Listen to what I say. What is the destination? The eradication of infatuation, the eradication of hostility, and the eradication of delusion [11.1] are what is called the destination. And what is the path leading to the destination? Present-moment awareness directed toward the body [11.2]. This awareness is what is called the path leading to the destination.

In this way, I have taught to you the destination and the path leading to the destination. That which should be done out of compassion by a caring teacher who desires the welfare of his students, I have done for you.

There are secluded places [11.3]. Meditate [11.4], do not be negligent! Don't have regrets later! This is my instruction to you.

SUTTA 12

निब्बुतसुत्त

Quenched

Nibbuta Sutta; Aṅguttaranikāya 3.55

ONCE, A MAN CALLED JĀṆUSSOṆI APPROACHED THE FORTUNATE ONE. EXCHANGING GREETINGS, HE SAT DOWN NEXT TO THE FORTUNATE ONE AND SPOKE.

"It is said, 'Unbinding [12.1] is conspicuous [12.2], unbinding is conspicuous.' In what regard, friend Gotama, is unbinding conspicuous? In what regard is it palpable, leading the practitioner to *come and see* [12.3], and to be personally realized by the wise?"

The Buddha replied, "Jāṇussoṇi, an infatuated, hostile, and deluded person comes to the realization that through the overwhelming power of infatuation, hostility, and delusion, he has become mentally exhausted, and that he is hurting himself and others. And that person becomes depressed and distressed. He realizes that if infatuation, hostility, and delusion were eradicated, he would no longer hurt himself, he would no longer hurt others, and he would no longer experience depression and distress. It is in this way, Jāṇussoṇi, that unbinding is conspicuous. Because a person realizes the absolute eradication of infatuation, the absolute eradication of hostility, and the absolute eradication of delusion, unbinding is conspicuous, palpable, leading the practitioner to *come and see*, and to be personally realized by the wise."

SUTTA 13

सङ्खतलक्खणसुत्त

Signs of the Fabricated

Saṅkhatalakkhaṇa Sutta; Aṅguttaranikāya 3.47

THE BUDDHA SPOKE AS FOLLOWS.

There are three signs that something is fabricated. What are the three? Its arising is evident. Its vanishing is evident. And its alteration while persisting is evident. These are the three signs that something is fabricated.

SUTTA 14

असङ्खतलक्खणसुत्त

Signs of the Unfabricated

Asaṅkhatalakkhaṇa Sutta; Aṅguttaranikāya 3.48

THE BUDDHA SPOKE AS FOLLOWS.

There are three signs that something is unfabricated. What are the three? No arising is evident. No vanishing is evident. And no alteration while persisting is evident. These are the three signs that something is unfabricated.

SUTTA 15

आनापानसतिसुत्त

Present-Moment Awareness with Breathing

Ānāpānasati Sutta; Majjhimanikāya 118

THIS IS WHAT I HEARD. THE FORTUNATE ONE WAS ONCE STAYING IN SĀVATTHĪ, IN THE EASTERN PARK OF MIGĀRA'S MOTHER'S PALACE, TOGETHER WITH MANY HIGHLY DISTINGUISHED SENIOR DISCIPLES. THE VENERABLE SĀRIPUTTA, THE VENERABLE MAHĀMOGGALLĀNA, THE VENERABLE MAHĀKASSAPA, THE VENERABLE MAHĀKACCAYA, THE VENERABLE ĀNANDA, AND MANY OTHERS WERE THERE.

At that time, the senior practitioners were teaching and instructing the novice practitioners. Some were teaching ten, others twenty, thirty, or forty novices. So, these novices gradually realized increasingly excellent progress.

Now, at this time, the Fortunate One was surrounded by the community of practitioners, sitting in the open air. This was on the day of assembly, during the Pavāraṇā ceremony [15.1], on the fifteenth night of the month, when the moon is full. The Fortunate One, surveying the utterly silent community, said, "I am pleased with this progress. In my heart I am pleased with this progress. So, you should energetically exert yourselves still more, mastering what you have not yet mastered, experiencing what you have not yet experienced, realizing what you have not yet realized. I will return here to Sāvatthī on the full moon day of the white water lily month, the fourth month."

When the practitioners living in the countryside heard this, they left in due course to go see the Fortunate One. There, the senior practitioners still more intensely taught and instructed the novice practitioners.

Then, on the day of assembly, on the night of the full moon of the fourth month, the Buddha was surrounded by the community of practitioners, sitting in the open air. Surveying the utterly silent community, the Fortunate One gave the following discourse.

—

This assembly is free from mindless chatter, this assembly is free from trivial prattle. It is established purely in the heart of the matter [15.2]. Such is the nature of this community, such is the nature of this assembly, that it is deserving and worthy of the world's offerings and respect as an incomparable field of merit. Such is the nature of this community that a small offering to it becomes great, and a great offering becomes even greater. Such is the nature of this community that the world rarely ever sees something of its kind. Such is the nature of this community that it would be worth traveling many miles just to see an assembly of its kind.

There are practitioners [15.3] in this community who are accomplished, *arahants*. They have destroyed their habituated impulses [15.4], fulfilled the training, done what had to be done, put down the burden, reached the ideal state beyond rebirth, completely destroyed the bonds of existence [15.5]. These accomplished ones have been completely liberated through sound knowledge. There are indeed practitioners of such a kind in this community.

There are practitioners in this community who, by means of destroying the five lower bonds, spontaneously reappear elsewhere [15.6], becoming unbound there, not to return from that world. There are indeed practitioners of such a kind in this community.

There are practitioners in this community who, by means of the destruction of the three bonds and the gradual elimination of attraction, aversion, and delusion, return to this world only once, as once-returners, bringing distress to an end. There are indeed practitioners of such a kind in this community.

There are practitioners in this community who are stream-enterers [15.7], no longer subject to frustration, steady, bound for awakening. There are indeed practitioners of such a kind in this community.

There are practitioners in this community who live applying themselves to the practices of cultivating the application of present-moment awareness in the four areas [15.8], the four sound efforts [15.9], the four bases of success [15.10], the five natural strengths [15.11], the five developed powers [15.12], the seven factors of awakening [15.13], and the preeminent eight-component course [15.14]. There are indeed practitioners of such a kind in this community.

There are practitioners in this community who live applying themselves to the practices of cultivating friendliness, compassion, joy, and equanimity [15.15] and of cultivating the perception of impermanence and impurity. There are indeed practitioners of such a kind in this community.

There are practitioners in this community who live applying themselves to the practice of cultivating present-moment awareness with breathing. When present-moment awareness with breathing is persistently practiced and cultivated, it is rich in results and of great benefit. This practice perfects present-moment awareness in the four areas. When present-moment awareness in the four areas is persistently practiced and cultivated, the seven factors of awakening are perfected. When these seven factors of awakening are persistently practiced and cultivated, this perfects higher knowledge and release [15.16].

1. *Place and Posture*

And how is present-moment awareness with breathing persistently practiced and cultivated so that it is rich in results and of great benefit? Now, go to the woods, to the root of a tree, or to an empty hut, sit down in a cross-legged position, and straighten your body. Establishing present-moment awareness right where you are, breathe in, simply aware, then breathe out, simply aware [15.17].

2. *Sixteen-Point Practice*

BODY

1. Breathing in long, know directly [15.18] *I am breathing in long.* Breathing out long, know directly *I am breathing out long.*
2. Breathing in short, know directly *I am breathing in short.* Breathing out short, know directly *I am breathing out short.* You should train as follows [15.19]:
3. I breathe in, sensitive to the entire body. I breathe out, sensitive to the entire body.

4. I breathe in, quieting the bodily formation. I breathe out, quieting everything that constitutes the body.

FEELING

You should train as follows:

5. I breathe in, sensitive to delight. I breathe out, sensitive to delight.
6. I breathe in, sensitive to ease. I breathe out, sensitive to ease.
7. I breathe in, sensitive to mental reactions. I breathe out, sensitive to mental reactions.
8. I breathe in, calming mental reactions. I breathe out, calming mental reactions.

MIND

You should train as follows:

9. I breathe in, sensitive to the mind. I breathe out, sensitive to the mind.
10. I breathe in, gladdening the mind. I breathe out, gladdening the mind.
11. I breathe in, composing the mind. I breathe out, composing the mind.
12. I breathe in, releasing the mind. I breathe out, releasing the mind.

MENTAL QUALITIES AND PHENOMENA

You should train as follows:

13. I breathe in, observing impermanence. I breathe out, observing impermanence.
14. I breathe in, observing dissolution. I breathe out, observing dissolution.
15. I breathe in, observing cessation. I breathe out, observing cessation.
16. I breathe in, observing relinquishment. I breathe out, observing relinquishment.

It is in this manner that present-moment awareness with breathing, when persistently practiced and cultivated, is rich in results and of great benefit.

3. *The Four Areas of Present-Moment Awareness*

And how does present-moment awareness with breathing, when cultivated and persistently practiced, constitute mastery of present-moment awareness in the four areas?

BODY

1. When attending to the bodily phenomena as described, the practitioner dwells observing the body *in and as* [15.20] *the body,* ardent, fully aware, and attentive, having given up longing and discontentment toward the world. I am speaking here of a certain kind of body among bodies; namely, this inhalation and exhalation of the breath. This is why the practitioner abides at that time observing the body *in and as the body,* ardent, fully aware, and attentive, having given up longing and discontentment toward the world.

FEELING

2. When attending to the sensations of feeling and perception as described, the practitioner dwells observing feelings *in and as feelings,* ardent, fully aware, and attentive, having given up longing and discontentment toward the world. I am speaking here of a certain kind of feeling among feelings; namely, thorough attentiveness to the inhalation and exhalation of the breath. This is why the practitioner abides at that time observing feelings *in and as feelings,* ardent, fully aware, and attentive, having given up longing and discontentment toward the world.

MIND

3. When attending to the mind as described, the practitioner abides observing mind *in and as mind,* ardent, fully aware, and attentive, having given up longing and discontentment toward the world. I am *not* saying that there is awareness of breathing for a person who is not fully aware and is forgetful. This is why the practitioner abides at that time observing mind *in and as mind,* ardent, fully aware, and attentive, having given up longing and discontentment toward the world.

MENTAL QUALITIES AND PHENOMENA

4. When attending to thoughts as described, the practitioner abides observing mental qualities and phenomena *in and as mental qualities and phenomena,* ardent, fully aware, and attentive, having given up longing and discontentment toward the world. Having seen, having realized, the abandonment of longing and discontentment, the practitioner becomes a person who observes with care and equanimity. This is why the practitioner abides at that time observing mental qualities and phenomena *in and as mental qualities and phenomena,* ardent, fully aware, and attentive, having given up longing and discontentment toward the world.

It is in this manner that present-moment awareness with breathing, when cultivated and persistently practiced, constitutes mastery of present-moment awareness in the four areas.

4. *The Seven Factors of Awakening*

And how does mastery of present-moment awareness in the four areas, when cultivated and persistently practiced, constitute mastery of the seven factors of awakening [15.21]?

PRESENT-MOMENT AWARENESS

1. When practicing in the manner described, present-moment awareness [15.22] becomes established and continuous. And when it does, the awakening factor of present-moment awareness is aroused. At that moment when it is aroused, the practitioner cultivates the awakening factor of present-moment awareness. Cultivating it, the practitioner brings the awakening factor of present-moment awareness to fulfillment.

INVESTIGATION INTO QUALITIES

2. Abiding aware in this way, the practitioner examines and investigates each mental quality with insight and undertakes a thorough inquiry into it. Doing so, the practitioner arouses the awakening factor of investigation into qualities [15.23]. So aroused, the practitioner cultivates the awakening factor of investigation into qualities. Cultivating it, the practitioner brings the awakening factor of investigation into qualities to fulfillment.

ENERGY

3. In the practitioner who examines and investigates each phenomenon with insight and undertakes a thorough inquiry into it, invigorating energy [15.24] is aroused. At this moment, the awakening factor of energy is manifested. So manifested, the practitioner cultivates the awakening factor of energy. Cultivating it, the practitioner brings to fulfillment the awakening factor of energy.

DELIGHT

4. In the practitioner who has aroused invigorating energy, there is born unfleshly delight [15.25]. At this moment, the awakening factor of delight is manifested. So manifested, the practitioner cultivates the awakening factor of delight. Cultivating it, the practitioner brings to fulfillment the awakening factor of delight.

TRANQUILLITY

5. For the practitioner who has aroused delight, the body is quiet, and the mind is quiet. At this moment, the awakening factor of tranquillity [15.26] is aroused. So aroused, the practitioner cultivates the awakening factor of tranquillity. Cultivating it, the practitioner brings to fulfillment the awakening factor of tranquillity.

CONCENTRATION

6. For the practitioner whose body is calm and who is at ease, the mind becomes concentrated. At this moment, the awakening factor of concentration [15.27] is aroused. So aroused, the practitioner cultivates the awakening factor of concentration. Cultivating it, the practitioner brings to fulfillment the awakening factor of concentration.

EQUANIMITY

7. With the mind concentrated in this way, the practitioner becomes a person who observes with thoroughgoing care and equanimity [15.28]. At this moment, the awakening factor of equanimity is aroused. So aroused, the practitioner cultivates the awakening factor of equanimity. Cultivating it, the practitioner brings to fulfillment the awakening factor of equanimity.

Cultivated and persistently practiced in this way, present-moment awareness in the four areas fulfills the seven factors of awakening.

5. *Penetrative Insight and Release*

How do the seven factors of awakening, when cultivated and persistently practiced, fulfill penetrative insight and release? Each of the factors of awakening, rooted in detachment, dispassion, and dissolution, ripens in relinquishment. It is in this way that the seven factors of awakening, when cultivated and persistently practiced, fulfill penetrative insight and release.

This is what the Fortunate One said. Exalted, those practitioners delighted in the words of the Fortunate One.

SUTTA 16

महासतिपट्ठानसुत्त

The Application of Present-Moment Awareness

Mahāsatipaṭṭhāna Sutta; Majjhimanikāya 10

THIS IS WHAT I HEARD. ON ONE OCCASION, THE FORTUNATE ONE WAS STAYING IN THE REGION OF THE KURUS, WHERE THERE WAS A VILLAGE CALLED KAMMĀSADHAMMA. THERE, THE FORTUNATE ONE SPOKE TO THE MENDICANTS.

The direct path [16.1] for the purification of beings, for the overcoming of sadness and distress, for the cessation of unease and depression, for finding the way, and for the direct realization of unbinding is this: the application of present-moment awareness in four areas. What are the four areas? Now, being ardent, fully aware, and mindful, and having put down longing and discontentment toward the world, you should live [16.2] observing the body *in and as the body,* live observing feelings *in and as feelings,* live observing mind *in and as mind,* and live observing mental qualities and phenomena *in and as mental qualities and phenomena.*

I. THE BODY

FIRST PRACTICE: PRESENT-MOMENT AWARENESS WITH BREATHING

How should you live observing the body in and as the body [16.3]? Now, go to the woods, to the root of a tree, or to an empty hut, sit down in a cross-legged position, and straighten your body. Establishing present-moment awareness right where you are, breathe in [16.4], simply aware, then breathe out, simply aware. Breathing in long, know directly *I am breathing in long.* Breathing out long, know directly *I am breathing out long.* Breathing in short, know directly *I am breathing in short.* Breathing out short, know directly *I am breathing out short.* Train as follows: *I breathe in experiencing the whole body. I breathe out experiencing the whole body. I breathe in quieting everything that constitutes the body. I breathe out quieting everything that constitutes the body.*

Just as a skilled acrobat or his apprentice, when making a long turn, knows directly *I am making a long turn* or, making a short turn, knows directly *I am making a short turn,* so do you, breathing in a long breath, know directly *I am breathing in a long breath* or, breathing out a short breath, know directly *I am breathing out a short breath.* Train in this manner: *Experiencing the whole body, I breathe in and out; quieting everything that constitutes the body, I breathe in and out.*

In just this manner should you live observing the body, either your own or others' [16.5], in and as the body. Live observing the nature of arising within the body, or the nature of cessation within the body, or both simultaneously. Even just realizing that *this is a body,* the practitioner makes awareness present. To just the extent that you directly know and are simply mindful are you one who lives unattached, not grasping at anything whatsoever in the world. This is how a practitioner lives observing the body in and as the body.

Second Practice: The Four Postures

Furthermore, when walking, know directly *I am walking;* when standing, know directly *I am standing;* when sitting, know directly *I am sitting;* or when lying down, know directly *I am lying down.* However your body is disposed, know that directly.

In just this manner should you live observing the body, either your own or others', in and as the body, and so on, as in the previous practice. This is how a practitioner lives observing the body in and as the body.

Third Practice: Full Attention

Furthermore, when going here or there, do so with full attention; when looking here or there, do so with full attention; when bending over or stretching out, do so with full attention; when getting dressed, do so with full attention; when eating, drinking, chewing, and tasting, do so with full attention; when defecating or urinating, do so with full attention; when walking, standing, sitting, sleeping, being awake, speaking, remaining silent, do so with full attention.

In just this manner should you live observing the body, either your own or others', in and as the body, and so on, as in the previous practices. This is how a practitioner lives observing the body in and as the body.

FOURTH PRACTICE: CAREFUL CONSIDERATION OF REPULSIVE BODILY FEATURES

Furthermore, investigate your body from the soles of the feet upward, and from the hair on the head downward—this body wrapped in skin, full of various kinds of repulsive features. Investigate as follows: *In or on this body of mine, there is head hair, skin hair, nails, teeth, flesh, tendons, bones, marrow, kidneys, heart, liver, diaphragm, spleen, lungs, intestines, bowels, stomach, excrement, bile, phlegm, pus, blood, sweat, fat, tears, oils, saliva, mucus, joint fluid, and urine.*

Just as if there were a sack filled at both ends with various kinds of grains, such as rice and seeds, and someone with eyes to see, opening that sack, would investigate them as follows—*This one is a piece of rice, this one is a seed*—just so should you investigate your body from the soles of the feet upward, and from the hair on the head downward.

In just this manner should you live observing the body, either your own or others', in and as the body, and so on, as in the previous practices. This is how a practitioner lives observing the body in and as the body.

FIFTH PRACTICE: CAREFUL CONSIDERATION OF THE ELEMENTS

Furthermore, you should investigate your body just as it is, however it is disposed, as consisting of elements [16.6], as follows: *In this very body of mine there is the earth element, solidity; the water element, liquidity; the fire element, combustion; and the air element, currency.*

Just as a skilled butcher or butcher's apprentice, having slaughtered a cow and divided it into pieces, would sit down at an intersection, just so should you investigate your body just as it is, however it is disposed, as consisting of the four elements.

In just this manner should you live observing the body, either your own or others', in and as the body, and so on, as in the previous practices. This is how a practitioner lives observing the body in and as the body.

THE NINE CREMATION GROUND CONTEMPLATIONS

SIXTH PRACTICE: Now, imagine that you were to see, in a cremation ground [16.7], a corpse that had been discarded for several days and become swollen, discolored, and festering. Making your body the focal point, reflect: *This body of mine is of the same nature as that one; it will become just like that one; it, too, is not free from death.*

SEVENTH PRACTICE: Next, imagine that you were to see a discarded corpse that had been devoured by various wild animals. Making your body the focal point, reflect: *This body of mine is of the same nature as that one; it will become just like that one; it, too, is not free from death.*

EIGHTH PRACTICE: Next, imagine that you were to see a discarded corpse, a skeleton retaining some flesh, still bound by tendons. Making your body the focal point, reflect: *This body of mine is of the same nature as that one; it will become just like that one; it, too, is not free from death.*

NINTH PRACTICE: Next, imagine that you were to see a discarded corpse, a fleshless skeleton smeared with blood, still bound by tendons. Making your body the focal point, reflect: *This body of mine is of the same nature as that one; it will become just like that one; it, too, is not free from death.*

TENTH PRACTICE: Next, imagine that you were to see a discarded corpse, a skeleton completely devoid of flesh, still bound by tendons. Making your body the focal point, reflect: *This body of mine is of the same nature as that one; it will become just like that one; it, too, is not free from death.*

ELEVENTH PRACTICE: Next, imagine that you were to see completely disconnected bones, strewn here and there—hand bone, foot bone, anklebone, calf bone, thighbone, hip bone, ribs, backbone, shoulder bone, neck bone, jawbone, teeth, skull. Making your body the focal point, reflect: *This body of mine is of the same nature as that one; it will become just like that one; it, too, is not free from death.*

Twelfth Practice: Next, imagine that you were to see a discarded corpse, bones as white as pearl. Making your body the focal point, reflect: *This body of mine is of the same nature as that one; it will become just like that one; it, too, is not free from death.*

Thirteenth Practice: Next, imagine that you were to see a discarded corpse, bones piled up and decayed. Making your body the focal point, reflect: *This body of mine is of the same nature as that one; it will become just like that one; it, too, is not free from death.*

Fourteenth Practice: Next, imagine that you were to see a discarded corpse, bones reduced to powder. Making your body the focal point, reflect: *This body of mine is of the same nature as that one; it will become just like that one; it, too, is not free from death.*

In just this manner should you live observing the body, either your own or others', in and as the body. Live observing the nature of arising within the body, or the nature of cessation within the body, or both simultaneously. Even just realizing that *this is a body,* awareness is made present. To just the extent that you directly know and are simply mindful are you one who lives unattached, not grasping at anything whatsoever in the world. This is how a practitioner lives observing the body in and as the body.

II. FEELINGS

Fifteenth Practice: Now, how should you live observing feelings [16.8] in and as feelings? Experiencing an agreeable feeling, know directly *I am experiencing an agreeable feeling.* Experiencing a disagreeable feeling, know directly *I am experiencing a disagreeable feeling.* Or experiencing a feeling that is neither agreeable nor disagreeable, know directly *I am experiencing a feeling that is neither agreeable nor disagreeable.* Experiencing a material feeling, whether agreeable, disagreeable, or neither, know that directly. Or experiencing an immaterial feeling [16.9], whether agreeable, disagreeable, or neither, know that directly.

In just this manner should you live observing feelings, either your own or others', in and as feelings. Live observing the nature of arising within feelings, or the nature of cessation within feelings, or both simultaneously. Even just realizing that *this is a feeling,* awareness is made present. To just the extent that you directly know and are simply mindful are you one who lives unattached, not grasping at anything whatsoever in the world. This is how a practitioner lives observing feelings in and as feelings.

III. MIND

SIXTEENTH PRACTICE: Now, how should you live observing mind [16.10] in and as mind? Know a mind possessed of infatuation directly as a mind possessed of infatuation. Know a mind free from infatuation directly as a mind free from infatuation. Know a mind possessed of anger directly as a mind possessed of anger. Know a mind free from anger directly as a mind free from anger. Know a mind possessed of delusion directly as a mind possessed of delusion. Know a mind free from delusion directly as a mind free from delusion. Know an attentive mind directly as an attentive mind. Know an inattentive mind directly as an inattentive mind. Know an expansive mind directly as an expansive mind. Know a contracted mind directly as a contracted mind. Know an undignified mind directly as an undignified mind. Know a dignified mind directly as a dignified mind. Know a concentrated mind directly as a concentrated mind. Know a scattered mind directly as a scattered mind. Know a relaxed mind directly as a relaxed mind. Know a tense mind directly as a tense mind.

In just this manner should you live observing mind, either your own or others', in and as mind. Live observing the nature of arising within the mind, or the nature of cessation within the mind, or both simultaneously. Even just realizing that *this is mind,* the practitioner makes awareness present. To just the extent that you directly know and are simply mindful are you one who lives unattached, not grasping at anything whatsoever in the world. This is how a practitioner lives observing mind in and as mind.

IV. MENTAL QUALITIES AND PHENOMENA

Seventeenth Practice: Observing Mental Qualities and Phenomena in Relation to the Five Hindrances

Now, how should you live observing mental qualities and phenomena [16.11] in an as mental qualities and phenomena? You do so by observing mental qualities and phenomena in and as mental qualities and phenomena in relation to the five hindrances. How do you do this?

When there is an impulse within toward sensual desire, know directly *There is an impulse toward sensual desire within me.* When there is no impulse within toward sensual desire, know directly *There is no impulse toward sensual desire within me.* As for the arising of a previously unarisen impulse toward sensual desire, know that directly. As for the cessation of a previously arisen impulse toward sensual desire, know that directly. As for the non-arising in the future of a ceased impulse toward sensual desire, know that directly.

When there is hostility within, know directly *There is hostility within me.* When there is no hostility within, know directly *There is no hostility within me.* As for the arising of previously unarisen hostility, know that directly. As for the cessation of previously arisen hostility, know that directly. As for the non-arising in the future of ceased ill will toward others, know that directly.

When there is heavy lethargy within, know directly *There is heavy lethargy within me.* When there is no heavy lethargy within, know directly *There is no heavy lethargy within me.* As for the arising of previously unarisen heavy lethargy, know that directly. As for the cessation of previously arisen heavy lethargy, know that directly. As for the non-arising in the future of ceased heavy lethargy, know that directly.

When there is agitated worry within, know directly *There is agitated worry within me.* When there is no agitated worry within, know directly *There is no agitated worry within me.* As for the arising of previously unarisen agitated worry, know that directly. As for the cessation of previously arisen agitated worry, know that directly. As for the non-arising in the future of ceased agitated worry, know that directly.

When there is debilitating doubt within, know directly *There is debilitating doubt within me.* When there is no debilitating doubt within, know directly *There is no debilitating doubt within me.* As for the arising of previously unarisen debilitating doubt, know that directly. As for the cessation of previously arisen debilitating doubt, know that directly. As for the non-arising in the future of ceased debilitating doubt, know that directly.

In just this manner should you live observing mental qualities and phenomena, either your own or others', in and as mental qualities and phenomena.

Eighteenth Practice: Observing Mental Qualities and Phenomena in Relation to the Five Existential Functions Subject to Grasping

Furthermore, you should live observing mental qualities and phenomena in and as mental qualities and phenomena in relation to the five existential functions subject to grasping. How do you do this? Reflect as follows: (1) *This is an appearance. This is the arising of the appearance. This is the disappearance of the appearance.* (2) *This is a feeling. This is the arising of the feeling. This is the disappearance of the feeling.* (3) *This is a perception. This is the arising of the perception. This is the disappearance of the perception.* (4) *These are conceptual fabrications. This is the arising of conceptual fabrications. This is the disappearance of conceptual fabrications.* (5) *This is cognizance. This is the arising of cognizance. This is the disappearance of cognizance.*

In just this manner should you live observing mental qualities and phenomena, either your own or others', in and as mental qualities and phenomena.

Nineteenth Practice: Mental Qualities and Phenomena in Relation to the Spheres of Perception

Furthermore, you should live observing mental qualities and phenomena in and as mental qualities and phenomena in relation to the six internal and external spheres of perception. How do you do this?

Know the eye directly; and directly know visible forms. Know the ear directly; and directly know sounds. Know the nose directly; and directly know scents. Know the tongue directly; and directly know tastes. Know the body directly; and directly know tactile objects. Know the mind directly; and directly know thoughts. And in each case, when, on the basis of the two—eye, visible forms; ear, sounds; and so on—a bind is produced, know that directly. As for the production of a previously unproduced bind, know that directly. As for the cessation of a previously produced bind, know that directly. As for the non-production in the future of a ceased bind, know that directly.

In just this manner should you live observing mental qualities and phenomena, either your own or others', in and as mental qualities and phenomena.

Twentieth Practice: Observing Mental Qualities and Phenomena in Relation to the Factors of Awakening

Furthermore, you should live observing mental qualities and phenomena in and as mental qualities and phenomena in relation to the seven factors of awakening. How do you do this?

When the awakening factor of present-moment awareness is present within you, know directly *The awakening factor of present-moment awareness is present within me.*

When the awakening factor of investigation of qualities is present within you, know directly *The awakening factor of investigation of qualities is present within me.*

When the awakening factor of energy is present within you, know directly *The awakening factor of energy is present within me.*

When the awakening factor of delight is present within you, know directly *The awakening factor of delight is present within me.*

When the awakening factor of tranquillity is present within you, know directly *The awakening factor of tranquillity is present within me.*

When the awakening factor of concentration is present within you, know directly *The awakening factor of concentration is present within me.*

When the awakening factor of equanimity is present within you, know directly *The awakening factor of equanimity is present within me.*

In just this manner should you live observing mental qualities and phenomena, either your own or others', in and as mental qualities and phenomena.

Twenty-first Practice: Mental Qualities and Phenomena in Relation to the Preeminent Realities

Furthermore, you should live observing mental qualities and phenomena in and as mental qualities and phenomena in relation to the four preeminent realities. How do you do this?

This is unease: know this directly, just as it is. *This is the arising of unease:* know this directly, just as it is. *This is the cessation of unease:* know this directly, just as it is. *This is the path leading to the cessation of unease:* know this directly, just as it is.

In just this manner should you live observing mental qualities and phenomena, either your own or others', in and as mental qualities and phenomena.

Live observing the nature of arising within mental qualities and phenomena, or the nature of cessation within mental qualities and phenomena, or both simultaneously. Even just realizing that *these are mental qualities and phenomena,* the practitioner makes awareness present. To just the extent that you directly know and are simply mindful are you one who lives unattached, not grasping at anything whatsoever in the world. This is how a practitioner lives observing mental qualities and phenomena in and as mental qualities and phenomena.

FRUITS OF THE PRACTICE

Whoever cultivates these four applications of present-moment awareness for seven years can expect one of two results: penetrative insight right here and now or, if there is a remnant of the grasping tendency, the state of a non-returner.

Let alone seven years, whoever cultivates these four applications of present-moment awareness for six, five, four, three, two years, or even one year, can expect one of those two results.

Let alone one year, whoever cultivates these four applications of present-moment awareness for seven, six, five, four, three, two months, one month, or even half a month, can expect one of those two results.

Let alone half a month, whoever cultivates these four applications of present-moment awareness for seven days [16.12], can expect one of two results: penetrative insight right here and now or, if there is a remnant of the grasping tendency, the state of a non-returner. The basis for my assertion of the direct path for the purification of beings, for the overcoming of sadness and distress, for the cessation of unease and depression, for finding the way, and for the direct realization of unbinding is this: the application of present-moment awareness in four areas.

This is what the Fortunate One said. Exalted, the practitioners rejoiced at the words of the Fortunate One.

GUIDE TO READING THE TEXTS

SUTTA I

सकुणग्घिसुत्त

Wandering Beyond Our Proper Domain

Sakuṇagghi Sutta: "The Hawk"; *Saṃyuttanikāya* 5.47.6

WE ARE LIKE GHOSTS SLEEPWALKING IN A DESOLATE AND DANGEROUS DOMAIN. (HABITAT)

The first proposition states that we are oblivious to an aspect of our existence that is so immediate and foundational that the Buddha calls it our "native domain" and our "ancestral, natural habitat." Unconscious as we are, we grasp after the stream of sensory objects whizzing past us endlessly. Doing so is like clutching at clouds as you fall through space.

To get some bearing on the direction of this proposition, and on your "natural habitat," ask yourself this question: What is the *stuff* of my life? What kinds of things—objects, matter, phenomena—surround me? Have you ever carefully noticed? In this *sutta*, the Buddha posits that we have developed the poor habit of not really paying attention to the objects that constitute our lived experience, and that this lack of attentiveness makes us unconscious of the ways in which we relate to this existential *stuff.* In the proposition, I suggest that this unconsciousness renders us groundless, somewhat like wandering ghosts. In the *sutta,* the Buddha asks us to consider whether there might be harmful consequences in seeking our grounding in sensory fulfillment. Finally, he proposes that we learn to make ourselves at home in our "ancestral, natural habitat."

So, let's consider this proposition. Again, pose yourself the question: What is the *stuff* of my life, moment by moment? Putting aside the concept "life," and just paying attention for a moment, can you identify the actual phenomena that constitute your lived experience? Do you notice the appearance of forms—sights, sounds, scents, tactile feelings, and tastes? Just notice for a moment. Now, can you notice your reaction to any one of these, say, a particular sound? This sound together with our affective manner of being in relation to it is what the Buddha calls our "habitat" and "domain."

In the *sutta*, however, the notion of a domain is somewhat charged. The Buddha presents two possibilities. At any given moment, we may wander into hostile territory or we may rest secure at home. If we live in perpetual pursuit of the *stuff* arising ceaselessly around us, then we are lost. If we live with ardent and persistent clarity about the agitating nature of that *stuff*, then we remain at home, naturally settled and content.

The imagery used by the Buddha here points to the animalistic compulsion of humans both to wander off seeking pleasure in things (the quail) and to hunt down whatever appears within our scope (the hawk). At the same time, though, the simple narrative mode of presentation points to the childlike obviousness of the matters at hand.

In this *sutta*, the Buddha is asking you merely to *see* what is already apparent. Only once you have made your habitat clear to yourself will you have the degree of stability and insight required for further work. And only then will you cease to wander ghostlike in the field of insatiable sensory delight.

NOTES

1.1. *Death will gain access.* The Buddha often uses the term *māra*, "death," idiosyncratically. In ancient India, Māra was a mythological figure personifying death. So the text can be read as evoking an image of some sort of supernatural boogeyman-type being coming to get the incautious person. But who has ever seen such a being, other than on Halloween? More threatening, because more real, is *māra* as the insidious, impulsive grasping tendency of every normal human being. As we will see in "Threefold Knowledge" (*sutta* 3), the Buddha cautions against the easy leap of logic from natural process to divine being. In the following exchange, he clearly identifies *māra* with the same kind of potentially deadening involvement with phenomena as that which is posited in the present *sutta:*

> The venerable Rādha approached the Fortunate One . . . and said to him: "Sir, it is said, 'Māra, Māra.' In what way, sir, might there exist Māra?" [The Buddha answered:] "When there is form, Rādha, there might exist Māra, or the killer, or the one who is killed. Therefore, Rādha, see form as Māra [and so, too, feeling, perception, mental fabrications, and cognizance].
>
> (*Saṃyuttanikāya* 3.23.1)

1.2. *fivefold realm of sensual pleasure.* Thoughts are usually included as the sixth sense object (the mind being the sense organ, paralleling ear, eye, et cetera).

1.3. *foundation of present-moment awareness.* This translates *satipaṭṭhāna*, the Buddha's term for the practice of maintaining moment-to-moment clarity as we live our lives. The first term, *sati*, present-moment awareness, is one of the Buddha's most important technical terms. Briefly, it connotes the natural human capacity to be attentive to whatever is appearing in one's being in an open, clear, and nonintrusive manner. The second term, *paṭṭhāna*, refers to the application or foundation of that awareness. Although it is alluded to only in passing here, *satipaṭṭhāna* is as important to the Buddha's way as seated meditation. The practice is treated in detail in "The Application of Present-Moment Awareness" (*sutta* 16).

1.4. *four areas.* If you look carefully, the Buddha holds, you will notice four "places" or instances where your being *stands out, takes place*—literally *exists* (Latin: *exsistere*, "stands forth"). These four places are your body, your feelings, your mind, and particular mental qualities and phenomena. Moment by moment, vibrant activity is swirling around in each of these four locations—just have a look. Now, can you identify some other location where experience arises? The Buddha saw these four areas or locations as the primary points, the ground zero, of lived experience. All physical and perceptual forms of being, he held, are rooted in one of these places. This being the case, it is first of all here, in this fourfold field, where we must be at home. To be at home means to see with present-moment awareness (*sati*) just what is arising in these locations. The "just" means "without longing and discontentment," without, that is, attaching notions such as like and dislike, good and bad, right and wrong, to whatever it is. What is it like to *just see* that tension in your back, or that idea flashing through your mind? Just noticing, you'll get some sense of what it is like to finally be at home, in your own "ancestral, natural habitat."

"The Application of Present-Moment Awareness" (*sutta* 16) is devoted to this theme.

SUTTA 2

चूळमालुक्यसुत्त

Transfixed by Flamboyant Speculation

Cūḷamālukya Sutta: "A Brief Talk to Mālukya"; *Majjhimanikāya* 63

WE REMAIN TRANSFIXED THERE, ENCHANTED BY PLEASURE AND FLAMBOYANT SPECULATION. (DE-ORIENTATION)

Why do we persist in wandering ghostlike in the field of what St. Augustine refers to as "the delectable desolation"? The first *sutta* was explicit about part of the answer; namely, because of our unconscious, addictive inclination toward "pleasing, desirable, charming," et cetera, sensory phenomena. The present *sutta* identifies the role played by speculative questions in keeping us locked in an improper range of living. It also makes clear that the scope of the Buddha's project *does not* encompass what we normally take to be religion, philosophy, or "spirituality."

What counts as a legitimate question? Well, doesn't it depend on the scope of the matter at hand? The idea of proper range or "native domain" reappears here in a different context. Imagine that you are my music teacher. In the middle of a lesson on scales, I stop to ask you a question concerning German grammar. How would you react? Wouldn't you point out that the question is irrelevant and encourage me to concentrate on learning my scales? The structure of this exchange is essentially the same as that behind "A Brief Talk to Mālukya." But while the dissonance between subject matters in the present example—musical scales/German grammar—is apparent, it is not so obvious in the *sutta.* The reason is that we expect "religious" authorities such as the Buddha to have answers to the big questions of life and death, the kind that Mālukya is asking in the *sutta.* The dissonance arises from the facts that, first of all, such questions are really not questions at all and, second, the Buddha is not a religious authority. So, in this sense, the *sutta* serves as a corrective to certain presuppositions we are most likely bringing to our study of Buddhism.

We might alter the example some to correspond more closely to the tenor of Mālukya's questions. Imagine that I interrupt the lesson on scales to ask you, my music teacher, about the cosmic origins of music, or about whether the sound made by my instrument persists in some other dimension after it fades into silence. Now, these questions are really no more relevant to the learning of scales than is the one about German grammar. But because there is something intriguing about these questions, they seem legitimate; they seem, that is, to require answers. Questions like these stimulate the powerful human urge to weave narratives about the origins, dissolution, and death of the world and its beings, and what may lie beyond the world.

In the proposition, I use the term "flamboyant" to describe such speculations. I use that term because intriguing questions put themselves on display in a manner that demands our attention. They strut ostentatiously before our cognitive apparatus. How can you ignore speculation on life after death, the possibility of eternal damnation, theories of the supernatural, or the idea of an awesome force, of "God"? Once a question concerning such matters is posed, it comes to life, both personally and culturally, in the form of stories, or narrative strategies. These stories, of course, are called "answers" by those who hold them dear; and these answers are attempts to make sense of what is unknown. Since, in the Buddha's view, a primary constituent of human awakening is developing the natural capacity to "see things as they are," this equally natural human proclivity to spin narrative in the face of speculative matters is a serious obstacle. So a primary goal of Buddhist training is to cease grasping at the ungraspable. And a speculative notion is *speculative* precisely because of its ungraspable referent.

You may want to reflect for a moment on actual questions or speculative positions that you yourself hold dear. Generally, in our culture, such positions relate to ideas that are embedded in theistic worldviews, concerning God, creation, heaven and hell, angels, saints, Satan, and so on. Very often, Buddhists, too, hold speculative positions concerning matters such as *karma*, the roles of *bodhisattvas*, the availability of cosmic *buddhas*, the potency of *mantras*, and so on. Even purportedly nonreligious secularists hold speculative views concerning matters such as the origin of the universe, the supremacy of science, and the power of reason. One of the central points of "A Brief Talk to Mālukya" is that the speculative questions swirling around such matters are not only useless to the Buddha's path but counterproductive, and even destructive, to the human quest for happiness.

Now, having reflected, you may have discovered that what the Buddha would call a useless or speculative question is precisely one that you consider—and indeed is almost universally considered—a perfectly legitimate religious, philosophical, or "spiritual" query. So we need to ask: On what basis does the Buddha determine the value of a question? As the Buddha tells Mālukya in the *sutta*, the determining factor for an unworthy speculative position is that it leaves "birth, . . . aging, . . . death; . . . sadness, regret, unease, depression, and anxiety"—in short, *dukkha* (see note 9.6)—undiminished. Even if you knew precisely how some supernatural being created the universe, the fact is that birth, aging, and human dissatisfaction would remain just as they are. Hence, speculations on, for example, the matter of cosmic creation are not only useless but also destructive distractions from the important—and knowable—matters concerning awakening. So what kinds of questions are worthy of attention? The Buddha's answer is: those which lead "to what is beneficial, to the beginning of training, to disenchantment, to dispassion, to cessation, to peace, to direct knowing, to awakening, to unbinding." So do you have a question about the nature of phenomena? If so, the Buddha can provide you with, or lead you to realizing for yourself, an answer. Why? Because (1) there *is* an answer (it is determinate, and hence not a speculative question) and (2) knowing the answer leads to profound well-being and ease.

In delineating the types of questions that he is counting as legitimate, the Buddha is simultaneously demarcating the range of his teachings. We are used to thinking of a religious figure as someone whose realization encompasses the whole of life, from the creation of the cosmos through social norms, governance, gender relations, diet, et cetera, to the afterlife and the ultimate end. The Buddha emphatically states in "A Brief Talk to Mālukya" that his knowledge is of one thing.

From one perspective, this one thing is the destruction of *dukkha;* from another, it is "awakening" or "unbinding"—*nirvāṇa* (see note 12.1). Since the overcoming of unease/realization of unbinding is a purely human matter as opposed to a supernatural one, what must be known is knowable. How could it not be? It is in order to determine such matters that the Buddha teaches.

NOTES

2.1. *"Is the world . . . after death".* Mālukya's questions are flawed in at least four ways: first, they are laden with hidden presuppositions; second, they cannot be answered; third, they serve to proliferate storytelling; and fourth, they are distracting. Since many of our own questions and speculations about the big matters of life and death are structurally similar to Mālukya's, it will be worthwhile to look at these four flaws in some depth.

Presupposing. The questions, as posed, reveal such a "thicket of views," as the Buddha elsewhere phrases it, as to be incoherent (see the discourses to Vacchagotta: *Majjhimanikāya* 71–73). That is, each of the questions contains far-reaching assumptions about the matters at hand. The person asking the questions already has made up his or her mind about, for example, the existence of a "life force" (the term, *jīva,* is often translated as "soul"), or about the strict dichotomy of being/non-being, or about just what is designated by the term "world." In each instance, an active, if largely unconscious, conceptual schema is pushing the question along. This hidden schema gives the question a piñata-like quality: each time you take a whack at answering it, some more stuff—presuppositions, assumptions, axioms, personal idiosyncrasies, and so on—falls out. So, like a piñata, the question being posed may have a legitimate enough *appearance,* but in reality its substance is the hidden sugary stuff.

Indeterminate. Even given that the questions being posed were transparently coherent, they are not answerable. There is, in fact, a modern-day story along the lines of the question *Does a* buddha *exist after death?* A practitioner asked the teacher whether or not there was life after death. The teacher answered, "I don't know." The student, somewhat crestfallen, said, "But I thought that you were an enlightened master." "Yes," the master responded, "but not a dead one." The master in this story knows that any possible answer would be not an answer at all but a mere expression of a belief, or of a hope, or of something else other than real knowledge.

Narrative. A prescribed answer of the sort just mentioned is at heart a *story.* Apparently, one of the jobs of a religious tradition is to provide a story in the face of the unknown. Do you want to know how the world was created? How it will end? What happens when you die? Well, the place to find the answer is your religious text of choice—the Bible, the Koran, the Vedas, the Bhagavad Gita, even certain later Buddhist *sūtras* (in Sanskrit) and *tantras,* for that matter. The answer will, of course, come in the form of a story. No, the answer *is* a story. I don't say "just" a story, because we all know the tremendous power of religious narratives to spur people equally to acts of heartwarming compassion and to acts of monstrous violence. The problem with narratives is thus not that they are ineffectual; it is that they are pointing in the wrong direction. A Buddhist teacher I know has a stock answer to any question even hinting at the metaphysical: "You already know." That is, the answer is to be found in immediate experience. But, concomitant with such an (immediate, imminent) answer is, of course, the dissolution of the very (metaphysical) question.

Distracting. This last point shows the final reason that the questions being posed by Mālukya are flawed; namely, they are distracting. If I am caught up in *narratives* about the issues of life and death, I am not attending to the actual *processes* of life and death. All language, of course, has a certain metaphorical, figurative quality to it. But, in reading the *suttas* presented here, I think you will find that the Buddha's language, even when he is literally *telling stories,* always points directly to life as it is lived, to life as it is experienced immediately. Why? Because awakening is awakening to life. Awakening is awakening to the world, to being, to existence, *as it is.* This being so, to what should you be attending? Well, it's right in front of you. No story is required to see *that.* Just look!

2.2. *"you fool of a man".* Mālukya's demand that the Buddha answer such irrelevant questions reveals Mālukya's utter lack of the most basic understanding of the nature of "the training" and of the tenor of the Buddha's teachings. What has Mālukya been doing all this time?

2.3. *"shot by an arrow".* With this famous simile of the arrow, the Buddha illustrates in graphic and somewhat slapstick terms the absurdity of misapplied questioning and speculation. Although there may be situations in which the questions being posed here are pertinent (say, in a court of law), given the victim's immediate situation, these same questions are not only pointless but life-threatening. The simile is also suggestive of the therapeutic nature of the Buddha's teachings. The physician is, of course, the Buddha, and the victim is, well, you. The Buddha knows how to relieve you of the poison arrow of detrimental states of mind and ways of being, but certain of your entrenched views stand in the way of allowing the teachings to do their work. Do you know which ones?

SUTTA 3

तेविज्जसुत्त

Enchanted by "God"

Tevijja Sutta: "Threefold Knowledge"; *Dīghanikāya* 13

THE MOST ENTHRALLING BELIEF OF ALL IS THAT OF SUPERNATURAL AGENCY.
(DE-ORIENTATION)

Is there any theme in the history of the world's religions that even approaches the pride of place granted the discourse on "God"? Virtually all definitions of the term "religion" (as understood in the West), in fact, assume some strong form of supernatural agency: where there is religion, we find supernatural agents; where there are supernatural agents, we find religion. The Buddha, however, was unconvinced of the supposed importance of this issue, and thus he refrained throughout his life from posing the very question of God's existence. It is then probably not surprising that in thousands of dialogues with all manner of interlocutors, the Buddha nowhere formulates anything like a cohesive response to the issue of theism.

So why, you might ask, should a dialogue about a subject of no concern to the Buddha be included in a book about the Buddha's teachings? The quick answer is that this *sutta* addresses a matter of great importance to *us*. When thinking about the big issues of life and death, most of us begin with received ideas (stories) about God, the divine, the sacred, the holy, the absolute, and so forth. So the short answer—that the *Tevijja Sutta* addresses a matter of ultimate significance to *us*—might be sufficient in itself; but add to it the fact that the Buddha saw a grave danger in such ideas, and we have good reason to study the text. The longer, and more satisfying, answer to the question lies, of course, in a careful study of the text itself, which we will now undertake.

Before taking a closer look at the text, it might be helpful if I make explicit a basic interpretative schema that I am recommending for a reading of the *Tevijja Sutta.* This schema is based on what I see as the central methodological tack of the Buddha in the *sutta.* The Buddha's technique involves three moves:

1. The first move is to *put on display* the problem raised by his interlocutor. Seen narrowly, the problem is "the path to God"; more broadly construed, it is that of the very existence of some entity "God." The Buddha puts the problem on display by revealing it as an issue that is *not* central to our life situation, as the interlocutor erroneously assumes. Indeed, the Buddha holds, "God" not only is *not* rooted in life but *is* rooted in the believer's unreflective acceptance of certain ways of using language.
2. The second move is to *reorient* his interlocutor toward what *is* central to his life situation: his sensory apparatus.
3. Finally, in the third move, the Buddha provides his interlocutor with a *practice* whereby he may cultivate a state of being that approaches what he previously imputed to a supernatural being.

Through sustained dialogue, the Buddha helps his interlocutor to clarify *to himself* his very practice of speaking and thinking with, specifically, theistic language (that is, language that assumes supernatural agency). The Buddha enables him to see that his language is riddled with imprecise usage, unfounded claims, and vacuous notions; and that such language, furthermore, engenders an entanglement in delusion and unwarranted expectation. Once he has some understanding of the nature of his language, the interlocutor can see *for himself* just how his life had been oriented toward a counterfeit promise (of heaven, salvation, union, et cetera). The promise is counterfeit because it has no real capacity for being fulfilled *in life* but remains always in the realm of a particular story that was fashioned by the believer's inherited cultural milieu and transmitted via particular language usages.

The Buddha's method thus serves his broader aim as a teacher: to lead his partner in dialogue to full realization of "the way things are." Only once the interlocutor is aware of what he is doing when he speaks and thinks in the particular terms that he does can he free himself from entrenched tendencies and begin to cultivate the skill of penetrative insight (Pāli: *paññā;* Sanskrit: *prajñā*), the primary disposition gained through the Buddha's training.

This coupling of a dialogical method and careful attention to the *individual's* specific conceptual and affective confusions reveals, furthermore, the therapeutic nature of the Buddha's encounter with others. The disquiet exhibited in the question of the interlocutor in the *Tevijja Sutta* is relieved under the very examination of the Buddha. The interlocutor's question, rooted as it is in misknowledge (*avijja*), eventually ceases to have force. But if conversation with the Buddha amounts to a sort of talking cure, it is not because the interlocutor has been *convinced* of anything—say, some logical or conceptual error in his position. Rather, he is cured because he has simply *seen* his position for the first time. *Seeing* his position means gaining insight into the premises, suppositions, psychological dependencies, and emotional commitments that have been opaquely entrenched in that position all along. This insight liberates the interlocutor from the unconscious force exerted by culturally acquired pictures of the world.

The Buddha's technique is consequently inseparable from the ultimate aim of his teachings. A dialogical encounter with the Buddha is permeated by the same "flavor" as is the entirety of his *dhamma,* namely, insight and liberation. We may glimpse in this fact a possible reason for the Buddha's refusal to expound a *general* critique of theism—or of anything else, for that matter. The reason might be this: general critiques and theories lack the force to expose the affectively potent *individual* practices operating behind specific world-building strategies, such as one's employment of language, concept, and analogy.

Now, having discussed the Buddha's method, I would like to say something more directly about the issue at hand: God.

Emmanuel Levinas begins *Totality and Infinity* with these words: " 'The true life is absent.' But we are in the world. Metaphysics arises and is maintained in this alibi." This statement captures beautifully the Buddha's own impatience with, perhaps even bafflement about, speculative metaphysical notions such as God. In positing a path leading to communion with God, Vāseṭṭha and other theists are in essence submitting that "the true life is absent." When one understands "the true life" to refer to a religion's ultimate aim for a person—heaven, liberation, salvation, union—the various strategies of theistic religions (faith, devotion, prayer, et cetera) can be understood as means of ensuring that that which is absent *here* is fully realized *there*. *There*, of course, is always some presumed *beyond*, whether conceived in spatial, epistemological, cognitive, affective, or some other terms. In the second section of the *Tevijja Sutta*, the Buddha, like Levinas's imaginary interlocutor, insists: "But we are in the world." He does this by showing that *even if* there were a God and a path to God, such as the theists claim, and *even if* the Brahmans (or Christians, or Muslims, and so on) could *see* or *know* the path, they would *still* be incapable of treading that path to the heavenly communion they so sought.

Through the sustained practice that presupposes the meditation outlined in the *sutta*, the practitioner is radically reoriented toward what the Buddha calls "one's proper range" (*gocaro sako*). This is the field within which, according to the Buddha, human life is properly lived. The proper range is the scope given by immediate experience. This point may seem obvious, but a central contention of Buddhism is that we are *constantly* wandering outside that range and into the improper, detrimental range of storytelling, fantasy, fabrication, personal narrative, and metaphysical conjecture. Throughout the canonical texts, the Buddha holds that to be careless toward, or inattentive to, immediate experience is to be as good as dead. Immediate experience is not only our proper range but, if we are honest about the manner in which our lives actually unfold moment by moment, our *only* range—immediate experience is *all* that there is. The Buddha, in fact, used the term "the all" (*sabba*) to denote this range.

"God" fits into *the all* in a manner no different from the sound of rain striking the roof, the scent of a flower wafting through the air, the sensation of skin touching cold metal, or the taste of salt on the tongue. In each case, a specific process unfolds: a phenomenon arises out of the confluence of numerous conditions; it comes into contact with a sense faculty; a specific type of cognizance—sight cognizance, sound cognizance, scent cognizance, taste cognizance, touch cognizance, or thought cognizance—arises at the point of contact. "God," in this account, does indeed arise in the mind, but not as the entity posited by theistic traditions. "God" arises as a thought, a concept, a notion, an idea, et cetera, conditioned, like every other thought or idea, by cultural practices, linguistic usages, personal need, and so on. The Buddha calls such conditioned entities "fabrications" and notes that they exhibit in every instance the qualities of impermanence, non-substantiality, and unreliability. The notion "God," like the sound of rain, arises in accordance with the confluence of necessary conditions, persists as long as those conditions hold together, begins to disappear as those dissolve, then dies away when those have ceased. What is left at the end? Well, what follows the final step of the elaborate staircase leading to the absent palace?

So we may summarize the Buddha's view of theism as follows: Theological language has embedded within it such far-ranging yet indemonstrable metaphysical presuppositions that it never escapes from the realm of the purely speculative. And any usage of such speculative language is by nature a life-limiting, even life-denying, "thicket of views" (*diṭṭhigahana*). To answer "God" in the context of any religious or philosophical query, the Buddha suggests, is really not to answer at all; it is, rather, merely to subscribe to a program. Because no such claim about or view of that term is actually ever verifiable in any meaningful sense, such an "answer" is tantamount to toeing the party line, mimicking talking points, or repeating a rumor that one has heard.

For the Buddha, any solution to our human problem that is founded on aimless conjectures about the state of things will fail to fulfill its purported promise of human well-being. Whatever answer a person receives from others, and however fervently he or she may accept that answer, it does not change the fact that "there is birth, there is aging, there is death, there are sorrow, disappointment, unease, grief, and despair." As a "physician," as opposed to a savior, the Buddha is concerned only to *show* the way to overcome the illness—the unease—of human existence. This is, in fact, one of the meanings of the Pāli term that is routinely translated as "teacher" in English: *desika.* A teacher is a teacher precisely by virtue of being adept at *pointing* to the matters of real and immediate concern, *orienting* the patient to those concerns, and *prescribing* the practice that leads to their resolution.

NOTES

3.1. *Brahman.* The *Tevijja Sutta* begins with the Buddha staying in a mango grove near the Brahman village Manasākaṭa, in the region of Kosala, in eastern India. The term "Brahman" refers to the upper class in ancient Indian society. "Upper," however, does not necessarily mean wealthy. The Brahman class was superior, in large part, by virtue of its being in control of the religious texts, the Vedas, which played such a crucial role in the lives of the people. Brahmans ran the educational institutions that trained the officiants who, in turn, presided over the liturgical life of the people. The Sanskrit term *brāhmaṇā,* in fact, refers to the officiants' special ability to invoke and coerce the potency, the *brāhman,* that animates the tremendous forces of the earth, atmosphere, and heavens. The primary purpose of the religious rites was precisely to influence these forces away from ruin and toward repair.

Maybe there is a similar figure in your own religious or spiritual life—a priest, rabbi, minister, therapist, *roshi,* sensei, guru, author, parent, friend, teacher—someone who serves as an authority on matters of great concern and presides over meaning-creating rituals. Few of us have to look far to locate such a figure in our lives.

Since the pertinent point about Brahmans in this *sutta* is that they play a decisive role in the religious lives of people, I have translated the term as "religious authorities." The term *tevijja* in the title of the *sutta* alludes to the Brahmans' training in the three-part sacred text, the Veda (*te* = threefold, *vijja* = special knowledge). However, *tevijja* can also be taken to allude to the *Buddha's* threefold knowledge: knowledge of previous existence, knowledge of the destiny of beings, and knowledge of the origin and ending of *dukkha* (see *Majjhimanikāya* 71).

3.2. *"communion".* The term that I am translating as "communion," *sahavyatā,* means, more literally, "companionship, fellowship." T. W. Rhys Davids, in *Dialogues of the Buddha* (London: Sacred Books of the Buddhists, 3 vols., 1890–1910), and Maurice Walsh, in *The Long Discourses of the Buddha: A Translation of the Dīgha Nikāya* (Boston: Wisdom Publications, 1995), both translate the term as "union." As Walsh points out, "union" probably goes too far theologically, since it implies "mystical union rather than merely belonging to the company of Brahmā" (p. 43). But, as he also mentions, the dialogue concerns a dispute about doctrines, so it is not clear precisely what type of union is being referred to here. I think that "communion" captures a sense of togetherness and unity while preserving the "religious" nuance implied by the young Brahmans.

3.3. *"God".* "God" translates *brahmā.* With patient philological spadework, it might be possible to reconstruct a more exact notion of what the disputants had in mind for the term *brahmā*. But any theological intricacies that we might thereby uncover would be beside the point. The terms of the argument are broad. The Buddha does not require certain clarifications about how "Brahmā" is being understood before he begins his therapeutic questioning. It is enough for him that there is some notion of a supernatural deity who is "the all-seeing, the all-powerful, the Lord, the maker and creator, ruler, appointer and orderer, father of all that have been and will be" (*Dīghanikāya* 1.2.5). Thus, any and all notions of such a supernatural deity are under question here. So in order to de-exoticize the argument some, and to place it more squarely in the Western discourse on the matter, I translate "Brahmā" as "God."

3.4. *"what is proclaimed"*. There are three premises operating in the debate. For the young men engaged in argument, these premises amount to cultural axioms since the Vedic Brahman class, into which they were born, posited them as incontrovertible. The first premise holds that there exists an entity known as "Brahmā." This entity was understood to be an impersonal, indefinable potency that created the phenomenal world. Omnipresent, omnipotent, and omniscient, in some sense immanent and in some sense transcendent, "Brahmā" has been understood by Christian observers of Indian culture since the sixteenth century as remarkably similar to their own conception of deity—so similar, in fact, that the term "God" is generally considered an appropriate translation. So, in these terms, the first premise is: "'God' is given." The second premise at work for both disputants is that this entity is *directly* knowable; in other words, its existence is not merely a matter of inference. And the third premise holds that certain Brahman teachers know, and have revealed, the way to that direct knowledge of God. Vāseṭṭha and Bhāradvāja disagree only on which teachers have revealed the right path to the direct knowledge of God.

3.5. *"So what . . . does the dispute . . . concern"*. The Buddha's immediate reaction on hearing the nature of the argument shows that he is unable to discern any real disagreement. When we look at the basic structure of the argument, the Buddha's response seems quite reasonable. The argument runs: It is given that there is an *X*; this being the case, *X* is knowable; *P* and *T* teach the means of discerning *X*. The structure of the argument conforms precisely to how language functions in the everyday world when it is employed as a means of positing, locating, and describing existents. So the young Brahmans' argument is wholly commonsensical at the structural level. The Buddha's inability to see a substantive disagreement at this point is just a recognition that the argument, so far, is grammatically intact.

3.6. "'*they lead*'". With this comment, Vāseṭṭha stirs the Buddha into full counseling mode. (I always imagine the Buddha, head bowed and eyes closed, vigorously rubbing his temples as he asks, for the third time, "Do you say 'they *lead*'?") By comparing the path to God to a path leading to a village, Vāseṭṭha is now claiming more for his terms than the logical structure of everyday descriptive usage will allow. The idea of a village and a path leading to that village is a noncontroversial notion: everyone understands what it means. Even more crucially, village and path are technically verifiable referents. God and a path leading to God are neither noncontroversial nor obviously referential. The analogy thus exposes an unintentional misuse of language by Vāseṭṭha. For the Buddha, this misuse is symptomatic of an unhealthy confusion. If Vāseṭṭha wants to claim for a path to God that it *leads*, then the *question* of the proper path would never arise, it would simply require a straightforward act of verification, just as the proper path to the village is transparently known by the countless people who tread it.

As the dialogue continues, the Buddha endeavors to show his interlocutor that this transparency is not at all the case in regard to the path to God. I imagine that the Buddha's voice becomes gentler at this point, and that his countenance softens. The reason is this: in uttering the words that he does without any apparent inkling as to their problematic nature, Vāseṭṭha has shown himself to be *entranced* by a certain view or picture of reality. In this case, the picture is a theistic one, in which there is some notion of an anthropomorphic, supernatural creator deity. The combination of three factors points to Vāseṭṭha's entrancement with this picture. The first is the fact that the *idea* of "God" is utterly nonsensical to anyone who does not already share the quite particular system of reference (Vedic/Brahmanical, Christian, Deistic, et cetera) within which it is afforded meaning. The second factor is the fact that the wide-ranging consequences of this theistic picture (some notion of revelation, sacred scripture, bodily resurrection, heaven, et cetera) are so transparently dubious to anyone who is not already captivated by that picture. The final factor is Vāseṭṭha's apparent obliviousness to the very fact that he *holds* this picture, that there even exist alternative ways of seeing the world—that one may *choose*. Vāseṭṭha's situation is indeed self-enforced. Although the notions that form his view are culturally derived, he himself *holds* them in view with locutions precisely like "they lead, they lead."

Vāseṭṭha's simplistic equating of the path to the village with the path to God is so keenly noted by the Buddha because it marks the precise place where Vāseṭṭha's conceptual and emotional vulnerabilities are located. The Buddha thus begins a series of questions aimed at healing this area, thereby permitting Vāseṭṭha to gain some insight into the unconscious practice of holding a view in place.

3.7. "*'the direct path'*". If there is nothing even approaching an instantiation of anyone's having encountered some entity "God," then what does it mean to claim, as the theists do, that "this is the direct path, this is the straight path that leads to salvation, and leads one who follows it to communion with God"? The sentence certainly does not carry meaning in the obvious way that the claim that one can come across the path to the village does. Again, the Buddha is not concerned here with discussing matters of language theory, verification principles, rules of evidence, or valid syllogisms and logic. Since Vāseṭṭha has not shown himself to be held captive by any of these strategies of argument, such a concern would be misplaced. Vāseṭṭha, rather, has shown himself to be captivated by the *story,* told by Brahmans since time immemorial, about the existence and nature of "the all-seeing, the all-powerful, the Lord, the maker and creator"—the story about God. The Buddha is thus aiming at dismantling something much more instinctive than an intellectual apparatus. He is endeavoring to expose the language practice that supports Vāseṭṭha's conceptual and linguistic *storytelling.* So, in keeping with the nature of the argument—i.e., its being storylike—the Buddha proceeds to tell some stories of his own.

3.8. "*a single file of blind men . . . desolate*". The first story the Buddha tells employs a simile that highlights the problematic nature of Vāseṭṭha's usage of the verbs "to see" and "to know." Not only are the seven generations of Brahmans, their teachers, and the founding sages like a great file of blind men speaking blindly of what they do not see, but even if they did have the eyes to see—even if there were something such as "God" *to be seen*—they would still not know anything like a *path* to that supernatural entity. The Buddha next points out that although the Brahmans direct prayers to the sun and moon, they are not able to point out anything like a path *that leads* to those celestial bodies. That is, theists do not articulate any but the most figurative, analogical, and allegorical notions of seeing and knowing a path to God.

3.9. "*path to . . . the sun and moon*". Even if an entity is discernibly present, it does not necessarily follow that it makes sense to speak of *a way to* it. How much less so if the entity is merely postulated?

3.10. "*'the most beautiful woman'*". As if bringing Vāseṭṭha down, step by step, from his lofty imaginings to a more realistic view of life, the Buddha turns from this celestial image to one of love and desire in the human realm. We might perceive in this story an implicit hypothesis concerning the very presence of theistic notions in a culture. People, in this view, seek an agent such as "God" for the same reasons that the young man in the story seeks out the most beautiful woman in India: in response to a compulsive longing for satisfaction. The Buddha's first preeminent reality (see note 9.7) states that an invariable human experience is that *available objects* produce at best fleeting satisfaction; and that such satisfaction, on closer examination, is really just another, if a more subtle, register of pain. The solution chosen by the figure in the story is to imagine the perfect woman, affectively bond to her, and then seek her out for love. How can Vāseṭṭha not admit that such behavior is "ridiculous"?

At this point, the reader might object that whereas the young man in the story knows nothing about the woman he seeks, the religious authorities have in fact worked out the details about God. On this account, the young man presented by the Buddha is nothing but a straw man, a poor example of a believer, comparable to one of the all-too-common proponents of theism who are ignorant of the intricacies of their theological traditions. In another text (*Majjhimanikāya* 95.14–15), the Buddha gives us some idea about how he might respond to this objection. There, he mentions five bases for having conviction in a religious system: faith, inclination, oral tradition, careful consideration of the grounds, and reflective acceptance of a view. It is acceptable to make a "truth" claim on the basis of any one of these modes; but the truth being claimed must, in honesty and fairness, be limited to the scope encompassed by the particular mode of conviction. That is, the person who posits "God" on the basis of faith is "protecting the truth" (*saccam anurakkhati*) when he says, "Thus is my faith," and acknowledges that he has no warrant to make a more elaborate claim or come to a definite conclusion. Thus the person may not justly claim: "Only this is true, anything else is wrong." So while it may be true that a religious tradition has constructed an elaborate theology, far-reaching institutions, weighty authorities, intricate devotional practices, and complex, sophisticated doctrines in the name of some all-powerful creator deity—all of which, furthermore, are "fully approved of by society and tradition, well transmitted, well conceptualized, and well reflected on"—it does not change the "empty, hollow, and insubstantial" nature of the *universal* claim to truth required by theism.

3.11. *"staircase . . . leading up to a palace"*. The final analogy that the Buddha presents to Vāseṭṭha as a means of revealing to him the errors in his conceptualization of the path to God might be read as alluding to what the Buddha viewed as both the intricacies and the vacuity of theistic traditions. This analogy is a particularly apt way for the Buddha to conclude this portion of the dialogue because it points out what, in his view, is *really* waiting for the theist at the end of all his or her complex systems and doctrines. In the end, no matter how intricate and elaborate the staircase may be, the fact remains that it leads to empty space: there is no palace; *it is all staircase.* When one discovers this fact, what then?

3.12. *"'Come, . . . come'"*. Here, and in the three following paragraphs, the Buddha is intent on disabusing Vāseṭṭha of any belief in the magical quality of religious practices. The Buddha is concerned with more here than making the obvious observation that no amount of "cajoling" will have an effect in the world of real objects. He is, more important, lampooning the Brahmans' primary vehicle to "spiritual" power and social prestige—their liturgical language—as being equally ineffectual.

3.13. *"lie down . . . his head covered with a cloth"*. One way of understanding the problem in this and each of the other analogies given by the Buddha in the *Tevijja Sutta* is to consider that in each case someone was involved in an incorrect, hence fruitless, orientation: moving blindly *toward* some indeterminate place shrouded in darkness; searching *throughout* the land for the most beautiful woman; building a staircase *toward* empty space; calling out for help *to* the riverbank. And in the second and third riverbank analogies, the person is incapable of being oriented toward anything at all: he is bound, immobilized, or covered and prostrate *on the ground.* The Buddha has him just where he wants him! And he has the ever-consenting Vāseṭṭha figuratively in the same place. With Vāseṭṭha lying on the ground, now with his head shrouded, there will be no more cajoling, no more talk about a path to God.

In such a position, and for someone with his former conceptual commitments, *only* in such a position is Vāseṭṭha open to the teaching of the Buddha. The cause of the kind of disorientation experienced by the figures in his analogies, the Buddha explains, lies in the inability to attend carefully to the workings of one's sensory apparatus. The result of such inattentiveness is confusion: the person confuses non-substantial, ephemeral phenomena for phenomena capable of being grasped and of yielding abiding satisfaction. The Buddha equates this state of confusion concerning the sensory apparatus with being bound and chained.

3.14. *"five hindrances"*. In the Buddha's typology of beings, what is being described here is an "ordinary" person (*puthujjana*) as opposed to an "accomplished" one (*arahant*) or "awakened" one (*buddha*). A person is ordinary by virtue of his or her being entangled in the five hindrances.

3.15. *"communion"*. Communion, in the Buddha's view here, must presuppose *commonality.* Since it cannot be said that the religious authorities possess any of the qualities claimed for God, on what basis can communion be established?

3.16. *"you . . . know the path"*. Vāseṭṭha realizes that, like the Brahmans mentioned before, he is at a dead end. But while the Buddha has convinced his interlocutor of the vacuity of the Brahmans' claim to know the way to communion with God, he has not, apparently, completely dissuaded Vāseṭṭha from the notion "God." For Vāseṭṭha says that he has heard from others that *the Buddha* knows "the path to communion with God." The Buddha, for his part, does not ask for a complete repudiation of what is obviously a deeply held conviction. Rather, like a good doctor facing a stubborn patient, he prescribes for Vāseṭṭha a *practice* that will cure him once and for all of his misapprehension.

3.17. *"God/exceptional integrity"*. This play on *brahmā* is another example of the Buddha's love of linguistic inversion (see the middle of note 9.7; see also note 3.19).

3.18. *"'from home into homelessness'"*. Throughout the *suttas,* this phrase refers to a literal action: leaving one's home and becoming a wandering practitioner or mendicant. The contemporary reader can understand this phrase to signify a fundamental shift in one's approach to life: from complexity to simplicity; from reactive action to mindful action; from recklessness to self-restraint; from conditioned habituation to skillful watchfulness; from— What would *you* say?

The Buddha's instructions in this section constitute a succinct summary of the entire Buddhist path as it is presented in the earliest texts. Described as it was to people who had chosen the socially condoned option of mendicancy, the path is cast within a structure unsuited for people like, well, you and me. So how can we reconcile this ancient mendicant path with our present situation? Really, the entire history of Buddhism is an answer to this very question. If the Buddha's teachings had not continually been made relevant and practicable by each new cultural recipient, they would not have survived. Now, assuming that we are interested in considering the relevance of the oldest formulation of the teachings for us, and not in merely adopting some ready-made adaptation, such as those referred to in the introduction, it will be a useful exercise to consider how *we* might make sense of that path.

For example, you might begin by considering what *you* would call the "dust" of "the householder's life" (mind-numbing pressures? debilitating responsibilities? endless compromise?). Assuming that you do not necessarily want to abandon your "circle of relationships," as a mendicant would, how can you nonetheless preserve some of the intent of the Buddha's words here? Might this phrase be understood as calling for us to reevaluate our relationships with the people in our lives? The text says that the mendicant's life is "open and spacious." How can this statement be fruitfully refashioned? Perhaps it can be seen as pointing to the fruits of letting go of habituation (habitat, home!) and becoming increasingly "watchful," as the text further states. Perhaps it can be seen as saying something about becoming decreasingly reactive in our activities and interactions with others. Can the spaciousness of the homeless person's life then be understood as the natural contentment that arises out of this attentiveness? What might be some other ways that you could understand "go from home into homelessness"?

3.19. "this *is the path to communion*". In saying that the cultivation of these traits *is* communion with God, the Buddha is engaging in a kind of cultural-linguistic inversion. As on numerous other occasions, he is taking a notion (together with its exactly corresponding term) that is held sacrosanct by the Brahmanical communities and reoutfitting it to serve distinctly different—Buddhist—purposes. Once he or she has attained the qualities and skills engendered by the practice (such as expansiveness, unencumberedness, purity, friendliness, and equanimity), it is indeed possible that the practitioner will attain communion with *brahmā*—now used literally to mean "expansiveness, greatness, the supreme good."

SUTTA 4

केसमुत्तिसुत्त

Knowing for Yourself

Kesamutti Sutta: "Discourse in Kesamutta"; *Aṅguttaranikāya* 3.65

THERE IS A SAFEGUARD AGAINST THIS BEWITCHMENT: KNOWING FOR YOURSELF.

(DE-ORIENTATION)

The *Kesamutti Sutta,* more commonly known as the *Kālāma Sutta,* is considered throughout the Buddhist world past and present to be something of a Buddhist Magna Carta, granting religious seekers the liberty of free inquiry. In his typically elegant and austere fashion, the Buddha presents here a strategy for determining whether or not religious propositions are worthy of embrace. The structure that he provides can easily be extended beyond religious issues per se to include *any* types of dogmatic assertions—for instance, scientific, political, or aesthetic ones. Considering the ubiquity of such social and religious dogma even in a liberal democratic nation like our own—much less in a traditional society like ancient India—and considering, furthermore, the paralyzing effect that such dogma has on our thinking, this *sutta* certainly does have a liberating and perhaps even revolutionary quality to it.

But the *sutta* serves another purpose as well. Just consider the Buddha's inventory of inadequate strategies for determining the value of an idea—don't we recognize precisely our very practices? "You should not be convinced by unconfirmed reports, by tradition, by hearsay, by scriptures, by logical reasoning, by inferential reasoning, by reflection on superficial appearances, by delighting in opinions and speculation, by the appearance of plausibility, or because you think, *This person is our teacher.*" What is left? When we no longer accept the proclamations of religious teachings and teachers on the usual bases, how can we deal with the great matters of life and death? When we let go of all of that, the Buddha seems to be suggesting, there is only one terrifying alternative: deciding for yourself on the basis of your own experience. What experience? The most basic, visceral experience, of either trouble or ease. If the teaching—the practice, the doctrine, the idea, the theory—enhances infatuation, hostility, and delusion, then you must surely recognize it as having detrimental effects on your life, you must actually *experience* it as leading "to harm and trouble," and as being faulty and thus worthy of rejection. Conversely, if a teaching serves to reduce these "three poisons," as the Buddha often refers to them, then you certainly know that fact directly. Experiencing increased well-being and ease as a result of that reduction, how can you not determine for yourself that that teaching is beneficial? The Buddha's strategy thus places determination of value squarely on the shoulders of the individual. The criteria of value have thus become empirical; they are tied to verifiable experience rather than to systems and communities of belief.

A key phrase in the Buddha's strategy in the *Kesamutti Sutta* requires that the teachings under examination be "fully taken up" or "fully carried out." How should we understand this phrase? There seems to be an assumption in the *sutta* of sustained consideration of a view or teaching. But in most cases, religious teachings are speculative (God hears your prayers; eating meat leads to rebirth as a pig) and are thus incapable of verification. Such teachings can never be accepted on any grounds other than those identified by the Buddha as unreliable. Can the claim "God hears your prayers" ever stem from anything other than tradition, scriptures, opinions, or at best, the appearance of plausibility? So the Buddha's advice to the Kālāmas appears to dismiss speculative teachings out of hand.

The Buddha's project in the *Kesamutti Sutta* is not merely negative. In addition to providing the Kālāmas with a tool for dismantling dogma, he offers them a practice. (The practice, known as "cultivating the four boundless qualities," is the same one that Vāseṭṭha was encouraged to perfect in "Threefold Knowledge," *sutta* 3.) Maybe the Buddha presented this practice at this exact moment in the discussion as a way of showing the Kālāmas the type of thing he had in mind as a religious claim not dependent on tradition, hearsay, and so forth. When your heart is suffused with joy, then your heart is suffused with joy. What use, then, for "God loves you"? There is joy. Whether or not God is in his heaven, there is joy. Words become superfluous; speculative notions unnecessary.

NOTES

4.1 *"mendicants and religious authorities"*. This term translates *samaṇa-brāhmaṇā*. In the *sutta* literature, the Buddha is often referred to as a *samaṇa* by non-Buddhist interlocutors. In the opening paragraph of the present *sutta*, in fact, the Kālāmas refer to him as a *samaṇa*. A *samaṇa* was a wandering, alms-begging sectarian; in short, a mendicant. The term literally means "striver" or "seeker" and stems from the Sanskrit verbal root √*śram*, "to make effort." The two most widespread of the *samaṇa* groups in northeastern India at the time of the Buddha, the Jains and the Ajivikas, practiced severe forms of asceticism, even self-mortification. Although the early followers of the Buddha eschewed such practices, they nonetheless renounced family, rank, and social obligation for a life of wandering and meditation. Each *samaṇa* group revolved around a teacher, who taught methods of practice that were derived from premises opposed to those of the second group referred to in this section: the *brāhmaṇā*, or Brahmans. So the Kālāmas would have been exposed to an impossibly wide and contradictory range of claims, propositions, practices, and philosophies.

4.2 *"unconfirmed reports . . . our teacher"*. It might be an illuminating exercise to give some thought to the grounds for certain of your own views concerning the big matters of life and death. Do you assume that the universe has a beginning, for instance, or believe in continued existence after death, say, heaven or rebirth? Are such assumptions and beliefs grounded in any of the categories considered unacceptable by the Buddha? That is, in what is the idea of a beginning or origin to life rooted? Is it rooted in your tradition, in your precious scriptures, or in the words of a religious authority? Do beliefs of such provenance deserve the kind of loyalty that we usually extend to our religious convictions?

4.3 *"when you know for yourselves"*. The Buddha gives this basic test criterion to the Kālāmas as a means of evaluating the worthiness of any given teaching. In doing so, he seems to be dividing religious teachings into two types. Most religious claims—being precisely *religious* claims—are speculative in nature. Being speculative, such claims cannot pass the basic test of *being knowable*; thus the criterion "when you know for yourselves" serves the function of eliminating at the outset many of the teachings that the Kālāmas find so contradictory and perplexing. So, on the one hand, there are speculative teachings that can be believed or accepted but never authenticated as accurate or even reliable. As we saw in "A Brief Talk to Mālukya" (*sutta* 2), the Brahmans' assertions about God would count as an unverifiable teaching. In such instances, the only option available to the inquirer is recourse to the kinds of sources and strategies enumerated by the Buddha in the present *sutta:* reliance on tradition, recourse to scripture, and so on. On the other hand, there are teachings that *are* testable: like a scientific theory, such teachings are capable of being either verified or refuted in one's own experience. Many of the yogic-meditative teachings of the *samaṇas,* for instance, would fall into this category.

The Buddha's insistence on empirically testable data forces a displacement of authority. When a testable claim is posited, the arbiter of value is no longer tradition or scriptures, or even sophisticated mental operations such as inference and deduction. Taking seriously the Buddha's criterion requires you to test the teaching against your own situation, regardless of what your tradition and scriptures hold.

4.4 *"infatuation, hostility, and delusion".* These terms translate the Buddhist technical terms *lobha* (elsewhere also *rāga*), *dosa,* and *moha,* respectively. In the popular Tibetan depiction of the Buddhist cosmos known as the wheel of becoming, these three qualities are represented by a rooster, a snake, and a pig grabbing on to one another's tails at the very hub of the wheel. This depiction is consistent with the Buddha's view that infatuation, hostility, and delusion are fundamental driving forces operating at the very heart of existence. Elsewhere, the Buddha calls these qualities "the three roots of harmful action" (*Itivuttaka* 45) and "the three fires" (*Dīghanikāya* 33.1.10.[32]).

Taken together, infatuation, hostility, and delusion are referred to as *kilesa,* "stain, defilement, soiling." The Pāli term stems from the Sanskrit verbal root √*kliś,* "to torment, to trouble, to cause unease." Think about it: Doesn't the presence of infatuation, hostility, or delusion in any given instance of experience tend to spoil things? Doesn't that hostility you feel toward the driver who is tailgating you cause discomfort for *you* and perhaps, if you're not careful, trouble for both of you? Notice, though, that it is not necessarily obvious where, say, justifiable indignation ends and outright hostility begins. This fact points to a crucial feature of the *kilesas.* Each of these qualities lies on a continuum of *ordinary* human responses to any given event, person, or phenomenon. Infatuation, *lobha* or *rāga,* is on a continuum extending from virtually imperceptible attraction through enjoyment to raging lust; hostility, *dosa,* from preconscious aversion through umbrage to violent hatred; delusion, *moha,* from automatic, unconscious perceptual assumptions through open-minded uncertainty to schizophrenic-like hallucination. Infatuation, hostility, and delusion, then, can be understood as the points where the flavor so vital to a fulfilling life turns sour and becomes toxic. As we will see when we look at "Quenched" (*sutta* 12), the Buddha considers the eradication of infatuation, hostility, and delusion (and beyond) to be of such monumental importance that he equates it with *nirvāṇa* itself.

4.5 *"vast, expansive, boundless heart".* As noted in the commentary on this *sutta,* we encountered this practice in the *Tevijja Sutta.* The practice, merely alluded to here without explicit instructions, involves the intentional cultivation of four affective qualities that are considered crucial to social harmony and individual well-being. These four qualities are friendliness, compassion, joy, and equanimity. They are often referred to in later literature as "the four immeasurables" because of the "vast, expansive, boundless" scope of their application, namely, "the entire cosmos."

4.6 *"the four comforts".* A common understanding in the West is that Buddhism is a nonreligious tradition and, as such, can be easily assimilated by Christianity or Judaism. In a sense, the Buddha's comments here on the comforting nature of friendliness, compassion, joy, and equanimity provide support for this view. That is, the Buddha seems to be saying that certain practices are effective, and their ensuing qualities beneficial, regardless of a person's religious orientation.

SUTTA 5

सब्बसुत्त

The Location of Lived Experience

Sabba Sutta: "The All"; *Saṃyuttanikāya* 4.25.23

THE MEANS OF "KNOWING FOR YOURSELF" IS IMMEDIATELY AVAILABLE: IT IS THE SENSORIUM. (RE-ORIENTATION)

One of the consequences of applying the criteria recommended to the Kālāmas in the previous *sutta* is that we can no longer rely completely on external authority—books, teachers, tradition—as our source of knowledge. So to what should we turn? To answer this question, we need to remember that the Buddha's project as a teacher is narrowly proscribed. It is simply to show us the way to overcoming *dukkha.* So the knowledge that we require concerns precisely this matter of human unease. If we bear this fact in mind, the answer to our question becomes obvious. What is our source for knowing the nature of our unease? It is literally right in front of our noses; namely, our means to experiencing "reality." The Buddha refers to this means as "the all." It is the all because it comprises the totality of our *lived* "reality" (lived, that is, in distinction to our imagined, story-laden—deluded—sense of reality).

I put the term "reality" in quotation marks because the common-sensical idea of reality is that it is precisely that which stands apart from *my, your* experience. In the present *sutta,* the Buddha assumes a view different from this commonsensical one; he assumes, namely, that the perceptual apparatus (eyes, ears, nose, tongue, body, mind—let's call it "the sensorium"; see note 5.2) is precisely that mechanism whereby the raw material out there (unprocessed "reality") is cooked up (made real) as *my/your* experience. So imagine that you and I are standing next to each other. A scent wafts across my nose, now your nose. I gag and cough; you breathe deeply and sigh in pleasure. Was the scent the same or different? The Buddha asks us to consider the possibility that all of our experience is just as in this example. If we are engaged in the project of overcoming *dukkha,* then our total attention is directed toward what unfolds within our sensorium. Attending in this manner, we can become deeply knowledgeable about the quality, processes, and nature of our lived experience moment by moment. So in this view, your experience *is* your reality. And your experience is *your* reality. If that experience is pervaded by persistent dissatisfaction and unease, as the Buddha says it is, don't you want to know not about "reality" but about the nature of experience?

Let's explore the Buddha's notion of totality further by asking another question: Can anything really be said to lie outside the sensorium, the perceptual sphere? Of course, countless events are unfolding and countless things exist in the world without my being aware of them. The totality of all of these events and things in the past, present, and future is what we commonsensically understand as "the all." We call it the "universe" or "cosmos." But this all, this universe, is not the Buddha's concern. His concern is that *you* come to know *your* all, your universe, intimately. Know in each instance just where a phenomenon is arising (in the nose, in the mind); observe its duration, its gradual dissolution, and its disappearance. Wafting scent; apprehending nose; my experience; reality. Where does one end and the next begin? Looking in this manner, we come to know directly—for ourselves—the nature of the coextensive field of experience-reality.

NOTES

5.1. *What is the reason for that distress.* What *is* the reason for that distress? After reading the next note, we'll come back to this question.

5.2. *sensorium.* This phrase translates *visaya.* We encountered this same term in "The Hawk" (*sutta* 1), where it meant "habitat." Although we use separate English terms to capture the specific connotations, in the Buddha's usage the two terms—"sensorium" and "habitat"—are not different. Do you notice the appearance of phenomenal forms—sights, sounds, scents, tactile feelings, tastes, and thoughts? Just notice a sound for a moment. Notice *where* it appears. At first, you may be tempted to say, "The sound is coming from over there; it arises out there." But notice that the sound is knowable via the ear. This point may seem obvious—it *should* be obvious!—but we habitually think, speak, and act as if we really believed that the sound, the hearing, and the ear were thoroughly distinct events or objects. It takes only a simple act of observation to notice that the three form a single field of appearance. The field of appearance, where phenomena arise, persist, dissolve, and disappear, is what is referred to in the present *sutta* as the "sensorium."

5.1. *[Sequel:] What is the reason for that distress.* The Buddha asserts that your sense organs and their corresponding data compose the totality of your world. In this view, positing anything whatsoever that lies outside of this sensorium involves an error of apprehension. That is, when Vāseṭṭha's teachers, in "Threefold Knowledge" (*sutta* 3), claimed to possess knowledge of "God," they misconstrued just what they knew in knowing that "God." What they knew, according to the present *sutta,* were particular thoughts, ideas, concepts, visual imagery, and so on, arising in their minds. The error they made was to extrapolate from these *thoughts* an actual physical entity in the "external" world. If one of them had ever seen such an entity, then he could correctly say, "I have seen God." In the former case there is distress because the person lacks clarity and honesty (with himself particularly) concerning his very world. In the latter case, when you see God, you see God. No distress.

In short, we make all kinds of claims about the existence of things without ever looking at just how we know them. The Buddha's notion of "the all" simply asserts that we always know via one of the six perceptual organs. We have to be clear about that fact.

SUTTA 6

फेणपिण्डूपमसुत्त

Look: It Is a Magical Display

Phenapiṇḍūpama Sutta: "Like a Ball of Foam"; *Saṃyuttanikāya* 3.22.95

BUT THE MODES OF PERCEPTION ARE MIRAGELIKE, AND THE PERCEIVED LIKE A MAGICAL DISPLAY. (RE-ORIENTATION)

Practicing the *Sabba Sutta,* "The All," we become adept at recognizing the way perception unfolds. We start to see clearly the interrelationship of what we had erroneously taken to be purely separate events. My eyes, the act of seeing, and the forms that I see; my ears, the act of hearing, and the sounds that I hear; my nose, smelling, and scents, and so forth, suddenly appear to be a *single* fluid event. Where does one aspect end and the other begin? One consequence of internalizing the *Sabba Sutta* is that we begin to feel at home *within* our sensorium. We realize that this sensory field is where we have already been all along: right here. Where else could we ever be? Now, from within this perspective, we have what the Buddha calls "good vision," and so can "reflect on" and "carefully examine" those appearances. What do we see about the nature of all that arises? Of course, I don't need to tell you. Just look! Listen! Smell! Feel! Taste! Think! This kind of looking is called "direct seeing" or "careful examination."

In the present *sutta,* the Buddha is sitting with some of his followers on the banks of the Ganges River. Seeing a ball of foam floating up onto the riverbank, he reflects that, contrary to immediate appearances, *all* forms are fundamentally no different from this ball of foam. What is the nature of this ball of foam? It is, on closer examination, discovered to be "empty, hollow, and insubstantial." And all other forms—what is their nature? When considered more carefully than our rapid everyday perception allows—we might, for instance, require a powerful microscope—they, too, are "empty, hollow, and insubstantial." The Buddha's insight on seeing the ball of foam inspires him to make four further such similes: feeling is like a water bubble; perception is like a shimmering mirage; conceptual fabrications are like a woodless core; cognizance is like a magical illusion.

It is important to note that the Buddha is not denying the reality of each of these processes. He is merely clarifying the *nature* of their realness. In our everyday speech, don't we use "real" to indicate qualities of absoluteness, continuity, solidity, fixedness, and so forth? That sensation you feel on touching a hot cup of coffee is a real, felt sensation. There is no denying the fact. But in what sense is it real? The Buddha's examples seem intentionally to run counter to our common assumptions about the nature of "real." Like a water bubble, a feeling of "hot" *arises* when the necessary conditions are present; *persists* as long as these conditions hold together; *dissolves* as those conditions weaken; and *disappears* as they disintegrate. Why is this insight important? You can do an experiment. Practice viewing appearances, perceptions, feelings, conceptualizations, and thoughts in the manner recommended by the Buddha here. Is your habitual way of reacting altered at all? What qualities of being become present when you see forms as balls of foam and thoughts as magical illusions? When you view reality in this manner, what then?

NOTES

6.1. *appearance.* A central teaching of the Buddha is that what we commonly call a "person" is really just the continual arising, interaction, and passing away of the five impersonal events or processes mentioned in this *sutta:* appearance, feeling, perception, conceptual fabrication, and cognizance. The Buddha uses a strange word to refer to these processes: *khandhas.* The term has two basics senses: (1) bulk, mass, shoulder, trunk; and (2) constituent, aggregate, part. So, as the Buddha uses it, *khandhas* indicates the processes that constitute the bulk of what we call a "person." I thus translate this crucial Buddhist technical term as "the five existential functions." These functions or processes are precisely appearance, feeling, perception, conceptual fabrication, and cognizance. That the individuated self can be reduced to these *khandhas* is, of course, deeply counterintuitive to our experience. So the *sutta* following the present one, *Anattālakkhaṇa Sutta,* is devoted to a fuller account of this "no-self" teaching. But since the Buddha assumes that his interlocutors understand that his examples point not just to form, feeling, et cetera, but to the interlocutors' deepest sense of identity, it will be helpful to give a brief overview of the five *khandhas* in these notes.

"Appearance," or "materiality" (*rūpa*), is the "givenness" of the material world, including my own body. Materiality can be further analyzed as the four basic elements of earth, water, fire, and air. Bhikkhu Bodhi's translation of the four elements as "solidity, cohesion, heat, and distension" points to their actual function in forming and maintaining matter (see Bhikkhu Bodhi, *The Middle Length Discourses of the Buddha: A Translation of the Majjhima Nikāya,* Boston: Wisdom Publications, 1995, p. 1187, n. 129).

6.2. *feeling.* The Pāli term *vedanā* implies a range of meaning that covers both "sensation" and "emotion." As sensation, it is the visceral quality that arises when a sense faculty comes into contact with a sense object. For example, when the nose meets a scent, sensation occurs. When this interaction occurs, one of three visceral responses is possible, according to the Buddha. The scent may be experienced as pleasant, unpleasant, or neutral. This response may lie anywhere on a continuum from subconscious to overt. But can't you yourself verify that such responses do not end there, with visceral sensation? Doesn't such contact often give rise to emotions? Imagine walking in from a cold rain into a cozy, warm room. The change of temperature on the skin is experienced immediately as pleasant, and then this pleasure conditions emotions, such as relief or security. So it is this continuum from sensation to emotion that is meant to be captured in the term "feeling."

6.3. *perception.* "Perception" (*saññā*) is the awareness of the object as something particular and differentiated. The light and form hitting the eyes, causing whatever primal sensation and conditioning emotions, is discerned as "a painting."

6.4. *plantain tree.* Given its lack of a solid inner core, this tree is often used in Buddhist literature as a symbol of non-substantiality.

6.5. *conceptual fabrications.* "Conceptual fabrication," or "fashioning" (*saṅkhāra*), is the fuller appropriation of the (perceived) qualities of the object. The important point here is that this appropriation is based on personal proclivities, which in turn are products of specific conditioned factors via family, culture, genes, and personal experience. This term is often translated as "volition," since it is understood as an assertion of the will over the object being perceived to fashion it in a particular way. Being such an assertion, furthermore, such an act is considered "volitional" in that it serves to establish patterns of mental, verbal, and bodily (i.e., "karmic," or consequential) activity. But the term *saṅkhāra* simply denotes "putting together, forming, embellishing." In the Buddhist view, this sort of thing is precisely what we do *whenever* we see, hear, smell, taste, feel, or cognize an object. Every instance of seeing a painting, et cetera, is an instance of seeing the painting *as*, the "as" deriving from our side, not from the side of the object.

6.6. *cognizance.* "Cognizance" (*viññāṇa*) is present throughout the act of perception. It is the awareness that attends the seeing of the eye-object via the eye, the hearing of the ear-object via the ear, and so forth. It is important to note that cognizance, or consciousness, is understood here as being focused through one of the six vehicles of perception (eye, ear, nose, tongue, body, mind) and not as some kind of pervasive, ghostlike awareness.

6.7. *disenchanted.* When we unconsciously, unquestioningly view some object as being just as it "appears" to us, or just as we perceive it (and so on with the other *khandhas*)—in some objective, absolute sense—this view is evidence that we are enthralled or enchanted by the appearance, perception, and so on. The Buddha asks at the end of each section, in effect: Why do you persist in being caught up in the endless barrage of appearances, ideas, images, concepts, viewpoints, perspectives, judgments, and so on and on and on? The slow dawning that all of these things are like mirages or magical illusions or hollow tree trunks engenders a clear-eyed disillusionment, disenchantment, and loss of infatuation. No longer infatuated, we naturally experience a dispassionate withdrawal from our habitual involvement with these endless forms. This withdrawal is liberating; it frees us from our previous life-limiting enthrallment. When we are no longer *held* in thrall (from Anglo-Saxon *thræl*, "slave"), what then?

6.8. *kinsman of the sun.* An epithet of the Buddha.

SUTTA 7

अनत्तलक्खणसुत्त

No Sign of I, Me, or Mine

Anattālakkhana Sutta: "Evidence of Selflessness"; *Saṃyuttanikāya* 3.22.59

AND THERE IS NO SELF, NO INTEGRAL PERCEIVER, BEHIND THOSE MODES OF PERCEPTION.
(RE-ORIENTATION)

In the previous *suttas,* the Buddha tells us that in order to resolve our persistent lack of ease, it is crucial that we come to know *for ourselves* the nature of reality. The means of this direct, extradoctrinal, extra-authoritarian knowledge, he further tells us, is immediately available: knowing requires that we learn to attend to the sensorium, to the sense doors—the modes of immediate, moment-to-moment presence. Once we turn our attention to the sensorium and become accustomed to attending to matters as they unfold right there, the Buddha asks us to push our insight even deeper. He asks us to observe that the reality given through these modes of perception is analogous to a mirage, magical illusion, or woodless core. As we become accustomed to seeing in this manner, it dawns on us that the *khandhas,* the apparent constituents that make up our (apparent) personalities, are engaged in a dance with shifting, changing, indeterminate, phantomlike entities. It might be that, with this insight, the practitioner now has a sense of attainment, a sense of having finally resolved the important matter of understanding the nature of reality. There is a sense that "I" have understood, that "I" know. This sense of accomplishment gives rise to a feeling of stability, as if there were a firm, fixed position from which "I" look out at the world, seeing that it is really like a dream. Seeing this condition of reality, "I" nonetheless feel constant and real and not at all dreamlike.

It is precisely at this phase of clarity that the Buddha pushes us to deepen our insight. In the present *sutta,* he is speaking to the "group of five mendicants." These five men are mentioned in the introduction as the group of mendicants who had practiced with the Buddha early on in his quest but had eventually abandoned him as a backslider. We might imagine, then, that these five men had realized the ephemeral nature of reality. Nonetheless, the Buddha finds it necessary to point out to them something more: there is no self, no actual "I," behind or within this process of realizing, knowing, or simply being. So the fact that the Buddha is speaking this *sutta* to advanced practitioners may be seen as indicative of the deeply counterintuitive idea of no-self. Our being in the world—our very way of experiencing, thinking, and speaking—wants to reject such a notion as absurd or simply wrong, doesn't it? If nothing else, no-self certainly runs counter to our *normal* way of thinking and being. As an experiment, just try to speak without pronouns, or think and experience for a few moments devoid of a persistent underlying sense of "I, me, or mine" doing the experiencing.

By observing in turn that which we call "experience," "thinking," and "language," we may also gain a vantage point for understanding the Buddha's counterintuitive teaching of no-self. When you carefully examine your actual experience, thinking, and language, isn't each instance run through with the kind of shifting indeterminacy best described as "miragelike"? Just take a look. If "miragelike" is the case, then what sort of "self," not to mention idea or definition of "self," can be preserved in light of this insight? It would be useful to reflect at this point on what it is precisely that *you* are calling "self." The Buddha presumes his interlocutors hold a notion of self that is by definition self-contained, undivided, integral, *individual.* As such, the self would be a powerful controlling agent. Is that the case? Again, just look at your immediate experience. If what we call "the self" is not *the* driving force behind experience, if it is not an agent (from the Greek, *agein,* "to drive"), then what is it that we are referring to with the term "self"? Is anyone there?

NOTES

7.1. *deer park.* The deer park and locations like it were ideal gathering places for ascetics and mendicants in the day of the Buddha. Practitioners from many different sects would have met here to engage in discussion and debate. A great Buddhist monastery and *stūpa* were later built on the grounds of the deer park. The ruins of these buildings, and the deer, along with a modern zoo, are still there.

7.2. *the group of five mendicants.* See commentary here and "Reality" (commentary on *sutta* 9).

7.3. *The body.* Pāli and Sanskrit *rūpa,* which I am rendering here as "body," has the same wide lexical range as the English term. In brief, *rūpa* may refer to an external appearance (as in "Like a Ball of Foam," *sutta* 6) or to the human form (as in "The All," *sutta* 5). In the present *sutta,* the Buddha's aim is to refute unequivocally the view that some entity "self" is located somewhere within the various modes of being referred to as the *khandhas.* So in this context, "one's own body" should be understood. However, the insight that the Buddha is hoping to inculcate here also applies, of course, to other bodies; that is, to all material appearances.

7.4. *not . . . self.* This term translates the Pāli *anattā* and the Sanskrit *anātman. Ātman* (the prefix *an°* marks a negation) is a term of enormous significance in Indian thought. Whenever you read words such as "Soul," "Spirit," and "Self" (almost invariably capitalized) in English-language books dealing with any aspect of Indian religion or philosophy, you can be all but certain that the underlying term is *ātman.* The reason that *ātman* is of paramount importance to the "spiritual" quest in Indian systems of thought and practice is that it is "the *ātman*" that undergoes the summum bonum of these systems, namely *mokṣa,* or liberation. This importance notwithstanding, it is not at all clear—apparently not even to those who employ it—precisely to what *ātman* refers. In the seminal Indian works known as the Upaniṣads, for instance, the meaning of *ātman* seems to lie anywhere along a continuum from a homunculus residing in the human heart to formless awareness itself. In short, the candidate for "self" in the Indian literature ranges from some sort of solid object to some imperceptible, ghostlike non-thing. The Buddha would, of course, say that this ambiguity really just amounts to evidence for "no-self." That is, ambiguity concerning the nature of the self arises precisely because there is no such entity "self" that can be looked at, examined, and described. That being the case (is it?), what force does the term "self" have? This is not a rhetorical question.

(For a thorough treatment of the issues surrounding *anattā* and *anātman,* we are fortunate to have Steven Collins's *Selfless Persons,* Cambridge: Cambridge University Press, 1982).

7.5. *then it would not give us trouble.* The Buddha assumes a fundamental property of "a self" implied in the term "agent"; namely, the ability to control.

7.6. *permanent or impermanent.* Another axiom of the *ātman* position holds that the self is permanent or eternal. Doesn't this axiom hold, too, for our notion of self as, for example, a soul or spirit?

7.7. *impermanent distressful.* For the idea of permanence to make any sense, something must have a location: it must *be,* and it must be *somewhere.* The only realistic candidates for such a location, if not simply "the self," are the *khandhas.* But now a danger arises. Buddhists have been vigilant to this danger from the Buddha's day down to the present. Many Buddhists, past and present, have succumbed to this danger, whether consciously or not. The danger is that we begin to reify the *khandhas,* and view them as actual entities rather than as a mere conceptual schema providing a rough parsing out of existential processes. (One of the most enduring responses to this danger of reifying the *khandhas* is the widely recited work known as the *Heart Sūtra.*) So here the Buddha disabuses the mendicants (and us) of the possibility that any or all of the *khandhas* can either replace or house an *ātman:* when the Buddha's interlocutors answer "impermanent" to his question about the *khandhas,* they are in fact denying a foundational premise of those who hold the view of "self" as stated in the previous note. Furthermore, when the five mendicants acknowledge that even if there was something like an integral self within one or all *khandhas,* that self would, by nature (given impermanence), be "distressful." This admission amounts to a denial of another major axiom of the *ātman* doctrine; namely, that the self is inherently blissful.

7.8. *This is not mine, I am not this, this is not my self.* The Buddha implies here that this statement can be used as an antidote to our habitual "I-making" and as a means of penetrating reality as it is. That is, by cultivating the understanding that "this perception (or material/body, feeling, conceptual fabrication, cognizance) is not mine, I am not this, this is not my self," we begin simultaneously to weaken our sense of self and see how things really are—devoid of self, essence, spirit, or soul.

SUTTA 8

भरासुत्त

Just Put It Down

Bharā Sutta: "The Burden"; *Saṃyuttanikāya* 3.22.22

TO HOLD ON TO THE MIRAGELIKE PERCEIVER, THE PHANTOM SELF, IS A STULTIFYING BURDEN. (RE-ORIENTATION)

As the final move in our re-orientation process, the Buddha recommends this: *Just put it all down!* Conceptually, philosophically, logically, and most of all, psychologically, letting go of our sense of "a self" is, obviously, easier said than done. So in the present *sutta*, the Buddha offers us a strategy that counteracts the powerful effects of conceptualizing, thinking logically, and so on, about "self." The Buddha's strategy is simply to cease all such effort. When a psychological compulsion arises to assert "I, me, mine," just view that compulsion as a burden, and put it down. How? It's easy. But it's also difficult. It's easy because it requires no effort whatsoever; in fact, it requires the opposite of effort. But this is hard to do because we humans are virtuosos of agitated effort, aren't we? Do we ever cease to do? In the *Bharā Sutta,* the Buddha explains what he means by "putting down the burden."

NOTES

8.1. *This is what I heard.* A formulaic statement preceding many *suttas.* This statement reveals the oral nature of the earliest transmission of the texts and points to the role of the early councils in fixing the wording of those texts. The earliest followers of the Buddha were, in fact, called "hearers"

(Sanskrit: *śrāvakas;* Pāli: *sāvakas*). At the first council, the Buddha's closest disciple, Ānanda, purportedly recited his memory of the Buddha's teachings. The other close followers would then approve of or amend, based on their own memories of what the Buddha said, Ānanda's version. Later, Mahāyāna authors would use this opening phrase to lend innovative literary creations an air of authenticity.

8.2. *The five existential functions subject to grasping.* Here, the Buddha is modifying "the existential functions" (*khandhas*) with "subject to grasping" (*upādāna*). Why this modification? The *khandhas* are bare functions of a person's existing in the world: the body and appearances simply are the case, feeling simply feels, perception simply perceives, conceptual fabrications are simply manufactured, and cognizance is simply aware. Looking at your own experience, however, you may understandably reply that this "simply" is not so simple. Appearances are alluring, and the body does grasp at appearances; feeling is certain of its response to stimuli, and does attempt to hold on to or push away its object; perception is convinced of its view, and does endeavor to hold its object in place; conceptual fabrications do spin out a compelling, enticing version of events; and cognizance does assume the indubitability of its knowing. So the fivefold *khandha,* though a bare existential apparatus, can easily become a grasping machine.

Two additional texts from the same subsection of the *Saṃyuttanikāya* as "The Burden" (the *Khandha* subsection) may help clarify the Buddha's meaning here. In the *sutta* called "Ways of Regarding Things" (*Saṃyuttanikāya* 3.22.47), the Buddha says that grasping is merely the function of a person's being "unskilled and undisciplined." Such lack of skill and discipline allows for the sense of "I, me, mine" to arise. Because of this "I am," there occurs "a descent of the five faculties" (eyes, ears, nose, tongue, and body). For a person who is skilled and disciplined, by contrast, no notion of "I, me, mine" occurs, and although the faculties "remain right there," they do not become entangled in the phenomenal world.

In the *sutta* immediately following "Ways of Regarding Things," called "Aggregates," the Buddha more explicitly clarifies the distinction between the phrases "existential functions" (*khandhas*) and "existential functions subject to grasping." There, he says that the difference lies in whether or not the *khandhas*—our modes of being in the world—possess "impulse." "Impulse" translates *āsava,* another central Buddhist technical term. Common renderings of this term are "impurity," "defilement," "taint," "canker," "effluent," "intoxicant," "influx," "stream," "corruption," "current," and "flow." Some more unfortunate translations are "evil influence," "Evil Canker," "depravity," and "sin." The term is formed from the verbal root √*su,* "to flow," plus the prefix *ā,* "outward," yielding the meaning "to flow out." In everyday language, *āsava* is used to denote, for example, the flow of a river, the secretion of tree sap, the intoxicating extract of certain plants and flowers, and the ooze discharged from a sore. In the present context, the Buddha transfers the term from the natural world to the psychological. Here, the five existential functions are subject to grasping when impulse—urge, drive, compulsion—is present.

8.3. *The person.* This term translates *puggala.* This may seem a strange choice of words on the Buddha's part after his having strenuously refuted the notion of a self. An entire school of Buddhism arose in India around the third century B.C.E. partly on the basis of the Buddha's use of this term precisely in "The Burden." This school called itself the Puggalavāda, or Personalists (literally, "those who hold the doctrine 'person' "). The Puggalavādins, in brief, held that there is in fact some entity properly designated as "person" but that it exists neither within nor external to the *khandhas.* As such, the person is inexpressible and indeterminate, though nonetheless real. One concern of the Puggalavāda, apparently, was to preserve moral determinism and ethical responsibility (if there is no responsible *agent,* how can we speak of moral culpability?).

My own view is that the Buddha is using the term "person" harmlessly. He is merely conforming to conventional speech. But, in using just this term, I think that the Buddha is giving a subtle but crucial teaching: *Don't think that the obvious lack of an inherent self, person, soul, life force, or whatever you want to call it absolves you of the responsibilities of being a person. And don't pretend not to know what "person" means. We all know what it means; and we know perfectly well to what it refers. It refers to so-and-so from such and such a family. You know who that person is.*

SUTTA 9

धम्मचक्कप्पवत्तनसुत्त

Reality

Dhammacakkappavattana Sutta: "Turning the Wheel of the Teaching";

Saṃyuttanikāya 5.56.11

WHEN WE REFLECT ON THESE PROPOSITIONS, FOUR PREEMINENT REALITIES BECOME OBVIOUS. (MAP)

The *Dhammacakkappavattana Sutta* is held almost unanimously by both scholars and Buddhists to give an account of the very first instance that the Buddha communicated his realization to others. The title itself alludes to such an inauguration of his teaching. In the biographies of the Buddha that developed in the decades and centuries after his death, the Buddha is shown to have been reluctant to express his newfound understanding to anyone, thinking it too demanding to comprehend. By resisting this urge to remain silent, the Buddha was acting as a world-conquering monarch—as a king who unleashes his war chariots on neighboring kingdoms in an act of usurpation. In ancient Indian literature, such a ruler is said to be a "wheel-turning king." This term would have created an image in the minds of those hearing it of a terrifying, violent force. While the Buddha, of course, aims to conquer a domain completely different from geographical territory, the use of this metaphor is instructive. It shows that from the earliest period, Buddhists conceived of this *sutta* as signifying an event of immense significance and scope. The *sutta* thus presents itself from the outset as both a primary document and a foundational teaching. Whether or not this traditional view can be unequivocally substantiated by modern textual-historical scholarship (there is really no way to determine definitively the relative ages and proper sequence of the various *suttas*), it would certainly not be difficult to trace most of the Buddha's subsequent teachings to some aspect of the teachings found here. Similarly, it could be shown without much difficulty that the doctrinal foundation established here has supported the numerous expressions of Buddhist doctrine appearing throughout the teachings' twenty-five-hundred-year history. So the *Dhammacakkappavattana Sutta* is, for all intents and purposes, indeed both a primary and a foundational Buddhist text.

The *Dhammacakkappavattana Sutta* is bare-bones. Many commentators have seen in its structure a basic medical model for treating illness: diagnosis, cause, prognosis, and prescription. What need does such an economical model have for elaboration? The point of a medical model is to get to the heart of a matter bearing on life and death, and to do so *now*. Similarly, the *sutta* aims simply to present "things as they really are," as the Buddha says elsewhere (*Saṃyuttanikāya* 5.56.1), so that the practitioner may become well *now*. The *Dhammacakkappavattana Sutta* "announces, teaches, establishes, reveals, expounds, and exhibits" (*Majjhimanikāya* 141) features so fundamental to human existence that the Buddha utilized a word he would rarely repeat in any other context during his forty-five years of teaching. This word, *sacca*, is routinely translated as "truth." Unlike the English term, which stems from the Anglo-Saxon word for "faith" (*treowthu*), the Pāli *sacca* (Sanskrit: *satya*) derives from the Sanskrit present participle *sat* via the verbal root √*as*, meaning "to be." So the Buddha claims to be expounding in this *sutta* something quite different from an article of faith. He claims to be simply revealing matters to "be the case"; the Buddha is claiming to be merely pointing out matters that are verifiable to everyone. Now, the reader of the *sutta*, of course, should not take it on faith that these matters are in fact verifiable. So you have to ask: Are these matters—unease, its origin, its cessation, and the path to its cessation—verifiable in my experience? In another *sutta* (*Saṃyuttanikāya* 5.56.5), the Buddha asserts that anyone who "fully awakens to things as they really are" will, as a matter of course, fully awaken to the knowledge propounded in the *Dhammacakkappavattana Sutta*. This statement accentuates the commonplace nature of the view being expounded in the *sutta*, but it also suggests that we are commonly asleep to that view.

It may enrich your reading of the *sutta* to ask: If this *sutta* stands at the beginning of the Buddha's teaching, why present it as the ninth text in the book? You probably noticed that the *sutta* is addressed to "the group of five mendicants." These were people who had devoted their lives to ultimate realization. So it would enhance your reading of the *sutta* to reflect on the qualities that such practitioners may already have possessed by the time the Buddha approached them in the deer park. The Buddha sometimes referred to his followers as "hearers." So the five mendicants may be seen as a composite of the ideal hearer (reader) of the text in the present. What qualities, traits, and aspirations should such a reader possess in order to hear what is being said in the *Dhammacakkappavattana Sutta*? I hope that you'll give this question some thought as you read.

NOTES

9.1. *deer park.* See note 7.1.

9.2. *group of five mendicants.* See the commentary.

9.3. *"a tathāgata".* This term, with which the Buddha often referred to himself, is an unsolved conundrum both in the field of Buddhist studies in the West and among Buddhist thinkers themselves. Literally, it means a person who is either "thus come (*tathā* + *gata*)" or "thus gone (*tathā* + *āgata*)." The long *a* (*ā*) in *tathā* makes the meaning unclear even at this basic, and somewhat nonsensical, lexical level. But even if it was clear which of these meanings were indicated by the term, we'd still have to ask: So what does it mean? In some interpretations of the term, scholars have understood it to be a reference, on the Buddha's part, to following in the footsteps of prior *buddhas*—his arrival on the scene is patterned after theirs. But an important Buddhist technical usage of *tathā* is found in the abstract noun formation *tathatā* (also spelled *tathātā* and *tathatta*), "the state of being so." In translations of Mahāyāna works, *tathatā* is usually rendered as "thusness" or "suchness," as a way of referring to reality just as it is, before discursive analysis *of* it, and beyond the grasp of description. It is with this sense that I gloss it here as "a person who has come to know reality." This rendering is largely consistent with the interpretation just mentioned, but it exceeds it with the universally inclusive "a"; *a tathāgata* is *anyone* who "knows things as they are."

9.4. *"the middle way".* The middle way (*majjhimā paṭipadā*) is a central Buddhist technical term. The Buddha applies it in instances where extremes in thought and action are the normative courses. For example, in the present *sutta,* he mentions a common mode of human being, "clinging to sensory pleasure," and the common (for his present interlocutors) reaction to this mode, "exhausting oneself with austerities." Now, note that the Buddha is assuming here "a person who has set out on the path" for overcoming human unease. So it is not the case that each of these modes of being is somehow bad or sinful, or for that matter even *wrong.* The problem is simply that each is, on its own—hence, as an extreme—ineffectual. This view becomes clear when we look at the components of the eight-component course. These components seek neither to abolish the natural human capacity for being involved in sensory objects nor to disavow disciplined modifications to that involvement. The former would be impossible; the latter would be counterproductive. (On the eight-component course, see the following note.)

In other contexts, the Buddha applies the middle way strategy to modify extremes in conceptualization. For example, to conceive of "the person" as a constant, persisting entity is to take the extreme view of eternalism (*sassatavāda*). To hold the opposite view, namely, that there is absolutely no continuity in experience approaching anything like "a self," is annihilationism (*ucchedavāda*). Taking your own experience as the basis, which is the case? Based on the arguments in "Evidence of Selflessness" (*sutta* 7), there is no empirical justification for a strong view of "self" (as, for example, an unchanging, integral essence). But based on actual, moment-to-moment experience, there *is* justification for some commonsensical, process-oriented view of "self." So when neither extreme describes the reality, how should we conceive of "self"? The Buddha's answer is, *Take the middle way.* The middle way strategy in this case is that there is continuity without a continuous entity. The process that the Buddha uses to account for this case, "dependent origination," is treated in "Gotama's Discourse" (*sutta* 10). The point here is that the middle way strategy is applied to reconcile limiting, conceptual dichotomies in order to account more accurately for reality. (The Buddha makes this case in these terms at *Saṃyuttanikāya* 2.12.17.) As this example shows, the middle way is also a strategy for reconciling the extreme ontological standpoints of *is* and *is not.*

9.5. "*eight-component course*". Several of the Buddha's followers were once asked why they trained under him. They replied that they did so in order to come to "a full understanding of unease (*dukkha*)." When they checked this answer with the Buddha, he approved but indicated that something more needed to be said. They should also mention that "there is a path, there is a way for the full understanding of this unease" (*Saṃyuttanikāya* 5.45.5). This path, of course, is the eight-component course. And the *na-*

ture of this path, the Buddha says elsewhere, is that it "slants, slopes, and inclines toward unbinding (*nirvāṇa*)," just as the Ganges River flows toward the ocean. The claim, then, that the Buddha couches in this image, is that the way to overcoming human pain and unease is natural and assured. Yet, just in case his listener takes this assurance for granted, he goes on to emphasize the absolute necessity of a single quality: diligence (see *Saṃyuttanikāya* 5.45.140–148). But really, this quality, too, is commonsensical: a way naturally and assuredly leads to its destination, but the wayfarer has to keep to it with diligence.

The eight components of the path are subdivided into three main aspects of Buddhist training: understanding (1, 2), conduct (3–6), and attentiveness (7, 8). The Buddha elaborates on the path in a *sutta* called "Analysis," at *Saṃyuttanikāya* 5.45.8, as follows. (As you read through the components of the path, it would be useful to consider how each could conceivably play out in your life. What changes would be required in daily life to fulfill each? What would have to be added to, or subtracted from, the way you live? What impact would these changes have on your life? Also, how does each of the factors of the path follow from, or relate to, the others? For example, does your basic view of the world affect your basic intentions toward the world; and do these intentions affect your speech?)

1. Sound* View: The practitioner has insight into existential unease (*dukkha*), its origin, its cessation, and the way leading to its cessation.
2. Sound Inclination: The practitioner tends toward renunciation, kindness, and harmlessness.
3. Sound Speech: The practitioner refrains from lying, slander, harsh speech, and frivolous speech.
4. Sound Action: The practitioner refrains from taking life, taking what is not given, and sexual misconduct.
5. Sound Livelihood: The practitioner refrains from any forms of livelihood that

* The term that I have translated as "sound" (*sammā*) is routinely rendered as "right." The Pāli word stems from the Sanskrit prefix *sam* ("together with," like Latin *con°*) + the verbal root √*añc* ("to turn to, to go toward"). So the general sense of *sammā* is to be fully inclined toward something. "Right" works if we understand by it the way that a sailboat is righted (correctly, properly positioned), or the way that the cold goes right through you (thoroughly). Unfortunately, most of us probably hear moralistic or judgmental overtones (right as opposed to wrong) when we here "right." "Sound" (from the Anglo-Saxon *sund* > the German *gesund*, "healthy") better captures the intended sense of the eight components as "whole" (a sound body), "stable, secure" (a sound institution), "reliable" (a sound argument), and "undisturbed, deep" (sound sleep).

would compromise fulfillment of all other aspects of the eight-component course.

6. Sound Effort: The practitioner (a) strives to *prevent* harmful mental states from arising; (b) strives to *overcome* those harmful, unwholesome mental states that have arisen; (c) strives to *generate* beneficial mental states that have not arisen; and (d) strives to *maintain* and *fully develop* beneficial, wholesome mental states that have arisen.
7. Sound Awareness: The practitioner, "being ardent, fully aware, and mindful, and having put down longing and discontentment toward the world, lives seeing the body *in and as a body*, lives seeing feelings *in and as feelings*, lives seeing mind *in and as mind*, and lives seeing mental qualities and phenomena *in and as mental qualities and phenomena*."
8. Sound Concentration: The practitioner attains the four states of meditative absorption (*jhāna*).
   a. Detached from sense desires, detached from detrimental mental states, accompanied by applied and sustained cognizance, the practitioner enters and dwells in the first meditative absorption, which is filled with delight and ease born of detachment.
   b. With the quieting of applied and sustained cognizance, gaining inner tranquillity and unity of mind, beyond applied and sustained cognizance, the practitioner enters and dwells in the second meditative absorption, which is filled with delight and ease born of concentration.
   c. With the fading away of delight, dwelling in equanimity, attentively present and clearly aware, the practitioner experiences embodied ease and enters and dwells in the third meditative absorption, of which the noble ones say, "Happy is the person who dwells with equanimity and present-moment awareness."
   d. With the abandonment of ease and tension, and with the vanishing of previous longing and discontentment, the practitioner enters and dwells in the fourth meditative absorption, which is beyond ease and tension, and possesses the purity of equanimity and present-moment awareness.

I. **Understanding** (1, 2) We all have some basic understanding of life. We have formed our particular understanding through the influence of our environment and through our experiences. This understanding underlies the general direction and quality of our lives. As such, it may be largely unconscious, or at least unarticulated. How is the world? How are people? What's the point of it all? Our *view* has an answer. When our view, our understanding, penetrates the preeminent realities of life, that is called "sound view." With a little self-reflection, it is not difficult to see the relationship between view and *inclination*. If I view people as generally threatening, I will impulsively be inclined to treat them as such. The Buddha considers our inclination to be sound when we tend toward letting go of infatuation, hostility, and delusion.

II. **Conduct** (3–6) Our disposition, how we comport ourselves in the world, follows from our understanding of things. When someone's thought (understanding), speech, and action are disjointed—when he or she says one thing but does another—we say that the person is being hypocritical. So we tacitly and commonsensically assume harmony among these three modes of being. If your fundamental view of life is sound (that is, you understand the preeminent matters), your inclination toward others will be sound (not hostile, et cetera). This being the case, how could you speak harshly to or about others? Wouldn't your *speech* naturally become gentle, or at least well intentioned? Furthermore, having insight into fundamental realities of our human situation, are you really going to fritter away your time chattering, gossiping, or yammering like a hyperactive monkey? And knowing what you know about things, won't you watch your *actions* more carefully, making sure that you don't cause too much damage to yourself and others? When we take such matters seriously, our choice of *livelihood* becomes crucial. Our lives, after all, are of a single fabric, aren't they? Finally, an important form that our conduct takes is cognitive in nature. (In Indian systems of thought, actions [*karma*] are held to be performed by means of the body, speech, *and* mind.) So healthy mental activity requires sound *effort* regarding our cognition (as well as our bodies and speech). Has anger arisen? Well, the soundest effort regarding that angry cast of mind is to overcome it. Is joy present in the mind? The sound thing to do then is to maintain it and fully develop it.

The Pāli word that I am translating as "conduct" is *sīla*. This term is normally rendered as either "virtue" or "morality"; but these English words not only ring too, well, virtuous and moralistic but also miss the point. The Sanskrit root of the term is √*śīl*, which means "to do, to practice, to be intent on, to cultivate." So each of these factors of the path, when persistently practiced, slowly becomes our custom, our way of being. What matters is not the virtue inherent in our actions but the soundness of them in relation to overcoming persistent unease.

III. **Attentiveness** (7, 8) Only once we have acquired a mature, clear-eyed view of the nature of human existence, and only once we have thereby formed healthy ways of acting in the world, can we get on with a disciplined, transformative practice. The practice prescribed in the Buddha's eight-component course is of a single piece but with two modes of application—dynamic and reflective. The Pāli and Sanskrit term used to summarize this practice is *samādhi*, routinely translated as either "concentration" or "meditation." But what do those English words mean? The root underlying *samādhi* is √*dhā*, meaning simply "to put, to place." Added to this root are the prefixes *sam* and *ā*, each of which signifies solidification and unification of the verbal action. Hence, *samādhi* yields "to place firmly together." Whenever we direct our attention toward an object, that is *samādhi*—we are literally placing our thought or awareness right there. Elsewhere, the Buddha takes this everyday directedness of attention one step further by defining *samādhi* as "the one-pointedness of mind" (*cittekaggatā*). He then adds that such one-pointedness has as its basis sound present-moment awareness and as its equipment sound effort (see *Majjhimanikāya* 44.12). So in its Buddhist technical usage, *samādhi* is a laserlike concentration of attentiveness; it is a complete unification of mind, which yields a profound state of being collected, gathered together, whole. (Perhaps it is *samādhi* that we are pointing to when we say to a nervous or distraught friend, "Pull yourself together.")

In the seventh and eighth components of the path, the terms are respectively *sammāsati* (sound present-moment awareness) and *sammāsamādhi*. Based on the intent of the actual practices, I am translating *samādhi* here as "attentiveness." Attentiveness, unlike the colloquial senses of "concentration" and "meditation," is a spontaneous human quality. Whereas you have to make an effort to concentrate or meditate, you really don't have to do anything special to have attentiveness—it's always already there. Just look.

In the dynamic mode, attentiveness is directed toward what the Buddha calls "the four areas." These areas are the energy fields where our lives vibrate moment by moment, namely, body, feeling, mind, and phenomena. Attentiveness toward these areas may be applied during meditation, but they mainly constitute a manner of being aware in the midst of our daily lives, moment by moment, active or inactive, agitated or at rest, and everywhere in between. Applying such awareness constitutes sound awareness.

As the final component of the path, the Buddha describes four levels of meditative absorption to be realized by the practitioner. These four, which constitute concentration, are cultivated during seated practice. The Pāli term that I am translating here as "meditative absorption" is *jhāna*. The Pāli is derived from the Sanskrit *dhyāna*, which becomes the Chinese *chan'na*, later shortened to *chan*, then the Korean *son*, and finally the Japanese *zen*. Zen is known as the "meditation school" precisely because of this appellation. But what do we mean by "meditation"? Rather than answer that question, which will put us on a trajectory toward Latin etymology and Christian monastic practice, let's ask: What did the Buddha mean by *jhāna*? In its everyday (unsound) application, *jhāna* simply denotes being engrossed in an object, for instance, being lost in thought or absorbed in a book or a television show. So *jhāna* is something that we all know firsthand.

But as he so often does, the Buddha takes this common human proclivity, analyzes its properties, and then distinguishes its everyday (unsound) application from a more refined, practice-oriented (sound) one. Let's look more closely at the first *jhāna* as an example:

Detached from sense desires, detached from detrimental mental states

The attainment of the first *jhāna* requires, first of all, the elimination of particular mental qualities. In *sutta* 3, the Buddha mentions harmful sense desires as "forms perceptible to the eye, which are pleasing, desirable, charming, agreeable, arousing desire, and enticing; sounds perceptible to the ear, . . . scents perceptible to the nose, . . . tastes perceptible to the tongue, . . . tactile objects perceptible to the body, which are pleasing, desirable, charming, agreeable, arousing desire, and enticing." He then mentions detrimental mental qualities as the impulses toward (1) desire, (2) hostility, (3) heavy lethargy, (4) agitated worry, and (5) debilitating doubt.

accompanied by applied and sustained cognizance

This statement alludes to the practice, cultivated during seated meditation, of placing one's attention on an object. As we will see in "Present-Moment Awareness with Breathing" (*sutta* 15), the Buddha's preferred object is simply the breath. So "applied cognizance" means to bring one's attention to the breath, and "sustained cognizance" means to keep it there. The application of this practice is precisely what allows detachment from sense desires and detrimental mental states (elsewhere called "factors of abandonment") on the one hand and fulfillment of beneficial qualities ("factors of possession") on the other. Two of these beneficial qualities are referred to next in the formula for the first *jhāna* as

delight and ease born of detachment.

(Three other "factors of possession" are applied and sustained cognizance and the one-pointedness of mind that they allow.) "Delight" is a translation of the Pāli word *pīti*. In its weak form, *pīti* is simply the mild euphoria or enthusiasm that accompanies us when we have an interest in some object. In its strong form, *pīti* indicates a rapturous exaltation of mind, body, and emotion. I render it here as "delight" to indicate a pervasive feeling of joy independent from any sense object. Similarly, "ease" translates the Pāli *sukha*, normally rendered as "happiness," to indicate a state of being that is not dependent on external stimuli.

9.6. *"this is unease"*. What is your reaction as you read through this list characterizing unease? At first, these examples appear to be platitudes. "Illness is unsettling"—isn't that statement banal? But looking further, might this section be seen as presenting a comprehensive, if terse, delineation of human dissatisfaction and pain? What the Buddha says here covers life pretty much from beginning to end: birth, aging, illness, and death; having what we don't want, not having what we do. (For the five components of grasping, see note 9.8.)

But what is meant by "unease" here? The most common rendering of the Pāli term *dukkha* is "suffering." So if you have read books on Buddhism before, you have almost certainly encountered the term "suffering" where I have "unease." However, probably very few people would describe their lives as being characterized by *suffering*. The notion of pain and anguish connoted by that term does indeed resonate in *dukkha*, but it is too drastic for a general and universal application. So the stock statement "Life is suffering," while not outright incorrect, is somewhat too drama-queenish. In getting a better feeling for the meaning of *dukkha*, let's place "suffering" at one extreme of the spectrum. At the other extreme, let's place qualities such as annoyance, tension, nondependability. So far, then, *dukkha* can be understood on one end of the spectrum as a subtle, perhaps barely discernible quality of being and, on the other, as severe mental or physical anguish.

A further nuance is added to the term *dukkha* when we bear in mind that, in the Buddha's view, even a "happy" moment is tinged by *dukkha*. That is because neither the moment nor the experience is stable. Since the quality of happiness arises in dependence on external factors, it fades away as those factors disassemble. And in that gap is felt the trace, however subtle, of underlying *dukkha*. Since, furthermore, our lives are successions of such moments, *dukkha* is said to be "pervasive." But Buddhists would go even further, to the point of what appears paradoxical, even contradictory: it is not only in the gap (due to impermanence and insubstantiality) that *dukkha* is present but even in the very experience of happiness.

Given this view, what should we call *dukkha* in our language? Our English term would have to have the following colorings (on an increasing scale of intensity):

faint unsettledness
irritation
impatience
annoyance
frustration
disappointment
dissatisfaction
aggravation
tension
stress
anxiety
distress
exasperation

vexation
pain
desperation
sorrow
sadness
suffering
misery
agony
anguish

(You may add to this list; there is virtually no end to it. And that is precisely the Buddha's point! It flows through life like water—each instant of life is colored to some degree by one of these qualities.)

Now, I think it is obvious that each of these qualities involves some degree of unease; so "unease" is how I translate the term for general usage. The lexical "opposite" of *dukkha* is *sukha;* and *sukha* straightforwardly means "ease, pleasure, happiness." Perhaps, then, *dukkha* can be taken to straightforwardly mean "unease, displeasure, unhappiness." We all know about *dukkha,* then, as it is glossed by the Buddha here.

9.7. *"preeminent reality"*. I hesitate to use this phrase since I intend it to replace one of the most venerable and beloved Buddhist-English-hybrid terms of all: "Noble Truth." I say "hybrid" because the term is neither quite English nor quite Buddhist. To be honest, "noble truth," much less "Noble Truth," has never made much sense to me. Whenever I read that phrase, I have to ask myself, In what sense can a Truth be Noble? And why the imposing Germanic capitals? "Noble" describes people, maybe animals, but not abstractions such as truth. Perhaps the idea is that realization of some truth is ennobling to a person, or that the particular truth is something sanctioned by noble people. Those explanations would be fine, but they raise a more serious question: Isn't the very notion of truth, given all the rest of the Buddha's teachings, a bit dicey? "Truth" just rings too boisterous to harmonize well with the rest of the *buddhavacana,* doesn't it?

The commonly used phrase "noble truth," and my suggested phrase, "preeminent reality," represent the Pāli *ariyasacca.* As I mentioned in the introduction to this *sutta,* the Pāli word *sacca* (Sanskrit: *satya*) derives from the present participle (*sat*) of the verbal root √*as,* meaning "to be." So something is "true" by virtue of its being in existence, of its being the case. This sense is actually that given by the Anglo-Saxon basis of the modern English word "truth," namely, *treowthu,* "faith, faithful." So if by "truth" we mean "being faithful to, corresponding to, reality," then it would be a satisfactory rendering of *sacca.* But since we so often use "truth" to indicate precisely matters that are neither obviously the case nor even coherent and that therefore must be taken on faith ("God is truth"; "the truth will set you free"; "universal truth"), it is wholly unsatisfactory. I would go so far as to say that the use of the term "noble truth" is historically and doctrinally irresponsible.

So far, I have given some reasons why we might want to rethink rendering *sacca* as "truth." But as I mentioned in the commentary on the *sutta,* the Buddha himself rarely used the term *sacca.* So why did he use it here? One explanation is that he didn't. K. R. Norman, a preeminent British scholar of Pāli language and literature, has convincingly argued that "the earliest form of this sutta [the *Dhammacakkappavattana Sutta*] did not include the word *ariya-saccaṃ.*" (This statement is his conclusion after a detailed philological investigation. Those wishing to take a deeper look may consult Norman's article, "The Four Noble Truths," in *Indological and Buddhist Studies [Volume in Honour of Professor J. W. de Jong],* Canberra, 1982, pp. 377-91.) In brief, Norman presents evidence showing that (1) the term *ariyasacca* is grammatically and syntactically not viable as found in the *sutta,* and (2) the earliest expressions of the fourfold set were what Norman calls "mnemonic" and "basic" formulations respectively: ***unease origin cessation path*** (without pronouns *dukkhaṃ samudayo nirodho maggo*); and ***this is unease, this is the origin of unease, this is the cessation of unease, this is the path leading to the cessation of unease*** (with pronouns, *idaṃ dukkhaṃ, ayaṃ dukkhanirodho,* and so on). When and how the phrase *ariyasacca* became attached to the fourfold set, Norman does not speculate. The fact is, obviously, somehow that term was added to the formula, and it stuck. Why? Who knows? Why has "Noble Truths" stuck in English?

Let's assume that the Buddha did use the term *ariyasacca.* After all, as Norman himself notes, the linguistic and chronological relationships among the various versions of the fourfold set are unclear. So why might the Buddha have used the term? My own view, which is purely speculative, is that he was being mischievously playful and ironic. There are many instances throughout the canon in which the Buddha engages in a practice that I call "linguistic inversion," whereby he takes a commonplace term and completely upends its meaning. An example of this practice is found in the *Dhammapada,* where the Buddha calls a person a "Brahman," a superior person, who in fact contradicts everything that an actual Brahman was. In the Buddha's view, a truly superior person possessed qualities (kindness, insight, equanimity, and so on) that (1) had nothing whatsoever to do with having been born into the "superior" (Brahmanical) class and (2) were rarely exhibited by those who were born into that class, i.e., the Brahmans. So the Buddha says, in effect: "Okay, you want to speak in terms of 'superior' and 'inferior'? Then the low-caste cowherd who cultivates calm and insight is superior, and the high-caste Brahman who doesn't is inferior."

The Brahmans had a special word that they applied to themselves, and to themselves alone: *ariya* (Sanskrit: *ārya*). They were the "Noble Ones." Their purported nobility derived in great part from the fact that they were the discoverers, revealers, possessors, upholders, and administrators of *sacca* (Sanskrit: *satya*), "truth." Contrary to the Brahmans' understanding of the notion, in the Buddha's usage, "the truth of the noble ones," *ariyasacca*, has nothing to do with supernatural entities and hidden forces of nature, and everything to do with readily apparent facets of human existence, *sacca*. But the Buddha, of course, is not mentioning mere random facets of existence; he is highlighting those features that are preeminent (another meaning of *ariya*), and those that stand out (also *ariya*), and those that are in the first order of importance (also *ariya*), those that are known by truly noble people (also *ariya*), the realization of which (*sacca*) ennobles a person. So for the Buddha, the *ariyasacca* are the preeminent realities, of which you and I must be fully cognizant if, as noble ones do, we are ever to come to ease in this world.

9.8. *"five existential functions subject to grasping"*. "The five components of grasping" is the Buddha's shorthand for what we commonly refer to as "person, self, identity, soul." The Buddha says that he looked everywhere in vain for the kind of stable, integral entity that is implied by such terms. You, too, can look. But where will you look? In your nose? ears? chest cavity? stomach? Perhaps your self can be found in your memories, thoughts, sense of identity. The more we look, the more absurd appears the commonly held notion of my being (having?) a self. For the Buddha, this persistent sense that I have of being a "person" is the result of erroneously imputing an *object* where there is really only *process*. This process, moreover, is perceptual in nature, having to do, as it does, with human existence (see "Evidence of Selflessness," *sutta* 7).

Although this process, like any other, is a seamless flow devoid of stops, it can, on analysis, be said to have innumerable aspects. The Buddha calls these aspects *khandhas*, meaning "clusters," "clumps," or "aggregates," and found it beneficial to identify five of them as possessing particular importance. These five are materiality, feeling, perception, conceptual fabrication, and cognizance. To get a view on this fivefold process of being, it might be useful to try an experiment. First of all, read the following explanation of the five components (A). This will give you some theoretical grounding in the process to which they point. Then analyze a perceptual act in terms of the components (B). This exercise should give you some practical insight into the process. Finally, consider the Buddha's pithy remarks concerning the fundamental nature of this process (C).

A. 1. **Materiality** (*rūpa*) is the "givenness" of matter, which consists of the four elements: earth (solidity), water (coherence), fire (energy), and wind (distension). In terms of the "person," *rūpa* is the body. Note that the Buddha is not concerned with the origin or end of the material world. The world just is—when you open your eyes, there it is. You must deal with it just as it is, regardless of how it came to be and how it might cease to be. Hence, the first instance that the Buddha marks out as a *khandha* is this primary givenness of the world that stands before our own material givenness. (In order to counter the idea that there is a pure, undefiled world out there that is corrupted by the *khandha* process, it is important to note that both the world and our experience of it are marked by conditionality from the outset of the *khandha* process. That is, my eyes are conditioned by numerous factors [genes, diet, experience, or *karma*], as is the painting with which they come into contact [constructed from parts, creative choices of the artist, intensity of light].)

2. **Feeling** (*vedanā*) is the qualitative continuum from the raw, unprocessed sensation that arises when a sense faculty comes into contact with a sense object to the emotional response conditioned by that sensation. For example, when the nose meets a scent, the scent may be experienced in varying registers of pleasantness, unpleasantness, or neutrality; and this experience triggers memories and emotions. It is important to note here that sensation concerns the quality of visceral friction and the feelings conditioned by that friction, and is not a matter of discriminating judgment or opinion.

3. **Perception** (*saññā*) is the processing of the object of sense *as* such and such: the sensation on the ear is "a dog's bark," on the skin is "a raindrop," on the tongue is "a chocolate cookie." Unformed materiality (vibrating waves hitting the ear and so on) settles into specific form. Perception, *saññā*, thus connotes a degree of sharpened focus, of something's coming into view as a particular kind of object.

4. **Conceptual Fabrication** (*saṅkhāra*) arises as the closer discernment concerning the (perceived) qualities of the object. The important point here is that this discernment is, to a great extent, based on personal proclivities, which in turn are products of conditioning (via family, culture, genes, experience). This term is often translated as "volition" since it is understood as an exercise of the will to fashion the perceived object in a particular way. But really the Sanskrit verbal formation from which the Pāli is derived simply denotes "putting together, forming, embellishing." In the Buddhist view, these terms describe precisely what we do whenever we see, hear, smell,

taste, feel, or cognize an object. Namely, we coconstruct the object by coloring our perceptions with qualities, judgments, and narratives deriving largely from our side and not from the side of the object itself. Because we react to the world as it is fashioned by us rather than to some world "in itself," *saṅkhāra* is an acutely important Buddhist technical term.

5. **Cognizance** (*viññāṇa*) can be understood as being simultaneously the mirror and the appearance reflected in the mirror. It is both our objectless awareness, which is standing always already present, and the awareness *of* the fully formed object (formed, of course, via the previous four *khandhas*). I think that *viññāṇa* functions in both of these senses within the *khandha* process. The English term "cognizance" nicely captures this double meaning since it connotes both "awareness itself" and "thinking about" that which is given in that awareness. So to give a specific example in terms of the *khandha* process: As a sentient being, I am aware. Sound waves hit my ears (*rūpa*). These waves are experienced as pleasant (*vedanā*). The perception forms that the waves are birdsong (*saññā*). As if automatically, particular memories, notions, and interpretations regarding the birdsong proliferate (*saṅkhāra*). I discursively think about those memories, respond to those memories, then think about those responses, and on and on (*viññāṇa*). Because of these intentional acts of thinking, *viññāṇa* is sometimes referred to as "*karmic* consciousness." That is, such thinking is itself a conditioned action that gives rise to further mental, verbal, and bodily activity. Finally, it is important to note that cognizance is understood by the Buddha as being manifest through a particular mode of perception—eye cognizance, ear cognizance—and not as some kind of pervasive, ghostlike "consciousness." (It is for this reason that I chose not to render *viññāṇa* in its usual manner as "consciousness.")

B. Now, having gained some theoretical understanding of the *khandhas*, identify each element in an actual act of each of the six modes of apprehension (seeing, hearing, tasting, bodily feeling, smelling, thinking). Here's an example. Observe the arising of a sound.

1. Note, first of all, the very presence of your ear and of the physical world. What you are noticing is, of course, the givenness of materiality (*rūpa*).
2. Simply and directly notice the next sound that arises. Note the bare sensation (*vedanā*) engendered by the friction from the interaction of that sound and your ear. Does this contact produce a sensation that is pleasant, unpleasant, or neutral? How does this sensation condition how you feel mentally, physically, emotionally?
3. Notice that seemingly simultaneous with contact comes a particular perception (*saññā*) concerning the nature of the sound object. It is a passing car; it is the chirping of a bird; it is your daughter's voice; it is someone coughing; and so forth.
4. Carefully observe what you did (*saṅkhāra*) with that perception. Did you start to weave some sort of story concerning the sound? Did you color it with

names, views, opinions, value judgments? In short, did you engage, to any degree, in manipulation and contrivance of the sound? Can you, in this manner, discern to what extent you played a role in cocreating the sound?

5. Notice the reflective, mirrorlike quality of simply being aware of sound. (Glass, perhaps, is a more suitable metaphor than a mirror, since glass is both transparent and reflective.) Notice that "within" this spacious awareness a particular object of sound awareness stands fully formed. Can you just be aware of this entire unfolding? This "just," you may notice, requires simply leaving "it" alone. ("It" is the raw sound together with your fashioning of the sound. How could you possibly separate each of these out from the other? How can you discern where "you" end and "it" begins?)

C. Finally, what do you make of the Buddha's characterization of this entire process? Was (is) what he says here clarified in your own experience?

> Form is like a lump of foam;
> feeling like a water bubble;
> perception is like a mirage;
> conceptual fabrications like a plantain tree;*
> and cognizance like an illusion.
>
> However one may ponder the self
> and carefully investigate it,
> it appears hollow and void
> when one views it carefully.
>
> (*Majjhimanikāya* 3.22.95)

An abundance of questions might arise out of this exercise. Many of these questions are of a potentially revolutionary and transformative nature because of the real-life consequences they engender. For example, is it necessary to posit a stable, integral self, soul, or identity in order to account for your moment-to-moment experience? What might be the source, role, and function of the persistent feeling of "I, me, mine" that runs throughout our experience? Doesn't this exercise in the *khandhas* strongly suggest that all we can honestly claim for moment-to-moment existence is that there is a continual unfolding of a *process,* physical and psychological in nature? If so, what challenges does this view (insight?) have for the theistic framework for living held dear, I imagine, by so many readers?

9.9. *"craving".* What is the origin of the unease we experience in our lives? The Buddha's answer is: The fact that you demand too much from the world. We ask—entreat, implore, intensely desire—that the world's objects

* That is, it consists of endless layers, like an onion, with, finally, no core.

yield abiding pleasure, satisfaction, and security. But how can they? Their fundamental nature is impermanent, non-substantial, and unreliable. "Asking too much" is an old-fashioned meaning of the verb "to crave" (from Anglo-Saxon *crafian*). The Pāli term behind this translation is *taṇhā*, from the Sanskrit *tṛṣṇā*, meaning "thirst." So what is the origin of human unease? It is the perpetual demands that we make on the world, and the parched state of being that arises from an apparently unquenchable thirst for sensory pleasure.

9.10. *"cessation of unease"*. This phrase refers to *nibbāna/nirvāṇa*

9.11. *"As long as"*. It is worth reflecting on the intensity of effort required by the Buddha—and by us?—to penetrate the four preeminent realities. The pervasiveness and regularity of unease in our lives must be *fully recognized;* the surging waves of craving that originate this unease must be *abandoned;* the ending of this unease must be *realized;* the way to this ending of unease must be *cultivated.* Given this "as long as," what would it mean for you to fully recognize unease, to abandon craving, to bring an end to unease, and to cultivate the way?

9.12. *"three sequences and twelve aspects"*. That is, the three realizations associated with each of the four preeminent realities.

9.13. *"So you really know!"* . . . *Koṇḍañña-Who-Knows.* With a literary flourish, the drama of this conclusion accentuates the importance of the *sutta.* It thus functions rhetorically to remind the hearer or reader of the power of the Buddha's realization, and of that power's universal relevance. Who knows, maybe when you deeply realize the teachings given here, *your* cosmos will really respond by becoming tremulously radiant, brilliant, and majestic. Who knows? Maybe you will become like good Koṇḍañña: [your name]-Who-Knows.

SUTTA 10

गोतमसुत्त

The World

Gotama Sutta: "Gotama's Discourse"; *Saṃyuttanikāya 2.1.10*

AS DO THE EMERGENCE AND CESSATION OF OUR INCESSANT "WORLDING." (MAP)

Someone asked the Buddha why the world was called "the world." This person was wondering what the term itself indicated about that which we refer to as "the world." The Buddha replied with a mischievous yet meaningful etymology. He said that it is called "the world" (*loka*) because it is "disintegrating" (*lujjati*) (*Saṃyuttanikāya* 4.35.82). He then elaborated by saying that *whatever* is subject to disintegration is "the world." And what is disintegrating? The eye is disintegrating, the visual object is disintegrating, and the visual cognizance ensuing from the contact of these two is disintegrating. The same is true for all of the other senses, including the mind. Now, a necessary condition for something to disintegrate is, of course, its arising. So how does this perpetually disintegrating world come to be in the first place? We have already seen that the Buddha abstains from answering indeterminate questions. So this question cannot fruitfully be about the origin and end of the cosmos. We have also become familiar with the Buddha's view that our own minds play a crucial role in forming "the world." So this question cannot fruitfully be about some universally constant, mind-independent object, *the* world. In another mischievous moment, the Buddha reiterated to a group of his followers his position that the end of the world cannot be known, seen, or reached by travel. Nonetheless, he added enigmatically, without reaching the end of the world, there will be no end to your human unease. Having said this, he got up from his seat and disappeared. Dumbstruck and bewildered, the group asked an advanced student, Ānanda, to explain to them the Buddha's meaning. Ānanda's explanation was that "the world" is that through which we become perceivers and conceivers of the world. So by means of what are we perceivers and conceivers of the world? Well, again, have a look: we become perceivers and conceivers of the world by means of the eyes, the ears, the nose, the tongue, the body, and the mind (*Saṃyuttanikāya* 4.35.116). So where does the world end? The same place it begins. Where does it begin? Where it ends. Where's that? Just look, listen, feel.

The language that we use to describe our situation vis-à-vis the world is revealing of deeply held, yet largely unconscious, assumptions. We refer to ourselves as being "in the world," as if the world were some sort of receptacle common to all. We refer to the world as being "before" us, "out there," "in front of our eyes," and so forth. It is true, when I open my eyes, there's the world. I can describe that world in clear, unambiguous terms. But then you, standing next to me, open your eyes and describe, in equally clear and unambiguous terms, a world alternative to my own. So now what? Is there one world on which we may have infinite views? Or is there perspective only? That is, if you took away all individual perspectives, would there be a world left over? There is a Zen *koan* in which two students are sitting in a garden debating the location of a stone. One student says, "The stone is external to me." The second says, "No, the stone is within my mind." The master, who was listening to this debate from the distance, walks up to the two students. "You are both wrong," he tells them. "If the stone is outside of you," he says to the first, "how can you know it? And you," he says to the second, "if the stone is in your mind, then what a heavy head you must have!" So where is the stone? Where is "the world"?

In the present *sutta,* the Buddha answers this question by pointing not to a place or a thing but to a process. Similar to the four preeminent realities, the process behind the emergence and cessation of each of our lived worlds is apparent to anyone who attends—albeit with "complete attentiveness," as the Buddha says in the present *sutta*—to it. The Buddha refers to this process as "interdependent origination." By this term he means to point out the simple and observable fact that all phenomena are by nature dependent on incalculable other phenomena for their existence. Just reflect for a moment on any physical object at hand. What conditions must have been present to bring that object about? Think of the manifold causes and conditions that operated to bring that object into being. Think of the intertwining interplay of physical, social, environmental, institutional, factors involved. Of course, you'll have to bring yourself into the equation. What prior causes and conditions made your presence possible? Just taking one of those necessary prior conditions—the meeting of your parents, and the meeting of each of theirs and each of theirs and so on ad infinitum—we can see that the calculus of a single phenomenon in a single instance of being is incalculable and inconceivable. Maybe Carl Sagan summed it up best when he said, "To make an apple pie, first create the universe."

It is perhaps not difficult to see some of the far-reaching implications of interdependent origination for some of our own far-reaching notions of causality, agency, and human well-being. Don't we tend to think of causality in terms of direct cause-effect correlations: because *that* was (one glass too many), *this* is (a hangover)? Don't we often speak and think in ways that reveal an underlying belief that the specific cause of *this* effect can be pinpointed? The Buddha himself says that interdependent origination employs a logic that, on the face of it, appears identical to such commonly held views of causality: that being, this becomes; from the arising of that, this arises; that not being, this does not become; from the ceasing of that, this ceases. In the Buddha's view, however, *this* and *that* contain such a multitude of interconnected, interacting causes, effects, and conditions that the notion of a determinate, identifiable cause becomes incoherent. So what caused the hangover? Just consider the complex net of contributing circumstances surrounding that last drink. How far back would you have to go in your tracing of such contributing factors? The Buddha did, in his own way, answer this question: "A first beginning cannot be discerned" (*Aṅguttaranikāya* 10.61). Well, can it?

The implications of interdependent origination for our commonly held notions of agency should be clear from the discussion on causality. Assuming the complex interdependency of causes, conditions, and effects, where can an intrinsic determinate driving force—that is, an agent—behind a given course of action be located? On the one hand, to assert that "I" am the determinate force behind such and such a course of action and its results is to deny reality: just consider the multitude of conditioning factors and forces, including those instigated by other ostensible agents, in play in any given decision or course of action. To admit, on the other hand, that such factors are codetermining the course of action is to *deny* agency in the strong, commonsensical sense of the term. Because of the former state of affairs, the devil is able to fool with our best-laid plans. Because of the latter, "the devil" turns out to be shorthand for the incalculable real and potential interplay of conditions and actors in any given situation.

What do "the world" and the "worlding" process as understood in terms of interdependent origination entail for human well-being? Can any real satisfaction be found in such an instable environment? We can look closer to home for a suggestion. William Blake addressed this question when he wrote the following lines:

> He who binds to himself a joy
> Doth the winged life destroy;
> But he who kisses the joy as it flies
> Lives in Eternity's sunrise.

Binding, grasping, holding on, is just not possible given the fleeting nature of constructed phenomena. The result of attempting to do so is thus destructive. We can all verify this point for ourselves. So what does the second couplet mean? How do we live joyously in a world that, as the Buddha points out, is born, decays, dies, falls away, and reappears, moment by moment? How do we escape from the unease inherent in this world? The first step, says the Buddha in the present *sutta*, is to fully understand the process behind the world's arising and falling away.

NOTES

10.1. *full comprehension.* It is important to note the fact that the understanding of which the Buddha speaks is not intellectual and conceptual. The Buddha speaks here of a "complete attentiveness" toward the matter of this "troubled" world, which attentiveness, in turn, produces "penetrative insight" and "full comprehension."

10.2. *birth.* Birth, aging, and death describe both bodily processes over the span of life and mental, physical, and phenomenal processes unfolding moment by moment. The entire schema of interdependent origination can be understood in terms of this dual temporal frame of reference. The life-span frame, I think, is obvious; the momentary frame less so. It might help, then, to illustrate the more subtle workings of the schema with a common example. In order for destructive anger, for instance, to take its course through my mind, body, and speech, it must be born. This point must sound painfully obvious. But imagine being skilled in preventing the destructive anger from being born in the first place. Imagine the trouble, for yourself and others, that would be avoided. The value of the interdependent origination schema lies in its function as a liberating strategy. And this point, this practical application, is, perhaps, not so obvious.

10.3. *existence.* So destructive anger blindsided me, and I said or did something out of that anger that has caused serious trouble. So I want to know: From where did that anger come? Investigating that now disintegrated state ("aging-and-death"), I see that it was not eternally present in my mind-body continuum. I see that it arose at some particular point in time (birth). But it did not emerge out of nothing, did it? To what can this birth be traced? Investigating in this manner, I see that, for the anger to have been born, there must have been existence prior to its emergence. Elsewhere, the Buddha mentions three possible modes of existence: desire, form, and formlessness (*Saṃyuttanikāya* 2.12.2). So the birth of something, whether sensuous (desire), physical (form), or mental (formlessness) in nature, requires the condition of a state of existence. If this condition were not the case, wouldn't it be absurd to speak of "anger"? Out of what could this anger have emerged; into what could it have settled? The Pāli term *bhava* covers the range of each of these terms: "becoming" (emergence), "being" (settling), "existing" (as anger).

10.4. *grasping.* What creates the conditions that engender states of existence, out of which, in turn, particular thoughts, desires, and so on are born? The Buddha asserts that if we would but look with the proper attentiveness, we would see that grasping plays a decisive role in this process. Grasping, as we have seen, is the function of the fivefold process commonly referred to as "person" or "self." The Pāli term *upādāna* means "holding on to, attaching to, clinging to, nourished by." It can also be used as a noun: "fuel, supply." The Buddha mentions four basic trajectories of grasping activity. Grasping can be propelled toward "desire" (*kāma*), toward "speculative viewpoints," or "beliefs" (*diṭṭhi*), toward "customary morality and rituals of observance" (*sīlabbata*), and toward "notions concerning 'the self' or 'the soul'" (*attavāda*) (*Saṃyuttanikāya* 2.12.2). So in terms of our example, the formless mental state of anger has received its nourishment and fuel from grasping activity related to, for instance, a cherished viewpoint's being challenged or a sense of identity's being hurt.

10.5. *craving.* Without an underlying force, there would be no compulsion to grasp. That force is craving. As with the second preeminent reality, the term for craving here is *taṇhā:* "thirst," "longing," "intense desire," "yearning." So what sort of craving might lie behind anger? Perhaps I yearn for respect. So when someone makes a remark that challenges my sense of worthiness (*attavāda:* "view of self"), I become angry. Or perhaps I become angry while reading an article disputing a political viewpoint to which I subscribe (*dīṭṭhi:* "viewpoint, opinion"). In each instance, it is the underlying craving, however conscious or unconscious, that conditions the particular grasping. The Buddha identifies six specific trajectories of craving, namely, craving toward objects, sounds, scents, tastes, tactile sensations, and ideas (*Saṃyuttanikāya* 2.12.2). So in terms of our example, the anger aroused from reading the article challenging my political viewpoint is an instance of craving that flows from holding on to certain ideas.

10.6. *feeling.* I have become habituated to certain streams of craving because of the sensations, feelings, and emotions that they arouse. Doesn't it feel good to observe the duties related to, say, a loving God—duties that have been passed on to you from your parents? (This observance would be an example of *sīlabbata,* or grasping toward customary morality and rituals of observance.) The Buddha asserts that, if we trace our cravings further back, we will find they are founded on feelings. Elsewhere, he specifies that these feelings are derived from the interactions of the six sense organs (including mind) with their corresponding objects of sense (*Saṃyuttanikāya* 2.12.2).

10.7. *contact.* Feeling, of course, requires contact between a sensory organ and an object of sense. So when ideas arise concerning, say, my political beliefs, we can say that they have made contact with my conscious mind. Observe what happens when such contact is made. Doesn't it produce a certain sensation, one that can be described as pleasant, unpleasant, or neutral? And doesn't this sensation condition my physical-mental-emotional state?

10.8. *six sense fields.* What underlies sensory contact? The answer is quite readily apparent: the eyes, ears, nose, tongue, body, and mind (*Saṃyuttanikāya* 2.12.2). In Pāli, these faculties are called *āyatana,* which means "extensions, spheres, fields." A "sense field" is a totality, a sensorium, that, for analytical purposes, can be divided into three aspects: (1) the physical faculty, for instance the eyes; (2) that faculty's particular object of perception, such as the visual object; and (3) the particular type of awareness ensuing out of that contact, such as "visual cognizance."

10.9. *mind-body entity.* The Pāli term here is *nāmarūpa.* This term is commonly translated as "name and form." "Name," or *nāma,* refers to the mental qualities of feeling, perception, intention, contact, and attention. "Form," or *rūpa,* refers to the four "great elements," namely, earth (solidity), water (coherence), fire (energy), and wind (distension) (*Saṃyuttanikāya* 2.12.2). A confluence of these two is called "name and form," or a bit less opaquely, I hope, "the mind-body entity." Any such term, of course, is just a technical way of speaking of what, in everyday language, we refer to as a "person." So where are the six sense faculties grounded? Well, in a person, if by "person" we understand this shifting, swirling, evanescent interaction of psychophysical qualities and elements. Given such a view of the "person," where might our anger be located?

10.10. *cognizance.* What condition must be present for there to be a functioning "person"? Putting aside legal and philosophical complexities, doesn't it seem obvious that the answer is "cognizance"? The mental and physical qualities constituting the person require animated awareness for us to speak of a person in any meaningful sense. Again, the Buddha is not concerned here with an analysis that successfully negotiates the labyrinth of legal, biological, or philosophical intricacies. He is concerned with a commonsensical analysis that is founded on phenomenological actualities. So tracing your sense of yourself as a functioning mind-body entity—as a person—back another step, on what are "you" founded? Although it may sound counterintuitive, the present *sutta* asks you to consider the possibility that your very sense of self is dependent on identityless cognizant capacities. These capacities are called "cognizant" (*viññāṇa*) because they simultaneously involve both awareness and knowing; they are, namely, the capacities for seeing, hearing, tasting, smelling, tactile feeling, and thinking (*Saṃyuttanikāya* 2.12.2).

10.11. *fabrications.* That which we see, hear, smell, touch, taste, feel, and think—on what are they founded? We might answer reflexively, "On the thing, the sound, the scent, and so on, itself." But we have already seen that the nature of such phenomena is foamlike, miragelike, phantomlike, and so forth. So given our tendency to appropriate phenomena in quite individual and particular ways, the question becomes: On what is *my apprehension* of the thing, the sound, the scent, and so on, founded? The Buddha's answer is: On the active, intentional, and volitional tendency to fabricate. Such fabrication is threefold, namely, bodily, verbal, and conceptual (*Saṃyuttanikāya* 2.12.2). That is, I do not merely see or taste but form opinions about what I see or taste. I make meaning from, conceptualize, what I see or taste; and then I react to, respond to, add to, act on, that conceptualization. And I do so with my body, my speech, and my mind. So, in short, cognizance is dependent on this "making" activity called "fabrication."

10.12. *ignorance.* And what underlies such fabrication? Not knowing does. Not having direct knowledge of or penetrative insight into the preeminent realities of human existence underlies fabrication—not having insight into unease, its cause, its ending, and the path to its ending (*Saṃyuttanikāya* 2.12.2).

SUTTA 11

परायनसुत्त

A Genuine Refuge

Parāyana Sutta: "Destination"; *Saṃyuttanikāya* 4.43.44

OUR GENUINE REFUGE FROM THIS WHIRLWIND OF WORLDING IS TO BE UNBOUND. (DESTINATION)

This teaching of the Buddha concerning human being and *the* human being, concerning mind, body, perception, desire, pleasure, grasping, awareness, causation, self and no-self, pain and its ending—to where does it lead? Every teaching carries some notion of a goal or an end. Precisely how this goal is posited depends on the premises of the teaching itself. If there is a notion of a personal, anthropomorphic creator God operating in the teaching, the goal is likely to be put in terms of an ultimate end, such as eternal heaven or hell. A tradition that posits an impersonal godhead will probably state the goal in terms of dissolution into or union with the Absolute. More-psychologically or -epistemologically oriented traditions—that is, those traditions that emphasize an understanding of the mind and the importance of particular knowledge—tend to state the goal in terms of liberation from a limited self or release from the constraints of ignorance.

Everyone knows that the goal of Buddhism is *nirvāṇa* (Pāli: *nibbāna*). But we have to wonder just what this term means, particularly since it is typically left untranslated. When pressed, both Buddhists and scholars of Buddhism translate it something like "an extinguishing, a blowing out, a quenching." The Buddha, in fact, had many names for what he conceived as the goal of his teaching. In the *suttas* immediately preceding the present one, for instance, he calls it

the far shore
the subtle
the very difficult to see
the unaging
the stable
the undisintegrating
the unmanifest
the unproliferated
the peaceful
the deathless
the sublime
the auspicious
the secure
the destruction of craving
the wonderful
the amazing
the unailing
the unbinding
the unafflicted
dispassion
purity
freedom
the unadhesive
the island
the shelter
the asylum
the refuge

Whew! Toward what, exactly, could such terms possibly be pointing? The present *sutta*, together with the three following *suttas*, addresses precisely this question. But be warned: they do not do so precisely. Concisely, yes, but certainly not precisely. You will notice that these *suttas* are unusually brief and suggestive. So we should consider the possibility that this very brevity is an aspect of the "answer" to the question posed by the Buddha at the outset of the present *sutta:* "What is the destination?"

NOTES

11.1. *infatuation, . . . hostility, . . . delusion.* See note 4.4.

11.2. *Present-moment awareness directed toward the body.* See "The Application of Present-Moment Awareness" (*sutta* 16) for full details.

11.3. *secluded places.* The text, reflecting the ascetic milieu of Buddhism's origins, actually says "There are these roots of trees, these empty huts."

11.4. *Meditate.* "Present-Moment Awareness with Breathing" (*sutta* 15) deals with the Buddha's instruction on meditation in minute detail.

SUTTA 12

निब्बुतसुत्त

Conspicuous Unbinding

Nibbuta Sutta: "Quenched"; *Aṅguttaranikāya* 3.55

TO ERADICATE INFATUATION, HOSTILITY, AND DELUSION. ERADICATED, QUENCHED, UNBOUND. (DESTINATION)

Imagine working for several hours in ninety-degree heat with high humidity under a blazing sun. As your body temperature rises, your body loses its normal ability to dissipate or evaporate the intense heat through the pores of the skin. All of a sudden, you feel like you are having a heart attack. You become nauseated and heavily fatigued. As your strength wanes, you get a severe headache. Your muscles cramp, your pulse pounds, and you are overcome with a disorienting dizziness. You start hallucinating. Noticing your bizarre behavior, someone recognizes that you are experiencing heatstroke. That person comes over to you, takes you by the arm, and leads you into the shady area under a great tree. He or she pours cool water onto your burning skin and over your sweltering head, and fans you. You drink water. Slowly, the pent-up heat begins to be sweated out, and then it evaporates. Your pulse slows down. Your headache disappears. Your muscles relax. You can see and think clearly again.

You are cooled, quenched, calmed, deeply, deeply refreshed.

These words all capture the meaning of the Pāli term in the title of the present *sutta: nibbuta.*

Fire is one of the Buddha's most useful similes. Obviously, before electricity, fire served functions that were crucial to human survival, such as cooking raw meats and generating warmth. The hearth was also the center of domestic rituals that we today would call "religious" but that earlier peoples would have considered as crucial to existence as eating and staving off the bitter cold. In these rituals, deities were propitiated to bring protection, increase wealth, ward off evil, prevent disease, and postpone death. In the Buddha's India, fire was deified as *agni,* a term related to the Latin *ignis* and, from that term, the English word "ignite." The dominant tradition of the Buddha's day was that recorded in the Vedas; and the primary practice of the Vedas was *yajña,* the fire sacrifice. Thus, *agni,* the "resplendent force" (*deva*) of fire, was of paramount importance:

> You, Agni, shining in your glory through the days,
> are brought to life from out of the waters and from the stone;
> from out of the forest trees and herbs that grow on the ground,
> you, sovereign lord of all, are generated pure.
>
> (Ṛgveda 2.1.1–2)

As expressed in this verse, fire, *agni,* was thought to be omnipresent. It was, moreover, by means of *agni* that the priests' sacrificial offering was carried past the fire altar into the atmosphere and then to the heavenly realm beyond.

The Buddha, of course, rejected the Vedas outright. But he apparently viewed fire as a doubly potent symbol. First, as we have just seen, "fire" would have resounded with ultimate significance in the minds of virtually all of his interlocutors. I can imagine the Buddha playing with this symbol by saying to one of those conversation partners: "You believe that *agni* is omnipresent? Okay, then consider this:"

> All is aflame . . . the eye is aflame, forms are aflame, and visual cognizance is aflame; the ears are aflame, sounds are aflame, and aural cognizance is aflame; the nose is aflame, scents are aflame, and olfactory cognizance is aflame; the tongue is aflame, tastes are aflame, and gustatory cognizance is aflame; the body is aflame, tactile feelings are aflame, and tactile cognizance is aflame; the mind is aflame, thoughts are aflame, and mental cognizance is aflame.
>
> (*Saṃyuttanikāya* 4.35.28)

"So, yes, I agree: the world's on fire. What has set it aflame, you ask? Well, just look at your own experience: infatuation, hostility, and delusion."

Second, the Buddha must have perceived in fire's very manner of being a close approximation to how the human mind actually functions when active, and what it undergoes when it is released, or unbound. In a well-known dialogue with the mendicant Vacchagotta, the Buddha asks:

> "If a fire were burning before you, Vaccha, would you know that?"
>
> "Yes, I would," responds Vacchagotta.
>
> "And would you be able to say on what that burning fire is dependent?"
>
> "Yes; on grass and kindling."
>
> "Now," the Buddha continues, "if that fire burning before you were extinguished, Vaccha, would you know that?"
>
> "Yes, I would," responds Vacchagotta.
>
> "And would you be able to say to which direction the extinguished fire went; for instance, to the north, south, east, or west?"
>
> Somewhat perplexed, Vacchagotta answers, "No. Such a case does not apply. The fire burned because it was sustained by the fuel—grass and kindling. When the fuel is used up and is not replenished, then we have to consider that the fire is extinguished."
>
> (*Majjhimanikāya* 72)

So, fire burns, consumes, perhaps even rages and destroys, *as long as* there is fuel to sustain it, as long as, we might say figuratively, it grasps at its fuel. When it ceases to grasp at its fuel, because there is no fuel, what becomes of it? Maybe we should not so quickly answer that "it just becomes nonexistent." What is "it" in this case? What has become of the chemical components that had previously constituted "fire"? Does it make sense to ask where your angry mind goes when it is no longer present? The mind is still present, it is just no longer agitated by (permeated by? becoming?) what we call anger. So how might the mind be like fire?

NOTES

12.1. "*'Unbinding'*". In his remarkable book *The Wings to Awakening* (Barre, Mass.: Dhamma Dana Publications, 1996), Thanissaro Bhikkhu makes an argument for translating *nirvāṇa* (Pāli: *nibbāna*) as "Unbinding." Many people in the modern West are familiar with the term *nirvāṇa* via popular culture, if not from Buddhism itself. As I mentioned in the commentary on this *sutta, nirvāṇa* is commonly understood to designate some sort of extinguishing, or blowing out. Secondary works on Buddhism often repeat the Buddha's own example of the blowing out of a flame. (There are countless etymological and philological intricacies associated with the verbal formation [prefix] *nir* + √*vā*, from which *nirvāṇa* is derived. Readers interested in exploring these matters in depth can do no better than to consult Steven Collins's *Nirvana and Other Buddhist Felicities: Utopias of the Pali Imaginaire,* Cambridge: Cambridge University Press, 1998, particularly pages 191–203. I also recommend Thanissaro Bhikkhu's *The Mind Like Fire Unbound,* Barre, Mass.: Dhamma Dana Publications, 1993).

But "blowing out" may not be the only way of construing the term. There is evidence that from at least the fifth century, Buddhists themselves have understood the term *nirvāṇa* to suggest an unbinding. Many, I suspect most, scholars would reject this understanding as being based on "folk" (read "fanciful, hence wrong") etymology. It is true that in the Indian cultural realm, explanations of word origins can be quite, well, creative. This is not necessarily the bad thing that modern scholars make it out to be. If nothing else, we learn from a tradition's creative etymologies something about that tradition's self-understanding.

I am following Thanissaro Bhikkhu's lead in adopting the unusual term "unbinding" for *nirvāṇa;* so I will let him speak for himself in defending this choice. I am quoting him at such length on this (and for the second time: see my *The Dhammapada: Verses on the Way,* New York: Random House, 2004, pp. 113–15) because I think that his argument is worthy of wider recognition and consideration. His statement here certainly serves as a gentle budge away from what has become yet another axiomatic Buddhist-English hybrid (non)translation. And who knows, maybe it will help us to understand what *nirvāṇa* "is."

> The Buddha's choice of the word Unbinding (*nibbāna*)—which literally means the extinguishing of a fire—derives from the way that the physics of fire was viewed at his time. As fire burned, it was seen as clinging to its fuel in a state of entrapment and agitation. When it went out, it let go of its fuel, growing calm and free. Thus, when the Indians of his time saw a fire going out, they did not feel that they were watching extinction.

Rather, they were seeing a metaphorical lesson in how freedom could be attained by letting go. (*The Wings of Awakening*, p. 6)

[Now quoting a canonical passage; the Buddha said,] If a [practitioner] abandons passion for the property of form . . . feeling . . . perception . . . mental processes . . . consciousness, then owing to the abandoning of passion, the support is cut off, and there is no base for consciousness. Consciousness, thus unestablished, not proliferating, not performing any function, is released. Owing to its release, it stands still. Owing to its stillness, it is contented. Owing to its contentment, it is not agitated. Not agitated, [the practitioner] is totally "nibbāna-ized" right within.

(*Saṃyuttanikāya* 22.53)

[Thanissaro Bhikkhu again:] This being the set of events—stillness, independence, unattachment—associated with the extinguishing of fire and the attainment of the goal, it would appear that, of all the etymologies offered to explain the word "nibbāna," the closest one to its original connotation is that quoted by Buddhaghosa in *The Path of Purification* (8.247) [a premier authoritative source for the Theravāda; fifth century C.E.]. There, he derives the word from the negative prefix *nir* plus *vāna*, or binding: Unbinding.

Modern scholars have tended to scorn this derivation as fanciful, and they favor such hypotheses as "blowing out" [etc.]. But although these hypotheses might make sense in terms of modern Western ideas about fire, they are hardly relevant to the way nibbāna is used in the Canon. Freedom, on the other hand, is more than relevant. It is central, both in the context of ancient Indian theories of fire, and in the psychological context of attaining the goal: "Not agitated, [the practitioner] is totally unbound right within." . . . What kind of unbinding? We have already gained some kind of idea—liberation from dependency and limitations, from agitation and death. (*The Mind Like Fire Unbound*, pp. 41–42)

As I mentioned in *The Dhammapada*, I am going one small step further than Thanissaro Bhikkhu by writing "unbinding" in place of "Unbinding." "Unbinding," with its Germanic uppercase, seems too much like a static place or thing, like the Absolute, the Transcendent, the Holy, or God. The lowercase version helps to cut through this tendency toward reification and suggests instead an active *process*—a process that is, as far as I can tell, utterly, utterly human.

12.2. "*'conspicuous'*". The Pāli *sandiṭṭhika* and Sanskrit *saṃdṛṣṭi* parallel the Latin-derived English term "conspicuous": "open to view, in full view, visible, actual." Can the Buddha really be equating *nirvāṇa*, "unbinding," with the eradication of infatuation, hostility, and delusion? The effects of such an eradication certainly would be in full view—to you and to all of those whom your life touches.

12.3. *"come and see"*. "Come!" (*ehi*) or "Come and see!" (*ehi passa*) was the invitation that the Buddha extended to others who wished to join his order. Note that he does not require some sort of admission of faith or oath of loyalty. From the outset, he seems to be asking the follower to be open, probing, and discerning. I can imagine the Buddha saying to someone after a discussion about one of the topics in this book: "Would you like to know these things for yourself? Well, then, come and see!"

SUTTA 13

सङ्खतलक्खणसुत्त

What It's Not

Saṅkhatalakkhaṇa Sutta: "Signs of the Fabricated"; *Aṅguttaranikāya* 3.47

Binding is concomitant with the fabricated. (Destination)

What does it mean for something to be "fabricated"? The Pāli term in the title of this *sutta* is *saṅkhata,* which means "compounded, conditioned, constructed, created." In everyday usage, these English terms simply indicate that an object, a phenomenon, has been put together from parts, has been, that is, fashioned or fabricated. That description includes everything—everything perceivable, conceivable, knowable, felt, intuited; that is to say, everything (remember "The All"?). And in everyday terms, something's being fabricated probably seems harmless enough. For the Buddha, however, as we have seen repeatedly in this book, that characteristic is a source of real trouble. It is, in short, the very tethering of our binding.

In the great autobiographical *sutta* called "The Noble Quest" (*Ariyapariyesanā Sutta; Majjhimanikāya* 26), the Buddha says that he had come to realize there are really only two types of pursuits in life. We, who are subject to birth, persistence, decay, and death, can spend our lives seeking happiness in and through fabricated phenomena, which are by nature subject to birth, persistence, decay, and death. Or we, who are subject to birth, persistence, decay, and death, having understood the futility and danger of the former pursuit, can pursue "the untainted, unsurpassed refuge from bondage."

What does this statement mean? The answer, of course, has to be discovered personally by the one on the quest. As a pointer on the way, though, it may be helpful to consider that according to the first two verses of the *Dhammapada*, the place to begin looking is the mind itself. Why? Because the mind is the maker of all of our experience.

> Preceded by mind
> are phenomena,
> led by mind,
> formed by mind.
> If with mind polluted
> one speaks or acts,
> then pain follows,
> as a wheel follows
> the draft ox's foot.
>
> Preceded by mind
> are phenomena,
> led by mind,
> formed by mind.
> If with mind pure
> one speaks or acts,
> then ease follows,
> as an ever-present shadow.

The mind, in this view, literally makes "my" world, in that it actively fashions the various phenomena it encounters. We've seen in previous chapters the mechanisms involved in this fashioning. Just reflect for a moment on the role of the six sensory faculties (the sensorium) in forming their respective objects. A sound arises; my ear chases it, grabs hold of it, and together with my mind, shapes and molds it, consumes what it will, and discards the rest. Now another sound, and another. Now a taste, now a thought, and another, and another, and another. I respond, grab hold, forge, discard, grab hold again and again and again. Phenomena arise, change while persisting, and vanish, only to arise again. To do so is the very nature of the fabricated.

Is there no end to this exhausting activity?

SUTTA 14

असङ्खतलक्खणसुत्त

Just This

Asaṅkhataḷakkhaṇa Sutta: "Signs of the Unfabricated"; *Aṅguttaranikāya* 3.48

Unbinding is concomitant with the unfabricated. (Destination)

Consider for a moment the display that we call "reality." Isn't "reality" well characterized as a swirling, vibrating, ever-changing, phantasmagoric exhibition of sights, sounds, scents, tastes, tactile feelings, and thoughts? Consider, too, the fabricated nature of the display, how it's all put together from countless causes and conditions arising, interacting, and combining with other causes, effects, and conditions, in a manner, moreover, that fuses past, present, and future. Considering this shimmering display in concrete (no pun intended) terms of *things*, we can ask: What is a prior and necessary condition for the display to appear at all? This question isn't meant to be philosophical. It is intended to point to something quite, well, real. For there to be *things*, there must be the *space* in which they appear. If there were not the space that is my study, there would be no way and nowhere to place my desk, chairs, pictures, and so on. "The space that is my study" is, of course, a fabrication: physically, a study requires walls, ceiling, floor, a house surrounding it, et cetera; mentally, "study" requires concepts, ideas, naming, differentiation, and so on. But is space itself a thing, something fabricated? Is it an unfabricated non-thing? Is space even distinguishable from the things that appear in or are coterminus with it? Are the things, separately and in relation to one another, distinguishable from the space that they inhabit?

We could ask the same questions about the relationship between sound and silence. Sound is obviously a fabricated object. But what about silence?

These examples may take us a little way toward understanding the Buddha's contrasting of "the fabricated" and "the unfabricated" in the previous and present *suttas*. But they are inadequate for a real understanding. For unlike space in relation to things or silence in relation to sound, the unfabricated of which the Buddha speaks is not dependent on the fabricated. If it were, then that dependency in itself would render the unfabricated fabricated. So what does the Buddha mean by this distinction?

One way of understanding the distinction between fabricated and unfabricated is to consider that the Buddha is contrasting not concepts or things but ways of being. Wherever, whenever, however fabrication holds sway in our lives—that is called *saṃsāra*, "continuous becoming." Wherever, whenever, however it doesn't—that is called *nirvāṇa*, "unbinding."

> If, like a piece of metal when struck,
> you yourself do not resound,
> can it be that you have achieved unbinding
> —there is no anger found in you?
>
> (*Dhammapada* 134)

Imagine that someone has spoken certain upsetting or otherwise threatening words to you. In your brain—hence, in both your mind and your body—or more specifically, in the amygdalae (the two almond-shaped structures deep in our brains), an alarm has been set off signaling a challenge to your mental-physical well-being. The amygdalae are such an ancient, well-tuned warning device that this compels you to respond to the perceived threat before the more rational, judicious cortex can evaluate the appropriateness or even rationality of your amygdalae-driven automatic response. So you are impelled from within to act, speak, or think angrily to the perceived challenge, and to do so before you are able to reflect adequately on the consequences of your angry actions.

> As you become angry your body's muscles tense up. Inside your brain, neurotransmitter chemicals known as catecholamines are released, causing you to experience a burst of energy lasting up to several minutes. This burst of energy is behind the common angry desire to take immediate protective action. At the same time your heart rate accelerates, your blood pressure rises, and your rate of breathing increases. Your face may flush as increased blood flow enters your limbs and extremities in preparation for physical action. Your attention narrows and becomes locked onto the target of your anger. Soon you can pay attention to nothing else. In quick succession, additional brain neurotransmitters and hormones (among them adrenaline and noradrenaline) are released which trigger a lasting state of arousal. You're now ready to fight.
>
> (http://mentalhelp.net)

. . . ready to argue, to feel hurt, become indignant, yell, hurl insults, sulk, flee. Now, the *Dhammapada* verse asks, what if instead of instinctually and habitually expressing the anger that is pulsing in you—instead, that is, of your *becoming* angry—the anger simply did not resound in you? This is not to say that you have repressed the anger. The anger still takes its all-too-natural course. Absent repression, how could it do otherwise? So what is this *way of being* that neither expresses nor represses fabricated states; neither grasps nor rejects fabricated objects; neither thinks nor suppresses fabricated thought?

SUTTA 15

आनापानसतिसुत्त

How to Meditate

Ānāpānasati Sutta: "Present-Moment Awareness with Breathing";

Majjhimanikāya 118

CULTIVATION OF PRESENT-MOMENT AWARENESS IS THE MEANS TO CONSPICUOUS UNBINDING. (GOING)

How did Gotama become the Buddha? How did he come to know "palpably . . . that which is to be realized by the wise"? How was he able to surmount the powerful detrimental surges of thought, speech, and action that overtake most of us most always? How did the Buddha overcome the seemingly interminable unease, stress, tension, and pain that characterize our human existence? How? In asking this question, there is no need to restrict it to the Buddha: How will *you* come to know "palpably . . . that which is to be realized by the wise"? How will *you* become a *buddha*?

It seems to be very simple. Just practice meditation. And it seems to be terribly difficult. Just practice meditation.

But what do we mean by "meditation"? Like Buddhism itself, the techniques, styles, and traditions that carry the moniker "meditation" have proliferated dramatically in recent years. While such wide availability of meditation certainly has many positive repercussions, it also has at least one problematic consequence: meditation has become something like foreign policy—everyone's an expert! In such an inclusive environment, how can we distinguish between, say, the countless varieties of stress-reducing, relaxation, autosuggestive, or even hypnotic techniques and that which the Buddha called "meditation"? This question can also be asked from within the variegated Buddhist tradition itself: What would constitute an amenable starting point for a cross-tradition dialogue on "Buddhist meditation"? This question has broader applications as well, encompassing most of the world's "religious" traditions. So what is it that the Buddha is calling "meditation"?

One of the Buddha's favorite metaphors for the practice that we refer to as "meditation" is *bhavanā*, "cultivation." He certainly had in mind the ubiquitous farms and fields of his native India when employing this image. Thus, unlike "meditation" or "contemplation," the Buddha's term is musty, rich, verdant. It smells of the earth. The commonness of his chosen term—it would have resonated with a farmer—suggested naturalness, everydayness, ordinariness. The term also suggested hope: no matter how fallow it has become or damaged it may be, a field can always be *cultivated*—endlessly enhanced, enriched, developed—to produce a favorable and nourishing harvest.

Now, while it is true that anyone may attempt to cultivate a field, not everyone will succeed. Cultivation, like anything else, requires specific skills. So the determinate question in identifying ability is twofold: What skills are required? And to what extent have they been cultivated? The task that concerned the Buddha, of course, was not the cultivation of fields but the cultivation of the mind. So the primary set of skills he taught involved the practiced cultivation of deep mental, emotional, and physical calm and penetrative insight into the actual nature of one's lived experience.

Once, when the Buddha was emerging from three months' seclusion, he made a comment that seems to me to be of real significance for our understanding of Buddhist meditation. I suspect that some of the Buddha's followers had been wondering just what he was doing for all that time deep in the cool forest. Perhaps followers of other teachers had been inquiring into the matter. In any case, the Buddha's followers apparently wanted to know what they should say when others inquired about the Buddha's activities. The Buddha's response was "Tell them that I dwell in concentration on, and present-moment awareness of, the breath."

"What?" I can imagine someone responding. "That's it? The Buddha became the Buddha by watching his breath!?" Is that possible? In this *sutta*, the Buddha says that it is indeed possible. How? By following the blueprint that he painstakingly drew for his followers. The present *sutta* is that blueprint.

NOTES

15.1. *Pavāraṇā ceremony.* A ceremony held at the end of the traditional rainy season retreat.

15.2. *This assembly . . . heart of the matter.* May all North American *saṅghas* take heed!

15.3. *There are practitioners.* What follows, in descending order, is a sort of gradation of practitioners: *arahants,* non-returners, once-returners, and stream-enterers.

15.4. *habituated impulses.* This term translates a central Buddhist psychological category, namely *āsava* (Sanskrit: *āśrava*). The *āsavas* are the three, sometimes four, forces that propel a person through *saṃsāra.* Because they are considered to be so deeply rooted in human existence, the English term "impulses" seems fitting. Like an impulse, an *āsava* occurs prior to overt cognitive functions and thus appears to be autonomous. The Pāli term has a strong connotation of "drive" and "compulsion." (For more on the translation of *āsava,* see note 8.2.)

More specifically, the *āsavas* are the impulse toward sense desire (*kāmāsava*), the impulse toward becoming (*bhavāsava*), and the impulse toward ignorance (*avijjāsava*). Sometimes the impulse toward views (*diṭṭhāsava*) is mentioned as a fourth *āsava.* The basic nature of these impulses is, in the Buddha's words, to "defile, bring renewal of being, give trouble, ripen in suffering, and lead to future birth, aging, and death" (*Majjhimanikāya* 36.47; see also *Sabbāsava,* "All the Taints," *Majjhimanikāya* 2).

15.5. *bonds of existence.* Each of the four types of practitioners enumerated in this section is defined in part by the bonds that he or she has cut or thrown off. The Buddha names ten such "bonds of existence." Five of these bonds are considered coarse or "lower bonds": (1) belief in an abiding personality, (2) doubt in the teachings, (3) misplaced confidence in the ability of rituals to lead to awakening, (4) attachment to sensuality, and (5) hostility toward others. Five are subtle or "higher": (6) craving for the world of form, (7) craving for the formless world, (8) conceit, (9) restlessness, and (10) ignorance. A stream-enterer is one who has destroyed the first three; a once-returner has additionally weakened the next two; a non-returner has completely destroyed the first five bonds; and an *arahant,* all ten (see *Dīghanikāya* 33.2.1 [7–8]).

15.6. *reappear elsewhere.* The Buddha lived in a culture that took rebirth (Pāli: *punabbhava,* "repeated becoming") as axiomatic. The terms "once-returner" and "non-returner" refer respectively to rebirth and cessation of rebirth in our worldly realm of form. Coupled with this general belief in rebirth is a pan-Indian cosmology that posits numerous potential "life-worlds" in an eternally oscillating universe. In this view, the universe undergoes an apparently endless (and beginningless, of course!) cycle of emergence, evolution, and destruction, oscillating perpetually between expansion and contraction, activity and calm. At the moment of greatest stillness and unity, emergence and expansion begin; at the moment of greatest activity and multiplicity, calm and concord. (See Richard Davis, *Ritual in an Oscillating Universe,* Princeton: Princeton University Press, 1991; and Randy Kloetzli, *Buddhist Cosmology,* New Delhi: Motilal Banarsidass, 1983.) The idea that a non-returner may "reappear elsewhere," that is, somewhere other than in our immediate world, is a logical extension of these two axioms.

What do you make of such ideas? The Buddha warned that such matters are "profound, difficult to perceive, difficult to comprehend." He also said that even though he himself has knowledge of such matters, he remains nonetheless "unattached to that knowledge." Letting go of such matters, furthermore, gives him "perfect peace."

Hmmm. In our culture, we don't want to let go of such matters, do we? Isn't it true that we consider it a sign of personal "depth" when someone involves himself or herself in questions concerning life after life or "the beyond"? Most of us, though, probably hold views (*āsavas,* remember?) that either have been received from others (parents, society) or simply make us feel at ease (heaven, reincarnation). But if we must speculate on these matters, it may be helpful to factor in some Buddhist positions. Taking interdependent origination into consideration, we might ask, for instance, how awareness in this instant could *not* contribute to a re-arising in another instant. "My" re-arising an hour from now in another room or, for that matter, in another world is wholly unremarkable—it's just the causal flow of interdependent causes, effects, and conditions taking its natural course. Taking into consideration the Buddhist notion of a "world," furthermore, how can we *not* speak of "arising in another world," since we do so continually? Moment by moment, worlds arise, persist, dissolve, disappear, and arise again. So the Buddhist view is that birth, life, death, rebirth, redeath, et cetera, are constantly churning (think *saṃsāra*).

This explanation will, I imagine, leave most readers unsatisfied. Some of us just want to know in clear, unequivocal terms: What happens when I die? Those readers may want to factor into their further speculation the following claim of the Buddha. In short, he seems to hold that it *is* possible to observe prior "moments" in an earlier stream-of-consciousness awareness (a.k.a. a previous life). But just imagine the degree of meditative mastery required for seeing the arising and passing of conscious awareness over such awesomely immense spans of time and space.

> When his concentrated mind is thus [i.e., through meditation] purified, bright, unblemished, rid of imperfection, malleable, wieldy, steady, and attained to imperturbability, [the meditator] directs it to knowledge of the recollection of past lives. He recollects his manifold past lives, that is, one birth, two births . . . a hundred births, a thousand births, a hundred thousand births, many aeons of world contraction and expansion. Thus, with their aspects and particulars he recollects his manifold past lives. . . . So, too, a [practitioner] recollects his manifold past lives.
>
> (*Majjhimanikāya* 39.19)

Until then, may you know the perfect peace of not worrying about it!

15.7. *stream-enterers.* The stream is the eight-component course. Just as a stream naturally inclines toward the ocean, and the ocean naturally inclines toward the depths, the path naturally inclines toward awakening.

15.8. *application of present-moment awareness in the four areas.* See "The Application of Present-Moment Awareness" (*sutta* 16).

15.9. *four sound efforts.* See note 9.5.

15.10. *four bases of success.* "Basis of success" translates the Pāli *iddhipāda,* which can also mean "basis of realization" or "basis of power." The second term, *pāda,* may also have the sense of "path, road, way." In each of the four cases, the basis or pathway referred to is a mental quality derived from concentration and effort. The bases are of such significance to the practice of meditation that the Buddha insists they can lead the meditator "from the near shore to the far shore," from, that is, *saṃsāra* to *nirvāṇa.* The four bases are (1) concentration due to resolution (*chanda*) accompanied by determined effort; (2) concentration due to energy (*viriya*) accompanied by determined effort; (3) concentration due to mind (*citta*) accompanied by determined effort; and (4) concentration due to examination (*vīmaṃsā*) accompanied by determined effort (*Majjhimanikāya* 16.26; see also *Saṃyuttanikāya* 5.51). In each instance, the effort must be balanced, neither too loose nor too tight (*Saṃyuttanikāya* 5.51.20). The term for "concentration" here, *samādhi* (see note 9.5), connotes a gathering together, collection, unification, of one's energies. The assumption, of course, is that our attention is normally dispersed in many different directions. Success in meditation, then, would require that we first become capable of focusing our attention.

15.11. *five natural strengths.* Five "faculties," "controlling energies," or "forces"—the Pāli term, *indriya,* carries all of these senses—that edify the practitioner in his or her practice. The five are: (1) confidence (*saddhā;* in the Buddha and his teachings); (2) energy (*viriya*); (3) present-moment awareness (*sati*); (4) concentration (*samādhi*); and (5) penetrative insight (*paññā*). (See also *Saṃyuttanikāya* 5.48.)

15.12. *five developed powers.* These five are the same as the five natural strengths (see the preceding note). As "powers," these qualities don't just serve as strong natural capacities but entail the additional capacity of enabling the practitioner to overcome opposing forces. (See *Saṃyuttanikāya* 5.50.)

15.13. *seven factors of awakening.* See note 15.21.

15.14. *preeminent eight-component course.* See note 9.5. The preceding lists of qualities, skills, and subjects constitute the thirty-seven "wings to awakening," on which see note 15.21.

15.15. *cultivating friendliness, compassion, joy, and equanimity.* See note 4.5.

15.16. *This practice perfects . . . higher knowledge and release.* In the discourse on Buddhist meditation, both throughout history and in the contemporary West, the practice of "watching the breath" is almost unanimously held to be a "beginner's practice," inevitably to be replaced by some more "advanced" practice. At best the practice is viewed as a necessary preliminary to serious meditation; at worst it is viewed as outright inferior. Today, Theravāda Buddhism alone holds the practice in high esteem. But that tradition's place in the overall Buddhist hierarchy of traditions parallels that of the practice itself: the ancient, pejorative appellation *hīnayāna* ("the puny vehicle") for schools such as the Theravāda reveals this estimation. But doesn't the Buddha's statement that "this practice perfects" unequivocally place *ānāpānasati* at the heart of Buddhist practice? It certainly seems to reveal his view that the practice possesses tremendous efficacious power. Not only is it rich in results, but it arouses, cultivates, and perfects all of the previously enumerated qualities and skills. So why is present-moment awareness with breathing so often looked down on?

15.17. *Establishing . . . simply aware.* In an isolated place, the practitioner sits down, assumes the meditation posture, and limits her or his awareness to the immediate presence of the body right in that place. The text thus implies a sort of implosion or collapsing of normally dispersed perceptual energies into the present time-space instance. Contrary to the Theravādin commentarial tradition, the Buddha's instructions do not call for the counting, following, placing, et cetera, of the breath. His instructions, in fact, clearly call for a present-moment awareness, or lucid-memory-in-the-present (*sati;* here *sata,* the past participle).

15.18. *know directly.* Note that the instructions call for a nonconceptual, nondiscursive knowing. This knowing is nondualistic. It is not a case of *me* standing over and apart from some thing—*breathing* or *the breath.* When "knowing directly," how can you distinguish among knower, knowing, and known?

15.19. *You should train as follows.* This statement is repeated throughout the text. The text actually reads *sikkhati,* "he trains, he trains himself." But this is an instance where I have transposed a text from the third person to the second person and, in this case, from the indicative to the optative. I've done this here in order to limit cumbersome English phrasing and to give the text a stronger sense of immediate relevance.

15.20. *in and as.* The text has the locative case for each noun, which can indicate either of these prepositions. Most translations give one or the other. I prefer to keep the apparent ambiguity in play. "In" the body sounds funny, but it suggests that the center of awareness has shifted. That is, it is not a case of the thinking organ being aware of some object, "the body." The awareness, rather, is precisely *in* the body—body aware of body. But even this "of" is problematic. We could just as easily (and just as misleadingly) say body aware *on* body, *through* body, *with* body. Prepositions are extremely bossy words. They force and reinforce on their users a profoundly dualistic view of the world: I am aware *of* such and such. In the present instance, though, it is a case of *bodyaware,* or *awarebody,* or *bodyawarebody,* period, no preposition required. The English "as," by contrast, serves the Buddha's meaning well. "Observing the body as the body" means that I regard the body not as "I-me-mine" but just *as* body. This "as" creates the distance required for me to forgo my (personal pronouns are bossy, too!) deep-seated tendency to personalize and claim ownership of the egoless processes of being.

15.21. *seven factors of awakening.* In the *sutta* recounting his final days, the Buddha tells his followers that the teachings will endure as long as they practice, develop, and cultivate that which he had "discovered and proclaimed" throughout his life. He then names thirty-seven "matters" divided into seven sets (*Dīghanikāya* 16.6.7). Elsewhere, the contents of one of these sets, the five natural strengths (see note 15.11), are termed "qualities that mutually contribute to awakening" (*bodhipakkiyā dhammā; Saṃyuttanikāya* 5.48.51). In the postcanonical literature, this latter term is routinely used to designate the combined seven sets of thirty-seven factors. The term for the group of seven factors listed in the present *sutta* is *bojjhaṅga,* "factors of awakening." The Buddha says that these factors lead the practitioner to "greatness and expansiveness" and to "the far shore," *nirvāna* (*Saṃyuttanikāya* 5.46).

Although there is some controversy over the matter (see, for example, Rupert Gethin, *The Buddhist Path to Awakening,* Leiden: Brill, 1992, pp. 343ff), I can see more benefit than harm in viewing the schema of the thirty-seven factors of awakening as both a comprehensive account and the final systemization of the Buddha's teachings. The only harm I see is that this view can't really be substantiated historically or textually with the degree of certainty that we might desire. The benefit is that the schema allows for a highly compacted compendium of the Buddha's teachings. Particularly in an oral culture, it was incumbent on teachers to organize their teachings for effective transmission and storage. Many of the schemas that we have encountered in the present book are examples of the Buddha's efforts in this regard. Given the fact that he taught for nearly half a century, it is perfectly sensible to suppose that the Buddha would have created an overall organizing schema for what had, by the end of his life, become a colossal body of teachings.

For those readers desiring a fuller treatment of the *bodhipakkiyā dhammā,* I can recommend two extraordinary books: Rupert Gethin, *The Buddhist Path to Awakening,* and Thanissaro Bhikkhu, *The Wings to Awakening* (Barre, Mass.: Dhamma Dana Publications, 1996).

Here is a summary of the thirty-seven qualities that mutually contribute to awakening. When reading through the list, please note that the Buddha seems to be insisting that each of these qualities be cultivated in conjunction with all of the others. He seems to view each quality as effective only when supported by the others. I have found it helpful to think of this schema in terms of two analogues. First, it is like a body, in that just as a joint requires muscle, bone, sinew, and so forth in order to function effectively, present-moment awareness requires concentration, energy, and so on to function properly. That is, none of the qualities can stand on its own. Second, the schema is also like an aptitude chart on which the various abilities required for virtuosity in some area are graphed. In this analogue, each of the qualities represents a skill operating in the service of fulfilling some capacity, for example, breathing technique for playing a flute. In the Buddha's schema, of course, each quality mutually contributes to our human capacity for awakening.

The Thirty-seven Qualities That Mutually Contribute to Awakening

(In each instance, the quality is to be "aroused, cultivated, and fulfilled.")

First Set: Application of Present-Moment Awareness (*satipaṭṭhāna*)
"Being ardent, fully aware, and mindful, and having put down longing and discontentment toward the world, the practitioner dwells"

1. observing the body *in and as the body*
2. observing feelings *in and as feelings*
3. observing mind *in and as mind*
4. observing mental qualities and phenomena *in and as mental qualities and phenomena*

(See "The Application of Present-Moment Awareness," *sutta* 16.)

Second Set: Sound Efforts (*sammappadhāna*)
The practitioner strives to

5. *prevent* harmful mental states from arising
6. *overcome* those harmful, unwholesome mental states that have arisen
7. *generate* beneficial mental states that have not arisen
8. *maintain* and *fully develop* beneficial, wholesome mental states that have arisen

(See "Turning the Wheel of the Teaching," *sutta* 9, and note 9.5.)

Third Set: Bases of Success (*iddhipāda*)

9. concentration due to resolution accompanied by determined effort
10. concentration due to energy accompanied by determined effort
11. concentration due to mind accompanied by determined effort
12. concentration due to examination accompanied by determined effort

(See note 15.10.)

Fourth Set: Natural Strengths (*indriya*)

13. confidence
14. energy
15. present-moment awareness
16. concentration
17. penetrative insight

(See note 15.11.)

Fifth Set: Developed Powers (*bala*)

18. confidence
19. energy
20. present-moment awareness
21. concentration
22. penetrative insight

(See note 15.12.)

Sixth Set: Factors of Awakening (*bojjhaṅga*)

23. present-moment awareness
24. investigation of qualities
25. energy
26. delight
27. tranquillity
28. concentration
29. equanimity

(See "The Application of Present-Moment Awareness," *sutta* 16.)

Seventh Set: The Preeminent Eight Component Course (*ariya-magga*)

30. sound view
31. sound inclination
32. sound speech
33. sound action
34. sound livelihood
35. sound effort
36. sound awareness
37. sound concentration

(See "Turning the Wheel of the Teaching," *sutta* 9, and note 9.5.)

15.22. *present-moment awareness.* The Pāli term is *sati.* This term is normally translated as "mindfulness." It refers to our natural capacity to rest our awareness on some object or event. Present-moment awareness, however, is *just aware;* that is, it is nonconceptual and nondiscursive in nature. In that sense, we can say that *sati* is awareness itself. Awareness is the very quality that constitutes human consciousness, just like water is the quality that constitutes a pond.

Present-moment awareness is the interminable receptivity toward whatever appears within our sensorium (seeing, hearing, smelling, tasting, tactile feeling, thinking). Postcanonical literature refers to it as "dry" (*sukkha*) attentiveness to whatever arises. That is, it is a bare or naked apprehension of things and events. A contemporary teacher, Henapola Gunaratna, somewhere calls it "mirror-thought," in that it merely reflects what appears, without grasping, rejecting, or coloring the arising phenomenon. When, for instance, anger arises, *sati* is merely aware of the bare process of feelings, thoughts, et cetera, unfolding in the mind-body continuum. Although this process is normally labeled "anger," present-moment awareness, being nonconceptual, does not name, express, or repress the anger: it simply remains present and receptive to it. In so doing, of course, "it" turns out to be no one, stable entity—anger—but a complex host of energies, concepts, physiological reactions, and so on. The practitioner who is cultivating present-moment awareness, furthermore, rapidly learns that being *just* aware of a given sensorial phenomenon tends to decrease the gravitational pull of that phenomenon. Thus, present-moment awareness engenders a less reactive, habituated way of relating to the world around us. During seated meditation, present-moment awareness is cultivated by placing and sustaining attention on the breathing process, as explained in the present *sutta.*

15.23. *investigation into qualities.* The word for this practice is *dhammavicaya.* When the practitioner is able to maintain awareness fluidly, moment by moment, he or she spontaneously realizes the fundamental qualities (*dhamma*) of phenomena. These qualities may be specific or generalized. In the preceding note's example, anger is a specific quality (*dhamma*). Investigation (*vicaya*) means that when anger has arisen, the practitioner knows—can see with penetrative insight—that that quality is marked by three characteristics: impermanence (Pāli: *anicca;* Sanskrit: *anitya*), non-substantiality (*anattā/anātman*), and unease (*dukkha/duḥkha*). More generally, but of the utmost significance for the practitioner, the Buddha identified five qualities that function to prevent success in meditation. In *sutta* 3, he called these qualities "hindrances, obstructions, obstacles, coverings, envelopings." The five hindrances are: (1) desire, (2) hostility, (3) heavy lethargy, (4) agitated worry, and (5) debilitating doubt. Whenever the practitioner is overcome by one of these qualities, it is imperative that he or she thoroughly investigate the quality. Investigating tiredness or lethargy, for example, means exploring its nature (heavy, dark, forceful, coercive, and so on) and its function (physically affecting, anesthetizing, all-enveloping). Because of the function of present-moment awareness and energy, the practitioner's investigation will be sharp and clear. So, paradoxically, the practitioner realizes that he or she "is" (what does that verb really mean in this case?) lethargic yet vibrant, sleepy yet alert. Knowing in this manner, one has a weakened tendency to be reactive toward whatever quality is appearing. During meditation practice, being skilled in investigation means that the practitioner has the capacity to see the nature of whatever is arising as being ultimately transparent.

15.24. *energy.* During meditation, persisting in present-moment awareness and spontaneous investigation requires concerted effort. With this effort, an internal energy (*viriya*) emerges. These two terms, "energy" and "effort," are both contained in the Pāli word *viriya.* "Virility" is a cognate English word that perhaps captures the full connotation of the original: potency, vigor, vibrancy, regenerativity, as well as effort and energy.

15.25. *delight.* The Buddha proposes that wherever tireless energy is fulfilled, extraordinary delight (*pīti*) is *naturally* (the text calls it "unfleshly") aroused. That is, this form of delight differs from ordinary delight in that it is not dependent on external objects or factors. It is, rather, a quality indigenous to psychophysical being when that being is transparently aware and energized. Delight, or joy, can be seen as a skill in that it is habituated during practice. (Really, the process of arousing, cultivating, and fulfilling a quality amounts to habituating. Think of the relationship between "habit" and "habitat"—being at home in.)

15.26. *tranquillity.* The Buddha asks the meditator to clarify this point for himself or herself: from the fulfillment of delight ensues "tranquillity" (*passaddhi*). Similar to delight, tranquillity ensues naturally when the other qualities are cultivated. That is, the meditator does not actually *do* anything to arouse tranquillity; it simply emerges on its own. In a sense, delight and tranquillity can be said to be always already present within the mind-body continuum; once the other factors are present, they simply manifest. Actually, the same may be said for calmness. Even though the meditator is focused on the breath, this focus does not *create* calmness; rather, the inherent condition of stillness, peace, calmness, is simply allowed to emerge.

15.27. *concentration.* This tranquillity *naturally* gives way to "one-pointed concentration" (*samādhi*). (The word *samādhi* as a major Buddhist technical term is discussed at note 9.5.) Within the seven skills system, the word refers to mental stability, non-distraction, and non-diffuseness of mental energy. The term literally means "to be collected (*dhi*) firmly (*ā*) together (*sam*)." In this sense, it is similar to our colloquial notion of "pulling oneself together." Unlike our common usage of "concentration," *samādhi* does not imply a purposeful, effort-filled mental state. Again, this skill is understood to be a natural, indigenous quality of awareness.

15.28. *equanimity.* This skill is necessary for balance. When the practitioner begins to experience delight, he or she may become excited. Conversely, when the practitioner becomes tired, discouragement ensues. A person skilled in equanimity (*upekkā*) is adept at cutting through these vicissitudes. Such a person proceeds evenly and remains in a state of emotional, physical, and mental balance and equipoise.

Outline of the Seven Skills

1. By keeping the attention on the breathing process during seated meditation, breath by breath, the student arouses, cultivates, and fulfills the skill of *present-moment awareness.*
2. This awareness is naturally cognizant of the nature of phenomena, the skill of *investigation of qualities.*
3. When the student persists in the cultivation of these two, he or she arouses, cultivates, and fulfills *energy.*
4. When the cultivation of these three is maintained, *delight* naturally ensues.
5. When this quality is cultivated and fulfilled, *tranquillity* naturally ensues.
6. When this quality is cultivated and fulfilled, *concentration* naturally ensues.
7. In order to maintain balance and avoid the disabling extremes of elation and depression, it is necessary to become skilled in *equanimity.*

SUTTA 16

महासतिपट्ठानसुत्त

How to Live as a Buddha

Mahāsatipaṭṭhāna Sutta: "The Application of Present-Moment Awareness"; *Majjhimanikāya 10*

APPLICATION OF THIS AWARENESS IN DAILY LIFE IS CONCOMITANT WITH LIVING AS A BUDDHA: *AWAKENED.* (GOING)

Buddhists and non-Buddhists alike have always been fascinated by the figure of the Buddha. The Buddha often referred to himself unostentatiously as a guide (*desika*) who, by virtue of having come to an understanding of reality (a *tathāgata*), awakened (a *buddha*) to the nature of our human situation. That's it. He was a teacher (*desika*) who was adept at pointing (also *desika*) to the matters of real and immediate existential concern, and at showing (also *desika*) the path to their resolution and fulfillment. That's it.

For many, however, that's not enough. As with virtually every founder of the world's "religious" traditions, Gotama the seeker is perpetually subject to the standard treatment of the pious follower: apotheosis. The godliness of the Buddha was and is expressed in iconography and narrative along with their corresponding devotional practices. The Buddha may have been a teacher, but he was infinitely more than that—he was and is a continual wellspring of power and aid. That, at least, is the logic of apotheosis. In the eyes of so many of his followers throughout history, the Buddha possessed and possesses what Pascal Boyer calls "a hidden causal essence." I mentioned this notion in the introduction; it will, however, be worthwhile to review it in the context of the present *sutta*.

> The notion of a hidden causal essence that cannot be observed yet explains outward form and behavior, is a crucial feature of our spontaneous, intuitive way of thinking about living species. Here, it is transferred upon a pseudo-natural kind, as it were: a sub-kind of human agents with different essential characteristics.

In other words, the Buddha, as a "spiritual" exemplar, possessed attributes that were qualitatively and quantitatively singular; otherwise he would not have been *enlightened,* he would not be *the Buddha.* It is, moreover, precisely these "essential characteristics" of the Buddha that made and make him holy, sacred, *spiritually* realized. A necessary corollary of this kind of thinking is, of course, the belief that an ordinary person cannot come to the understanding of reality that the Buddha did and, thus, cannot become a *buddha.*

What should we make of this all-too-human tendency to see uniqueness—specialness—in the, well, all-too-human? I find this inclination, exhibited by every stripe of the Buddha's followers, to be deeply counterproductive to his prescription for human well-being. And if the Buddha wasn't talking about human well-being, if he wasn't talking about being *a well human,* if he wasn't talking about *human being* pure and simple, if he wasn't talking about *reality,* if he wasn't addressing *this world,* and if he didn't have in mind *you and me* when doing so, then why *in the world* should we pay the slightest attention to the man? We don't need another omniscient soothsayer or savior to deliver us from . . . what, ourselves, our human destiny—do we? Can we really afford to fritter away more of our precious mortal existence on further enchanting stories about special beings, fantastic places, supernatural states of mind, and extraordinary *future* events? Maybe I am an incurable empiricist, but when they say "special," I furrow my brow and tilt my head. *Special? Hmmm. Show me.* If it's presentable, if it's humanly attainable and knowable, *if you can show me,* then it is not special. If it is specialness on margin (I'll see it in the afterlife), then I am not buying. How about you? The Buddha said that it was within his six-foot body, endowed with perceptions and conceptions, that he realized and declared the nature of reality (*Saṃyuttanikāya* 1.2.26). How could it be any different for you and me? How can a *buddha* be anything but an ordinary person, and anywhere other than *in life?*

We can also approach that question by simply asking: What value might there be in seriously entertaining the possibility that to be fully present in life, to be fully aware, fully awake, to our very experience of being, *is* to live as *a buddha*?

"Within this six-foot body." Why would the Buddha mention such an obvious fact? Do you remember the story about the quail and the hawk? In *sutta* 1, the Buddha tells a story about how we habitually wander ghostlike within a hostile and "foreign domain." In that *sutta,* he admonishes us to cease once and for all being snookered and hijacked like weightless phantoms every time some object that is "pleasing, desirable, charming, agreeable, arousing desire, and enticing" struts in front of us. The Buddha's admonishment, though, is not a puritanical harangue against the sins of pleasure: in subsequent *suttas* he cautioned us about the bamboozling power of aversion, hostility, and delusion as well as that of desire and attraction. So it is against this ghostlike rootlessness that the Buddha is admonishing us. But being as we are, do we have an alternative? Live within your "native domain," he says, within your "own ancestral, natural habitat."

> Death will not gain access to the person who lives within his or her native domain; within his or her own ancestral, natural habitat, death will not gain a footing. Now, what is your native domain, your own ancestral, natural habitat? It is the foundation of present-moment awareness in four areas. What are the four areas? Now, being ardent, fully aware, and mindful, and having put down longing and discontentment toward the world, live observing the body *in and as the body,* live observing feelings *in and as feelings,* live observing mind *in and as mind,* and live observing mental qualities and phenomena *in and as mental qualities and phenomena.*

This is your native domain, your own ancestral, natural habitat.

In this either-or scenario, we can, *at any given instant,* take a trajectory toward unease, pain, distress, discord, or take one toward ease, genuine pleasure, joy, compassion, harmony. It all depends on the strategies for living that we choose to adopt. As we saw in the diagram in the introduction, the first trajectory runs through infatuation, hostility, and delusion and ends in pain; and the second runs through clarity, insight, and present-moment awareness and ends in peace. You might look at these trajectories as two basic strategies for living. The first strategy is evidently deeply embedded in our human nervous system—just read the newspaper. The second strategy, therefore, and according to the Buddha, palpably goes against that all-too-human flow. At any given instant in our lives we are running either this program or that. At any given instant, that is to say, we are operating from either infatuation, hostility, and delusion *or* a clear view of things (even of those three qualities) unfolding out of our natural capacity for present-moment awareness.

As the title indicates, the present *sutta* is concerned precisely with the firm foundation and application of present-moment awareness in the life of the practitioner. Toward this end, the *sutta* can be seen as a meditation guide—it gives step-by-step instructions on how to establish, cultivate, and perfect a fluid, evenly distributed awareness of one's existence. But the *sutta* is more than a guide to meditation. This particular meditation—present-moment awareness in the four areas of existence—is interminable. How could it not be? As long as we live, our lives will unfold in these areas. To lose awareness of that unfolding is to become unconscious. Elsewhere, the Buddha put this fact in stark terms:

> Diligence is the path to the deathless.
> Negligence is the path of death.
> The diligent do not die.
> Those who are negligent
> are as the dead.
>
> (*Dhammapada* 21)

So the *sutta* is a guide to living diligently aware, fully present to your life as it unfolds moment by moment. It is thus a guide to both the *founding* and the *application* of present-moment awareness in daily life.

The Buddha's statement that he realized awakening within his six-foot body is thus no idle comment. Living in an awakened fashion requires that you be thoroughly grounded right here, where life unfolds moment by moment: *in your body.* But the Buddha added, "with its perceptions and conceptions"—that is, *in mind, in feelings, and in mental qualities and phenomena.* Since these four places mark the domain where our lives manifest, it is here where we belong, where we are first and foremost *at home.* This domain is our natural habitat, our ancestral home. The present *sutta* is thus the Buddha's guide to coming home.

NOTES

Title. (Mahāsatipaṭṭhāna): *sati.* The literal meaning of this principal Buddhist technical term is "memory." On the one hand, it is an extremely rich and complex term; but on the other, it is extraordinarily dry and simple. In the Buddha's day, Brahmans used the Sanskrit version, *smṛti,* literally "remembered," to designate "sacred" texts other than the Vedas per se, which were referred to as *śrūti,* "heard." Whereas *śrūti* has the connotation of "revealed [by the inspired poets, the *ṛṣis*]," *smṛti* carries a sense of "preserved [by tradition]." The former category encompasses the compositions used in the sacrificial liturgy; the latter includes a vast body of literature, such as legal codes, mythology, the epics, and so on.

The Buddha may have been playing somewhat on this commonly understood usage when he chose to use *smṛti/sati.* I can imagine him saying, "Okay, if the Brahmans want their precious *smṛti* to designate the pinnacle of 'that which is to be remembered,' then I will show them that which is truly worthy of holding in memory: it is *sati* itself." That is, that which is to be remembered (*sati*), is precisely that which remembers (*sati*). The treasure of memory is not a mere collection of words, however "sacred" or "holy"; it is not, in other words, the received corpus of orally transmitted texts. The treasure of memory, for the Buddha, is that to which the teachings point; namely, our capacity for remembering in and of itself. Living with this capacity fully and persistently engaged constitutes awakened living.

This being the case, "memory" obviously carries connotations for the Buddha that are not given in our own everyday usage of the term. We don't, for instance, ever use the term to denote a recollection or memory of or in the *present.* By definition, memory goes backward, toward the past; it remembers. So toward what can the Buddha be pointing us here? It would, of course, be counterproductive actually to answer that question. A few comments may nonetheless be in order. When you do the practices detailed in the present *sutta,* it is first of all crucial to keep in mind that you are not creating or somehow manufacturing *sati.* When the Buddha includes *sati* as an *indriya* ("natural strength"), he is indicating that it is a natural capacity, and as such already and always present. In that sense, *sati* can be understood as an elemental awareness, one that attends all instances of perception and cognition. So really, the idea of founding or establishing *sati* is somewhat paradoxical. It's a little like the idea that water can establish transparency. Transparency is indigenous to water. But imagine that a particular body of water becomes obscured by cloudy sedimentation caused throughout the day by various activities—loons landing on the surface, children swimming, someone skipping stones, leaves and branches falling. In such a case, is it correct to assert that the water is transparent? Well, not exactly. Yet at dusk, when the loons have flown for shelter, the children and the stone skipper have all gone home, and nature has come to rest, the sedimentation settles. And, significantly, it does so of its own accord. That is, when left alone, the water's transparency *naturally* results. Was the water transparent all along? Well, in typical Buddhist fashion, we can, we must, answer yes *and* no. Really, it's best just to leave this question as something to be examined in relation to the indigenous nature of your own *sati* quality of mind.

(Mahāsatipaṭṭhāna): *paṭṭhāna.* It is not at all clear whether the Pāli *paṭṭhāna* represents the Sanskrit term *upasthāna* or *prasthāna.* The first term has the sense of "placing oneself near [an object]," "coming into the presence of," "attending to." As such, it can also refer to the place or object that is being approached, made present, or attended to; hence, "sanctuary," "refuge," "dwelling," "abode," and so on. The second term, *prasthāna,* means "proceeding toward," "sending forth," "setting up." So the term as a whole signifies both the *place* where *sati* is made present and the *manifestation* of *sati* itself.

16.1. *The direct path.* What a remarkable claim the Buddha is making for this practice. The path outlined in the *sutta,* he says, is *ekāyana:* "narrow and unforked," "going in a single direction"—toward the cessation of unease, *nirvāṇa.*

16.2. *live.* The Pāli, *viharati,* also means "dwell," as I have translated it on several occasions in the present book. I render it here as "live" to give the sense of a continuous mode of being. We extend our cultivation of awareness in and of the four areas, developed in the actual meditative practice of *satipaṭṭhāna,* into our daily lives.

16.3. *How should you live observing . . . the body.* What follow are fourteen practices whose aim is to allow you to habituate yourself in your body. The need for such a habituation is, of course, astounding. You may ask: Well, is there really such a need? Are we not already at home in our bodies? Are we not already familiar with our bodies? On the basis of the present fourteen practices, the Buddha obviously held that we are in fact dangerously estranged from our own bodies. "Being at home in the body" requires a degree of awareness that, in its quality and fullness, calls for precisely the kind of cultivation described in the *sutta.* The fourteen practices are self-explanatory. Understanding them requires just that: practice. Some texts simply insist that the reader apply the logic of exploration and discovery. The present *sutta* is such a text. For those readers who nonetheless would like more detailed commentary than I offer here, I recommend Nyanaponika Thera's classic *The Heart of Buddhist Meditation: A Handbook of Mental Training Based on the Way of Mindfulness* (New York: Samual Weiser, 1962).

The fourteen-practice sequence takes the practitioner through the process of bodily being. It begins with the body sitting still, merely breathing in and out; and the practitioner knows just that. Next, the body is observed in its four states of walking, standing, sitting, and lying down. Then it is observed in more specific states of everyday agitation. Then the practitioner observes subtle inner aspects of the body. Finally, the body is dead. The practitioner considers the very stages of bodily disintegration that "he" or "she"—the body in and as body—will undergo. By the fourteenth practice, the body has become dust.

16.4. *breathe in.* This paragraph refers to the practice detailed in "Present-Moment Awareness with Breathing" (*sutta* 15).

16.5. *either your own or others'.* The text reads "either internally or externally, or both internally and externally." This phrase may sound strange in some instances that follow, but it's just a way of allowing for our human proclivity to observe how it is with others more easily than with ourselves.

16.6. *elements.* For a full explanation of these elements and their relation to meditation practice, see *Majjhimanikāya* 62.8ff.

16.7. *cremation ground.* Practices 6 through 14—almost half of the practices—involve a thorough consideration of the nature of bodily death, disintegration, and dissolution. Why?

> Spitting blood
> clears up reality
> and dream alike.
>
> (*Sunao*)

16.8. *feelings.* See notes 6.2, 9.8, and 10.6.

16.9. *immaterial feeling.* Literally, "fleshless." The Pāli term, *nirāmisa,* is usually translated in ways such as "spiritual," "not of the flesh," "unworldly." Besides being incomprehensible to me, such words miss the mark. In practical terms it makes no sense to speak of an "immaterial feeling," does it? All sensations and feelings obviously have a quality of materiality. They arise via contact between a sense organ and an external stimulus, and they are felt. Otherwise, how would we know them? In note 15.25, we saw that the awakening factor of delight is not dependent on external stimuli for its manifestation. It is *naturally* aroused as a result of the previously cultivated *internal* cognitive-mental qualities. There, too, the text uses *nirāmisa.* So I take the term *nirāmisa* in the present context similarly to mean that the feeling is not dependent on external factors, such as the feeling arising from grasping at an object of the sense.

As you undertake this practice, you will probably notice that quite acute sensations and feelings arise in instances of relinquishment and letting go of grasping. Might those sensations be viewed as "immaterial"?

16.10. *mind.* In the present context, the Pāli term, *citta,* has the sense of what we colloquially refer to as a "state of mind." It is the "center" of lived experience. Whereas in many instances *citta* is used to denote cognitive and reflective functions (e.g., attending to things, thinking, planning, fantasizing, pondering), here it seems to point to permeating affective qualities of mind. Largely because of this range of meaning, *citta* is often translated as "heart" or "heart-mind."

16.11. *mental qualities and phenomena.* Behind this somewhat cumbersome phrase is the ever-vexing multivalent Pāli term *dhamma* (Sanskrit: *dharma*). The range of the term goes roughly from "atom" to "cosmic structure." Along the way, it covers "thought," "quality," "teaching," "propriety," "correctness," "duty," "custom," "practice," "virtue," "function," and more. In the present context, the Buddha captures several basic meanings with the term: mental-physical-emotional feeling tones (practice 17), conceptualizing functions (practice 18), perceptual functions (practice 19), cognitive capacities (practice 20), and teachings (practice 21).

16.12. *for seven days.* Really?

PRONUNCIATION OF SANSKRIT AND PĀLI WORDS

a as in *but*
ā as in *father*
c as in chop
ḍ as *d*, as described for *t*
e as in *play*
e, o, ā, ī, ū receive the stress, as do *a, i,* and *u* followed by a double consonant or an *ṃ* (so, for example, *bhāra, Gotama, anattālakkhaṇa, Vāseṭṭha*)
g as in *gone*
i as in *it*
ī as in *queen*
kh, gh, ch, jh, ṭh, ḍh, ph, bh pronounced as the first consonant plus slight aspiration (note: *th* as in *Thomas,* and never as in *these; ph* as in *pajamas,* and never as *filly*)
ṇ, ṅ, ṃ, nasals, as in *song*
ñ as in *onion*
o as in *go*
p as in *pie*
ṛ as in *pretty*
ś as in *shiver*
ṣ as in *shiver* with tongue slightly back on the palate
ṭ as *t* with the tip of the tongue on the middle of the palate
u as in *foot*
ū as in *boot*

ACKNOWLEDGMENTS

Several people have contributed significantly to the production of this book. I would like to express my gratitude to them here. The care, joy, and abundance that my wife, Friederike Baer, and daughters, Alexandra and Mia, bring to my life daily provide the basic conditions for living the kind of life that, I believe, is essential to writing responsibly about Buddhism. My agent, Anna Ghosh, of Scovil Chichak Galen Literary Agency, has warmly supported and expertly guided this project from its inception. Judy Sternlight, my editor at Random House, brought the eye of a virtuoso reader to bear on the manuscript, which resulted in a better book. Sonam Kachru and Kai Riedl, my students, friends, and budding colleagues, will see in the book the reflection of some of our (endless) discussions and debates. The texts in the present volume were translated from the *Chaṭṭha Saṅgāyana Pāli Tipiṭaka,* Vipsassana Research Institute, Dhamma Giri, Igatpuri, India, 1990. I would like to express my appreciation to Rick Crutcher of Pariyatti (www.pariyatti.org) for making this multivolume set available to me. Finally, Andrew Olendzki of the Barre Center for Buddhist Studies and Christopher Queen of Harvard University generously offered their support at the outset of the project.

INDEX

ABOUT THE TRANSLATOR AND AUTHOR OF THE GUIDE

GLENN WALLIS holds a Ph.D. in Sanskrit and Indian Studies from Harvard. He is an associate professor in the Religion Department at the University of Georgia and director of the Center for Applied Meditation at the Won Institute of Graduate Studies, near Philadelphia. He is the author of *Mediating the Power of Buddhas* and the author of the Modern Library's *The Dhammapada: Verses on the Way*, as well as the translator and editor of numerous scholarly articles.

A Note on the Type

The principal text of this Modern Library edition was set in a digitized version of Janson, a typeface that dates from about 1690 and was cut by Nicholas Kis, a Hungarian working in Amsterdam. The original matrices have survived and are held by the Stempel foundry in Germany. Hermann Zapf redesigned some of the weights and sizes for Stempel, basing his revisions on the original design.